INTRODUCING RESEARCH IN EARLY CHILDHOOD

Sara Miller McCune founded SAGE Publishing in 1965 to support the dissemination of usable knowledge and educate a global community. SAGE publishes more than 1000 journals and over 800 new books each year, spanning a wide range of subject areas. Our growing selection of library products includes archives, data, case studies and video. SAGE remains majority owned by our founder and after her lifetime will become owned by a charitable trust that secures the company's continued independence.

Los Angeles | London | New Delhi | Singapore | Washington DC | Melbourne

INTRODUCING RESEARCH IN EARLY CHILDHOOD

POLLY BOLSHAW & JO JOSEPHIDOU

Los Angeles | London | New Delhi
Singapore | Washington DC | Melbourne

Los Angeles | London | New Delhi
Singapore | Washington DC | Melbourne

SAGE Publications Ltd
1 Oliver's Yard
55 City Road
London EC1Y 1SP

SAGE Publications Inc.
2455 Teller Road
Thousand Oaks, California 91320

SAGE Publications India Pvt Ltd
B 1/I 1 Mohan Cooperative Industrial Area
Mathura Road
New Delhi 110 044

SAGE Publications Asia-Pacific Pte Ltd
3 Church Street
#10-04 Samsung Hub
Singapore 049483

Editor: Delayna Spencer
Assistant editor: Catriona McMullen
Production editor: Victoria Nicholas
Copyeditor: Elaine Leek
Proofreader: Jill Birch
Marketing manager: Lorna Patkai
Cover design: Wendy Scott
Typeset by C&M Digitals (P) Ltd, Chennai, India
Printed in the UK

First published 2019

Library of Congress Control Number: 2018935686

British Library Cataloguing in Publication data

A catalogue record for this book is available from the British Library

ISBN 978-1-5264-0827-3
ISBN 978-1-5264-0828-0 (pbk)

TABLE OF CONTENTS

List of Tables vii
About the Authors ix
Acknowledgements xi

1 Introduction to research in early childhood 1

2 Beginning to think critically about research 15

3 Knowledge and truth in research 29

4 The language of research 41

5 Approaches to research about children 53

6 Approaches to research with children 65

7 Longitudinal research approaches 81

8 Cross-national research approaches 95

9 The ethics of research 109

10 How research is designed 123

11 Creative approaches to research 137

12 Your research journey has begun 149

References 161
Index 177

LIST OF TABLES

2.1 Brookfield's four processes for thinking critically 17
2.2 Using markers of quality to critique a source of information 24

3.1 Some different definitions of truth 31
3.2 The different factors that impact on our understanding of truth and what that impact might be 33

4.1 Some of the key vocabulary used in research 43
4.2 How to set out an effective glossary 45

5.1 Conducting research on children in controlled environments: positives and negatives 59

6.1 Benefits of researching with children 72
6.2 Some of the methods used by Clark and Moss (2011; Clark, 2017) for gathering children's perspectives 73

8.1 Strengths and limitations of conducting cross-national research 104

9.1 Ethical considerations at different stages of the research 112
9.2 The risk factors for all the participants in 'The Strange Situation' experiment 115
9.3 How methods can be disrespectful and how this can be minimised 117

10.1 How different disciplines might view the child 126
10.2 Benefits and limitations of data collection 132

11.1 How visual imagery has been used in previous research 139

12.1 How you are developing a researcher identity 158

LIST OF TABLES

ABOUT THE AUTHORS

Polly Bolshaw is a Senior Lecturer in Early Years at Canterbury Christ Church University (CCCU), who teaches predominantly on the BA (Hons) Early Childhood Studies programme. Prior to this, she completed the *New Leaders in Early Years* programme at CCCU and worked as an Early Years Professional in a Sure Start Children's Centre. Her research interests include research methods for undergraduate students, the experiences of people who work with young children and study early childhood, early childhood education for sustainability and services within the UK that aim to support children and their families. She is also the co-author of the blog Contemplating Childhoods https://contemplatingchildhoods.com/ along with Jo.

Jo Josephidou was a primary school teacher for 20 years before entering Higher Education as a Senior Lecturer in 2009. Initially she taught on ITE programmes at the University of Cumbria before joining the Early Childhood Studies team at Canterbury Christ Church (CCCU) in September 2014. She teaches on a variety of modules on this programme, including those that focus on developing students' early research skills. Jo has recently completed her doctoral research, which focuses on practitioner gender and the pedagogy of play. She is also the co-author of the blog Contemplating Childhoods https://contemplatingchildhoods.com/ along with Polly.

ACKNOWLEDGEMENTS

We are grateful to our many colleagues for their valuable comments and the encouragement and enthusiasm they have shown for our book.

The authors and the publisher are grateful for permission to reproduce the following material in this book:

Chapter 3, excerpts from Braun, V. and Clarke, V. (2013) *Successful Qualitative Research*. London: Sage. Reproduced with permission.

Chapter 4, excerpts from Thomson, P. (2015) 'Why is this reading so hard?' *Patter*, 13 April. Reproduced with permission of the author.

1 INTRODUCTION TO RESEARCH IN EARLY CHILDHOOD

INTRODUCTION

Welcome to the world of early childhood research! Whatever your starting point in terms of understanding research, this book will provide you with a firm foundation that you can build on as you continue in your studies.

This chapter will ...

- Build your understanding of what is meant by the term 'research'.
- Explore some of the purposes of research in relation to early childhood.
- Consider what research means to those studying early childhood, and why it is important for children, families and communities that research is carried out.
- Reflect upon the role that research plays in informing policy and the ways in which it may support you in identifying and developing quality practice within early childhood.
- Highlight the breadth of ways in which research is conducted in early childhood, which we will build upon in later chapters.

WHAT IS THIS BOOK ABOUT?

This book aims to introduce you to the concept of research in relation to early childhood. It focuses specifically on children aged from birth to eight years old and will encourage you to debate, discuss and analyse the process of research and how other people choose to conduct it.

The book starts by considering research in relation to early childhood quite broadly. We will discuss how it is important to make sure that you do not take sources of information and pieces of research on face value, but instead think critically about them. It then explores the ideas of knowledge and truth in research, and how our beliefs about these concepts shape how we know and what we know about children and their childhoods. Next, you will consider 'the language of research' and think about why it is important to build an understanding of specific research terminology. This terminology might be the same words that you come across in your everyday life but with a different meaning in an academic sense.

After that, we will compare and contrast research 'about' children and research 'with' children, by exploring what is meant by each of these ideas, and how they link to research designs like longitudinal studies and cross-national research. Following that, we begin to think about some of the specific aspects that researchers must bear in mind before carrying out a study, such as how to act ethically and how to choose the design of a piece of research, whether that is through using numbers, words or a more creative approach. Finally, we will ask you as the reader to begin to think about becoming a researcher yourself, and invite you to reflect upon how your knowledge about research in relation to early childhood has developed through reading and reflecting on this book.

WHAT DO WE MEAN BY RESEARCH?

The first question that we need to ask ourselves when considering research in early childhood is what we actually mean by the term 'research'. Think about the times you carry out 'research' in your everyday life: for instance, you may consider that using a search engine like Google to find out which bus you need to take to get into town is 'research', or what time films are showing at your local cinema. In your university studies, you may say that you are using a library search engine to 'research' a particular topic on which you need to write an assignment. We use the term 'research' to mean that which we want to find out about, explore or discover – something that we did not know before. We will build upon other research terms in Chapter 4 (The language of research), when we will consider how other familiar words may change their meaning within a research context.

We can also think about the idea of 'research' in an academic sense, which is what this book will focus on. We consider research in ECEC (Early Childhood Education and Care) to be related to investigations, studies and experiments that contribute to new information about young children, their lives, their families and their communities. In this sense, research is about creating new knowledge, rather than learning knowledge that has already been acquired or provided by someone else. For example, let's say a researcher wants to conduct research on what parents think about using health visitor services. They carry out a study by interviewing new parents and analysing the conversations they have with those parents. This helps them to come up with new knowledge, which researchers call 'findings', about common parental opinions of health visitors. This information might support and agree with what other researchers have found. Alternatively, it might contradict existing research-informed practice, and lead to changes in what health visitors do.

In this book, we define research in early childhood as being about asking questions that we have about children and their lives, and attempting to answer those questions by discovering new knowledge, opinions, perspectives and understanding. This fits with other definitions, including that by a charity called the National Children's Bureau (2015) who say that research is 'not just about exploring a subject, it is about creating new knowledge and understanding'. Others liken research to discovery, for instance Fraser (2004: 16) says conducting research is like discovery 'either because "no one has been there before" or because someone predicts what it is like there even though no one has been there'. Other authors note the importance of the role of enquiry within research, such as Lobe et al. (2007: 6), who explain 'research is designed to answer questions'. Although these definitions are all slightly different, you can see commonalities between them. Research is about generating knowledge and answers to questions – sometimes questions that have been asked before and sometimes questions that haven't. With regard to young children, this might relate to questions about what children's experiences are, why they have those experiences and what the impact of those experiences might be.

When we think about who conducts research, we might think about an individual who carries out studies on a very small scale or we might think of large organisations who seek to carry out bigger pieces of research with a greater number of participants spanning a large number of countries. For instance, undergraduate university students will typically conduct a small-scale piece of research called a *dissertation* in their final year of studies. They could be interested in exploring what children's views are on wearing a school uniform and give out questionnaires to one school class to help them gather opinions on this. Conversely, one organisation that collects data on a larger scale and which spans different countries is the Organisation for Economic Co-operation and Development (OECD). The OECD is an organisation of 35 member countries, including the UK, which monitors events and data in these countries in order to discuss what the implications might be of the findings of the data for those countries. The OECD can then use their data and research to advise governments across the world about what they should do or what policies they should introduce. The OECD's aim is to 'help governments foster prosperity and fight poverty through economic growth and financial stability' (OECD, 2017a).

Therefore, a piece of research can be something that is quite large, or something that is rather small. However, whatever the size of the research, we can relate it to the OECD's definition, which is that research in ECEC refers to 'studies and analyses on any issues related to the early education and development environment of children in ECEC centres' (OECD, 2012a: 1). It is important to remember that, whatever the size and scale of the research and whoever the researcher is, it is possible for the same research topic to be considered. Take as an example the research topic of the enjoyment that boys and girls derive from reading. Ashcroft (2017) is a student teacher who has written up a piece of research that he conducted as part of his university studies in *The SteP* (Student Teacher Perspectives) *Journal* about his study that explored how boys and girls differed in their attitudes to reading. It was carried out with quite a small sample of participants; his data comprised of 25 questionnaires completed by Year Three children from two classes in the same primary school. He found that boys were less enthusiastic about reading, and spent less time doing it. In contrast to this small study, in 2009 over half a million 15-year-olds from 65 countries took part in the Programme for International Student Assessment (PISA), including over 4,000 children from England (Bradshaw et al., 2009; OECD, 2009). The PISA study is administered every three years and compares educational systems across the world by assessing 15-year-old children through an internationally-approved test. The 2009 PISA study found that the number of girls reading for enjoyment was much higher than the number of boys (OECD, 2011), matching Ashcroft's (2017) findings. This shows how the same research topic can be considered both on a large and on a small scale, and either in one context or worldwide. We will consider the PISA study more in Chapter 8 (Cross-national research approaches).

TIME TO CONSIDER

Consider any information you already know about early childhood and how you know that information. What would you like to know about children? If you had to carry out some research, what questions would you ask to find out new knowledge about children and their lives?

IN WHAT DIFFERENT WAYS IS RESEARCH CARRIED OUT?

Later in Chapter 5 (Approaches to research about children) and Chapter 6 (Approaches to research with children), we will consider in much more detail how types of research can be categorised and the similarities and differences between different approaches. However, for now we will begin to consider in brief the various ways in which research can be carried out; this will be built upon in the subsequent chapters of this book. For instance, in Chapter 10 (How research is designed), you will become more familiar with the idea that research is typically either *quantitative* or *qualitative*.

In brief, quantitative research is typified by collecting measurable data that can be interpreted in a numerical way (that is, information that can be quantified) to come up with a 'right answer' to a research question. Conversely, qualitative research focuses on collecting data relating to attitudes, views and opinions on a particular topic, which means that rather than propose a 'right answer' to a question, it is instead likely to give one possible answer that would answer the question. The approach that a researcher chooses depends on the type of answer they want to their question. Sometimes, they will want to answer their question using quantitative ways of collecting information, whilst at other times researchers may use qualitative methods to come to conclusions about the world. There is not a right or wrong way to answer a research question – people have different perspectives about the best way to get new knowledge, which is something else that we will consider in this book in Chapter 3 (Knowledge and truth in research).

As well as distinguishing between quantitative and qualitative research, we can also think about different types of *research design*. The OECD (2012a) say that there are five main ways that research is carried out in relation to ECEC. These are:

- Policy research
- Large-scale programme evaluations
- Longitudinal studies
- Comparative, cross-national research
- Neuroscience and brain research

These five types are good to consider as a starting point to think about the different ways in which organisations and individuals collect information relating to early childhood. They are also useful to consider how different types of research may have an impact on young children and their families. The first four, in particular, we will reflect upon briefly now and will consider in more detail later in this book. The fifth main way of doing research, neuroscience and brain research, is not the focus of this book, but you can find out more in the OECD's (2012a) *Research Brief: Research in ECEC Matters* report, which is suggested as further reading at the end of this chapter.

Policy research

Baldock et al. (2005: 3) suggest that policies are 'an attempt by those working inside an organisation to think in a coherent way about what it is trying to achieve (either in general or in relation to a specific issue) and what it needs to do to achieve it'. In relation to early childhood, early years policies focus on government practices or courses of action that impact on young children's lives. One example of policy research in England is the research that was carried out to investigate the impact of offering free school meals to all primary school pupils (DfE, 2013). In three areas of England, all primary school-aged children were given free school meals, as a trial to see what the effect would be on the children's take-up of free school meals, eating habits, health and well-being, attendance, behaviour and academic performance. Overall, the pilot study found that universal free school meals led to 'a significant positive impact on attainment for primary school pupils at Key Stages 1 and 2' (DfE, 2013: 8) and suggested that 'outcomes are improved only through the universal provision of free school meals' (DfE, 2013: 115). Following this piece of research, in September 2014 the Coalition government (2010–15) announced that universal free school meals would be introduced for all children in Reception and Key Stage 1 in England and Wales. It would be easy to assume from this that recommendations from research are always taken on board by governments and others who commission it to inform policy, but this is not always the case. This is because there may be financial barriers to implementing the suggestions, as well as new research being published that may offer alterative solutions. Despite the fact that the pilot study also found positive benefits for Key Stage 2 children, the Coalition government did not decide to provide free school meals to children above Key Stage 1. Also, at the time of writing (shortly after the 2017 UK General Election), it is uncertain whether the offer for free school meals to all Key Stage 1 children will continue. Instead, it has been proposed that free school dinners will return to a means-tested system and free breakfast will be provided to all children in Key Stage 1 or Key Stage 2 instead. This is in part as a result of a pilot project evaluated by the Education Endowment Foundation (2016) that found there were academic, social and behavioural benefits for primary-aged children attending a breakfast club.

Large-scale programme evaluations

These are investigations of a programme that is already in place, which examines how effective that initiative is. The OECD (2012a: 3) state that researchers conduct programme evaluations in order to determine the effectiveness of a programme, to question ways in which a programme may be improved, to examine the ways in which it is accountable, to explore the extent to which it provides value for money and also to investigate how useful facets of the programme are. Within England, one example of a programme evaluation is the Effective Provision of Pre-School Education (EPPE) Project (Sylva et al., 2010). In order to evaluate what makes effective early years education and care, this piece of research used different types of data collection, such as observations, questionnaires and interviews, to investigate what the characteristics are of effective early years provision, and what the lasting effects of preschool may be on children's development. We will consider the EPPE Project in more detail in Chapter 7 (Longitudinal research approaches).

Longitudinal studies

These are studies that carry out data collection on the same participants at intervals over a period of time. These can be really useful for tracking children's learning and development and exploring how the different factors that play a part in a child's life can lead to differences in children's outcomes. Within the UK, several longitudinal studies tracking children's lives have taken place. One of the most recent is the Millennium Cohort Study.

RESEARCH IN FOCUS

The Millennium Cohort Study

The Millennium Cohort Study is an ongoing study that is following approximately 19,000 children born in 2000–2001. It covers a whole range of topics, such as 'parenting; childcare; school choice; child behaviour and cognitive development; child and parental health; parents' employment and education; income and poverty; housing, neighbourhood and residential mobility; and social capital and ethnicity' (Institute of Education, 2015). By collecting information in this way, researchers are able to consider, for instance, the relationship between children's development and their home environments. For example, using data from the Millennium Cohort Study, Sabates and Dex (2012) looked at the links between children's exposure to risks at home (including risk factors such as domestic violence, parental worklessness, parental alcoholism, overcrowding and teenage parenthood) and children's cognitive and behavioural development when aged between three and five. They found that growing up in homes with two or more risk factors was likely to disadvantage children in terms of both their cognitive and behavioural development. Being exposed to two or more risk factors was associated with a smaller vocabulary, and was linked to a greater likelihood of behavioural concerns such as conduct problems and hyperactivity. Having an understanding of these links may lead to greater support or early intervention for children who are in these situations, to minimise the adverse effects of these risk factors. We will consider the Millennium Cohort Study in more detail in Chapter 7 (Longitudinal research approaches).

Comparative, cross-national research

This is research that is carried out in more than one country, which allows us to identify what the differences and similarities might be in the experiences of young children and the provision for them. Policymakers can use this information to identify successful strategies employed by other countries, which can inform the decisions that the policymakers might take. It can also be used to identify where international organisations may want to prioritise action or identify what their future international goals might be. For instance, later in this book we will look at the role of Unicef, a charity whose aim is to improve children's lives worldwide by reducing the extent to which children are affected by violence, disease, hunger, conflict and natural disasters. Every year Unicef produces a report called *State of the World's Children*, which looks at global and national statistics of children to show how outcomes and experiences for children change worldwide. In their 2015 report, they found that 'the poorest 20 per cent of the world's children are twice as likely as the richest 20 per cent to be stunted by poor nutrition and to die before their fifth birthday' (Unicef, 2015a: 4). Thus, comparative, cross-national research can help us to identify what strategies are being used in some countries to equip children with good levels of nutrition, and provide knowledge that might help other countries reduce their child mortality rates. This type of research will be the focus of Chapter 8 (Cross-national research approaches).

Overall, we can see that there are different ways in which information on children and childhoods is being collected, and different ways in which new knowledge is being created. This leads to developments in policy, provision and practices, and hopefully leads to benefits for young children and the experiences that they have.

TIME TO CONSIDER

Think about the different types of research that the OECD (2012a) outline. Each of them helps us to think about why research may be important for children. In what different ways are they suggesting it might be important to carry out research on the lives of young children and their families?

WHY IS RESEARCH IMPORTANT IN EARLY CHILDHOOD STUDIES?

Tisdall et al. (2009: 4) give several reasons why they think that research in Early Childhood Studies (ECS) is important. Firstly, they say that 'research might open up new possibilities for children, and society more generally' (2009: 4). Think about this for a moment. By doing research, more about children's lives can be identified so that the experiences that they have can be improved.

RESEARCH IN FOCUS

Informing staffing in ECEC provision

Recently Save the Children (2015) published a study that said that 'a fifth of all children in England, and close to a third of the poorest children, are unable to read well when they leave primary school' (Save the Children, 2015: iv). As a result of this research, they made a recommendation that the government should 'ensure an early years graduate leads early education in every nursery by 2020, prioritising those serving disadvantaged children' (Save the Children, 2015: 7). This may open up new possibilities and opportunities for children in early years settings; there is the potential that outcomes for children in early years settings may be improved if there is a graduate in every setting. In addition, it may increase employment opportunities for adults who are considering careers within early childhood settings too, if these recommendations are taken on board.

Secondly, through research, questions may be asked about the way that we do things (Tisdall et al., 2009). Carrying out research and reading research enables us to think more critically about the way things are done. For instance, since 1870 and the passing of the Elementary Education Act 1870, it has been compulsory for children in England and Wales to attend school from the age of five. We can consider this to be 'the way things are done', or 'common sense thinking', which we will consider in Chapter 3 (Knowledge and truth in research). But research findings that identify benefits of starting formal schooling at age four or five are non-existent, whilst there is lots of evidence that supports the idea that children need more play-based opportunities to support their learning and development (Whitebread and Jarvis, 2013). Doing research into children's lives helps us to question what happens to children, and whether that is the best thing for them.

Thirdly, Tisdall et al. (2009) say that research can raise issues that might not have otherwise been considered and suggest options that would otherwise not have been conceived. In 2009, Tompsett et al. (2009) carried out research to find out what difficulties or conflicts of interest GPs may face when they have both parents and their children as patients, and have safeguarding or welfare concerns about the children (Tompsett et al., 2009). An unexpected finding was that GPs did not often refer to the views of their child patients. The researchers suggest 'more work is needed to improve communication and their involvement in decisions' (2009: 5) so that GPs are more likely to listen to children's feelings and wishes when making decisions about them.

Research can also offer the opportunity for representation, so that 'children's views and experiences are not only listened to but heard by other groups' (Tisdall et al., 2009: 5). Feeding their perspectives forward, through dissemination, can help bring about changes in both policy and society. Linked to this, Smith (2011: 17) suggests that research that aims to improve children's well-being needs to be given priority. She cites Dobbs et al. (2006), who conducted research to explore what 80 children in New Zealand thought about family discipline, including their experiences of physical punishment and what they thought was appropriate. One of the findings of the study was that the majority of participants (all aged between four and 15) did not think it was appropriate to use physical punishment as a form of discipline. Dobbs et al. (2006) argue it is important that notice is paid to children's perspectives on matters that concern them. We could argue in addition that the publication of their research allows their views to be heard by a wider number of people; this could change attitudes in relation to sensitive areas like using corporal punishment on children. Research that aims to consider children's perspectives is something that you will consider more in Chapter 6 (Approaches to research with children).

Many others, in addition to Tisdall et al. (2009), confirm the importance of research in early childhood education and care. The OECD (2012a) also give three main reasons why it is important this type of research takes place. Firstly, they suggest that if we evaluate ECEC programmes, then this may lead to improvements in provision, and also a greater degree of accountability of the programmes that are being delivered. They also believe that if more pieces of research are carried out then there would be more evidence to suggest the value of positive early childhood experiences. This could mean ECEC programmes attract a greater amount of investment from governments and justify why financial support is necessary. Finally, they believe that through research, the practices that take place within early years settings may improve, as they become based on what the evidence suggests gives the best outcomes for young children.

TIME TO CONSIDER

Think about the reasons given by Tisdall et al. (2009) and by the OECD (2012a) about why it is important that research on and with children and their families takes place. What links can you make between these? Which reasons do you think are the most important? Why else do you personally think that research in early childhood is important?

CASE STUDY

Rebecca: an early years practitioner in a baby room

Rebecca works in a baby room in a nursery. She is also currently working towards her Foundation Degree in Early Childhood Education and Care. She is not the room leader but she is a key person for some of the babies; she uses the Early Years Foundation Stage (DfE, 2017a) to ensure that she is providing the babies with an enabling environment and forming positive relationships with them. She is curious to know how research has had an impact on what happens in practice in the setting. She thinks about what happens on a day-to-day basis in the nursery, what is considered to be 'good quality' and what rules and regulations are in place. She considers how they might have been based on research that has been carried out.

Firstly, she considers her role as a key person. The Statutory Framework for the Early Years Foundation Stage (DfE, 2017a) states that every child must be assigned a key person – a person for that child to build a firm bond with, who ensures that the child has their individual needs met and works with the child's family to promote their learning and development at home. She looks at where the thinking has come from that children need a key person. The key person system was coined by Goldschmied and Jackson (2004: 25) as a way of acknowledging that children need to form special relationships with individuals, just as most adults would like 'a special relationship with some person on whom we can rely, a relationship which is significant and precious to us'. In 2001, the key person approach became a statutory part of 14 national standards for full day care for under-eights (DfES, 2001) and has remained a statutory part of early years provision ever since. Rebecca looks at the evidence provided by Tickell (2011a) to support her review of the Early Years Foundation Stage curriculum (Tickell, 2011b), in which it states that the key person approach is beneficial for building positive relationships between practitioners and parents. To justify the importance of using the key person approach in early years settings, Tickell (2011a) says that evidence around attachment theory shows why having a key person approach is important to ensure young children's security, and cites research that states that practitioners recognise how a child's key person can be a valuable support for their key children. Rebecca uses this information to develop her understanding of why the key person approach is a part of the EYFS, and reflects upon how her role as a key person has been informed by research.

Then, she considers the staff–child ratio within the baby room. Her setting, like all early years providers, follows the Department for Education's Statutory Framework for the Early Years Foundation Stage, which says that for every three children aged under two there must be at least one member of staff (DfE, 2017a). If Rebecca was working with two-year-olds, this ratio would increase to one member of staff for every four children, and (as a Level 3 practitioner) if Rebecca was working with children aged three or above, she could be responsible for eight children. She looks for research that justifies the adult–child ratio for children under two. Melhuish et al. (2015) suggest that although there is some evidence to link ratios and group sizes with children's outcomes, not all studies find that there is a link between a higher adult–child ratio and better outcomes for children. In contrast to this, the OECD (2012b) suggest that high staff–child ratios, alongside small group sizes, typically lead to better outcomes in children's learning and development, as well as promoting better working conditions for early years practitioners. However, Melhuish et al. (2015) do state that a ratio of 1:3 for under twos is recommended relatively consistently by researchers. This could explain why this is the ratio that is currently statutory in early years settings in England.

Finally, Rebecca considers the Foundation Degree she is currently studying, towards which her Local Authority is contributing funding. She looks at some of the findings from the Effective Provision of Pre-School Education (EPPE) Project (Sylva et al., 2010). This piece of research found that there was a link between the quality of early years settings and the level of qualification that staff in those settings had. Where early years practitioners had higher levels of qualifications, children had better outcomes because staff in those settings took more opportunities to engage children in 'intellectual challenges' and were most effective in how they communicated and interacted with children to develop their thinking skills (Sylva et al., 2003). As a result, Taggart et al. (2015) argue that since 2006 EPPE has been cited to justify developing the skill level of people working with young children. For instance it was referred to within the Nutbrown Review (2012), where Nutbrown highlights findings from the EPPE Project to show the importance of qualifications in the early years. The study was also used within the DfE's (2011: 11) Early Years Evidence Pack to illustrate that 'qualifications are a driver of quality', due to findings that when early years settings had trained teachers, by the age of five the children in those settings made better progress in their pre-reading and in their social development.

TIME TO CONSIDER

Think about what you know about early years provision for toddlers and young children. In what ways do you think that practice has been shaped by research that has been carried out in toddler and preschool rooms in early years settings?

FINAL REFLECTION

There are many different ways that research can be defined and many different ways that research can be carried out in relation to young children. In this chapter we have started to think about what these different ways may be. We have also begun to consider the reasons why it is important to conduct research in early childhood, and through Rebecca's case study, we have thought about how research impacts on the day-to-day lives of young children who attend early childhood settings, as well as those who work in them.

KEY POINTS

- Research in relation to early childhood is about how we ask questions about children and their lives and then answer those questions by collecting and making sense of data. This leads us to discover new knowledge, opinions, perspectives and understanding.
- Research is carried out in a variety of ways, using a variety of different methods of data collection. Some of these focus on collecting data that can be quantified and presented in a numerical way (*quantitative* data). Some of these focus on data that can't be quantified and instead are more likely to present information that can be described using words, that often relates to attitudes, views and opinions (*qualitative* data). Some pieces of research combine both types, using a mixed-methods approach.
- Some of the most common ways that research is carried out in relation to early childhood is through policy research, large-scale programme evaluations, longitudinal studies, comparative, cross-national research and neuroscience and brain research (OECD, 2012a).
- Research is important for a variety of different reasons, including because it allows us to think critically and question decisions that are currently made. It can lead us towards important information that we might not have considered and (perhaps most importantly) it may bring about new possibilities and thus better outcomes and life chances for children and their families.

FURTHER READING

Organisation for Economic Co-operation and Development (OECD) (2012) *Research Brief: Research in ECEC Matters.* Available at: www.oecd.org/education/school/49322250.pdf (accessed 2 January 2018).

This short report from OECD is a brilliant document that introduces the role that research plays in relation to early childhood education and care. It includes information about neuroscientific research in relation to young children.

Melhuish, E., Ereky-Stevens, K., Petrogiannis, K., Ariescu, A., Penderi, E., Rentzou, K., Tawell, A., Leseman, P. and Broekhuizen, M. (2015) *A Review of Research on the Effects of Early Childhood Education and Care (ECEC) on Child Development.* Available at: http://ecec-care.org/fileadmin/careproject/Publications/reports/new_version_CARE_WP4_D4_1_Review_on_the_effects_of_ECEC.pdf (accessed 2 January 2018).

This very comprehensive report reviews pieces of research that have looked at the impact of early years provision on children's development. You will find this report a useful introduction to the breadth of research that focuses on links between children's development and their early childhood settings.

2 BEGINNING TO THINK CRITICALLY ABOUT RESEARCH

INTRODUCTION

Having developed an understanding of what research is, let's now look at whether it can always be trusted.

This chapter will ...

- Support you in approaching sources of information with a critical eye and looking at issues from a range of perspectives.
- Consider why it is important to think critically and introduce one strategy that can help us do this.
- Identify several markers of quality that you can use to analyse pieces of research, such as their resonance, their truthfulness and integrity, the timeliness of their information, style, the provenance of the author and the relevance of the information presented.
- Look at some good and 'not so good' examples of pieces of research so that you can begin to evaluate them with your emerging critical eye.

HOW CAN WE BEGIN TO THINK CRITICALLY?

When students begin university, they often think that whilst studying they are going to be given a lot of answers. In reality, the opposite is true. Studying at university is more likely to give you more questions than answers, because through studying you are going to be introduced to lots of new pieces of information, which will naturally encourage you to think more about the world and perhaps question what you believe to be true. Questioning what you believe to be true is one way of *critical thinking*. Critical thinking is, essentially, the art of not taking what you read, watch or hear at face value. Often, students feel confident in thinking critically when presented with information that has come from peers whom they know are likely to exaggerate. For instance, when their peers make claims about how many hours they have spent in the library, they can effectively question whether what they are hearing is really true. However, they sometimes feel less comfortable doing the same thing when reading newspapers, academic texts or watching documentaries. It is important to evaluate sources of information, as otherwise it might be hard to decide which pieces of evidence are worth including in your assignment and which pieces you cannot trust. It is vital to understand that not all pieces of evidence are reliable. For instance, if you have a social media account, you might have seen that often people share stories which, upon a quick read, you realise are satire, hoax stories or 'fake news' (Berkowitz and Schwartz, 2016). Just as you question the information that you choose to believe on Facebook, it is also good to think critically about the sources of information that you reference and refer to in your academic work.

When we are reading academic pieces of information, it can be harder than when on social media to work out which information we need to take with a pinch of salt. This is why it is important to think in a critical way about everything we come across. Otherwise, we might be presented with misleading information and accept it as true. For instance, Ecker et al. (2014) refer to a newspaper headline published in 2011 in the UK's *Daily Express* which stated 'Air pollution now leading cause of lung cancer' (Rawle, 2013). If you were to take this information at face value, you would accept (although it might surprise you) the fact that somebody is more likely to develop lung cancer as a result of air pollution than, for instance, as a result of smoking, because that is what the headline suggests. However, within the main body of the article, it is actually stated that air pollution has been categorised as a 'leading environmental cause of cancer deaths' (Rawle, 2013). This means that although air pollution may be a main cause from an environmental perspective, that is different from being the leading cause of all instances of lung cancer when other risk factors – like smoking or being exposed to second-hand smoke – are taken into account. Ecker et al. (2014) suggest that the headline provides an inaccurate summary of the article, and uses it as an example of where a newspaper headline might be misleading. Thus, it is important when you approach a piece of information that you identify the things that you might assume on first glance are true and then question whether that really is the case.

Identifying assumptions that frame our thinking is the first of four steps that Brookfield (2015) uses to describe the process of thinking critically. He talks about thinking critically not in relation to reading newspapers, but instead in relation to how students engage with social media. For instance, he describes a *paradigmatic assumption* that texting using mobiles phones means that students' ability to spell correctly has diminished. Brookfield defines a *paradigmatic* assumption as one that we use to put the world into categories, and often we do not even realise that they are just assumptions, rather than a true fact. He also suggests that some people hold *prescriptive* assumptions, which focus on what people assume ought to happen. For instance, in relation to his paradigmatic assumption about texting, it could be thought that students ought to be discouraged from sending text messages and instead write out their thoughts on paper.

Secondly, he states, it is necessary to examine the extent to which the assumptions are accurate. For instance, it might be the case that some of the information is true, just not all of it. Or, it might be the case that the information has been exaggerated or distorted in some other way. Thirdly, he suggests the need to consider what our assumptions might be if we adopt a different perspective, so that finally we are led towards 'taking informed actions' (Brookfield, 2015: 48), which might be adopting a different point of view to the assumption we were originally drawn to. If we follow these four stages, then we will be led away from immediately taking information as gospel and away from regarding things as true that might need to be questioned.

Table 2.1 Brookfield's four processes for thinking critically

1. Identifying the assumptions that frame our thinking and determine our actions
2. Checking out the degree to which these assumptions are accurate and valid
3. Looking at our ideas and decisions (intellectual, organisational and personal) from several different perspectives
4. On the basis of all this, taking informed actions

Source: Brookfield, 2015: 48

TIME TO CONSIDER

Let us follow Brookfield's four steps, as outlined in Table 2.1, when reading a newspaper headline that relates to research with young babies. A headline was published in *The Sun* in 2011 (with headlines of a similar vein published in other tabloid newspapers) that stated 'Breast is not best' (Morton, 2011). Let's start by thinking about what assumptions we might draw from this headline. You might assume that research has been conducted that has found that breastfeeding is not as effective as bottle-feeding for babies. Now, let's consider the extent to which this headline is accurate and valid. It reported findings from a study published in a peer-reviewed journal by Fewtrell et al. (2011), that reviewed the evidence around breast-feeding exclusively until the age of six months ('exclusively' meaning that the baby received no formula milk and had not begun weaning). It found that there are some concerns with breastfeeding exclusively until six months, for instance due to a higher likelihood of iron deficiency anaemia, food allergies and coeliac disease. However, the researchers do not propose that babies should not be breastfed – they are just suggesting that other research indicates that there may be health implications for children if they are solely breastfed up until the age of six months. They argue that further research needs to be conducted to consider whether the Department of Health needs to change their recommendations around babies' nutrition. Thus, in relation to Brookfield's (2015) second step, a closer examination of the original

(Continued)

(Continued)

source that *The Sun* are referring to reveals it seems that there are limitations in the extent to which the headline is accurate. It might be considered that Morton (2011) has in fact made a prescriptive assumption that babies ought not be breastfed, because of the evidence that Fewtrell et al. (2011) present.

For step three, Brookfield (2015) suggests that we need to consider other ideas from different perspectives. For instance, the same research article was reported by BBC News (2011) with the headline 'Weaning before six months "may help breastfed babies"' and in *The Guardian* with 'Six months of breastmilk alone is too long and could harm babies, scientists now say' (Boseley, 2011). These headlines appear to portray the findings of Fewtrell et al.'s (2011) article in a more accurate manner. We may also wish to consult other sources for their perspective of the issue. The World Health Organisation (2015) suggests that 'infants should be exclusively breastfed – i.e. receive only breast milk – for the first six months of life to achieve optimal growth, development and health', which seems opposed to some of the findings that Fewtrell et al. (2015) present. We may also consider other academic responses to the article, such as from the Scientific Advisory Committee on Nutrition (SACN) (Williams and Prentice, 2011). They wrote a response to Fewtrell et al.'s (2011) article in the same academic journal, which disputed some of the claims that the original authors had made about how SACN has previously worked with the government about providing information about breastfeeding.

Finally, according to Brookfield's (2015) four processes of critical thinking, we are now in a position to take informed actions. Our first informed action might be that we cannot take for granted *The Sun's* headline that 'Breast is not Best'. You might have already held a paradigmatic assumption that we can't trust tabloid newspaper headlines, and not be surprised by that. However, to other people it might come as a shock that it is best to avoid basing your academic knowledge and assignments on newspaper sources. But it does not end there. Our second informed action might be that we cannot assume that information in peer-reviewed journals is accurate, as we know that the Scientific Advisory Committee on Nutrition (SACN) dispute what Fewtrell et al. (2011) suggest. That is just one example of why it is important to think critically about the material you come across, so that you challenge the assumptions that you might make on your first glance of accessing materials.

TIME TO CONSIDER

Have a look at an online version of a daily newspaper to find an article that relates to a report or piece of research that has been written about children or families. What assumptions might we be drawn towards when reading the newspaper article? Now, try to search online for the original piece of research or report that the newspaper journalists have read to inform their piece – they will often tell you the original piece of information that they are referring to, or include a hyperlink to it. What are the differences and similarities between how the information has been presented in the newspaper article and in the original report? To what extent do you think that the newspaper article is an accurate interpretation of the information? What assumptions might we come to about the topic now?

WHAT MARKERS OF QUALITY CAN WE USE TO HELP US THINK CRITICALLY?

Another way that we can think critically when information is presented to us is to consider markers of quality of pieces of information. In this section, you will consider how we can analyse a source's resonance, truthfulness and integrity, timeliness, style and relevance, as well as the provenance of the author, to help us think critically about it. Using these markers of quality is important for three main reasons. Taking them into account will help you decide whether a source is worth reading and thus worth referring to in your own academic work. Plus, if you have decided after looking at the source's markers of quality that it is worthy of using as evidence in your piece of work, then it will help strengthen your argument if your reader can see that the literature you are using to support your points is strong and credible. Also, in academic assignments it can be good to show critical analysis, and referring to markers of quality to highlight the potential strengths or limitations of a piece of evidence can be one way to do this.

As a starting point, we can think about key terms that we can use to describe a piece of information, which might help us to decide whether it is information worth reading or referring to. Think about what terms we might use to describe sources of information we think might be appropriate to use in an academic context. We might start off with words like objective, reliable, understandable, comprehensive, up-to-date and accurate. We might avoid using sources of information that we think are complicated, simplistic, biased, misleading or dated. Next, we can think about where we are most likely to find sources of information that fulfil those qualities. In terms of types of information, we might think about material either being 'scholarly' or 'popular', or somewhere in the middle. Scholarly sources of information are those aimed at researchers, students or academics, which often provide evidence to support their points, are written by people with expertise in the field, use academic language and often look at a topic in a high level of depth. We might consider peer-reviewed journal articles to be scholarly sources, as well as academic books and research reports. In contrast to these, popular sources of information are aimed at the general population, and thus might not be as in-depth, are less likely to have explicit evidence to back up their points and more likely to be written by people who don't have expertise in that area. Examples of more popular sources are blog posts, websites and newspaper articles. The academic nature of a university degree means that students should be tailoring their reading to scholarly, rather than popular, sources, as those are the ones that are more likely to be described by words like objective, reliable, understandable, comprehensive, up-to-date and accurate. However, we cannot assume that a source that we believe is scholarly, like a peer-reviewed journal article, is necessarily going to be worth reading, so we need to consider other markers of quality too.

Resonance

The word *resonance* can be difficult to interpret or link to the concept of thinking critically about sources of information. Traditionally the verb 'to resonate' relates to something making a sound. When we link this to research, we can think about it in relation to two aspects. You can consider how a piece of research has resonated with you as a reader – how does it sound? Does it strike a chord? Does it ring a bell? If you can connect it with something that you already know, or with your own experiences, then that might indicate that you already know other pieces of research, literature or theories that support it, which could be an indicator of the quality of the source. However, we need to be aware that we may have a subconscious bias towards information that resonates with us, because, as Goldacre (2009: 248) states not only do we 'overvalue confirmatory information for any given hypothesis', but we are also more likely to seek it out. We can also think about how a piece of research has had an impact on other research – how it has 'resonated' in the field with other authors. One way that we can do this is to evaluate the extent to which other people have cited the piece of research in their work. Software like Google Scholar tallies the number of times that a piece of research has been cited, which might indicate its resonance in the field. The larger number of times something has been referred to in other texts, we could argue the more that it resonates with other authors. Be wary, however, that the newer a piece of research is, the less time there has been for others to read it and to cite it, so resonance alone should not be taken as a marker of quality.

RESONANCE CHECKLIST

- Does it resonate with you, as the reader, and further your own knowledge?
- Have other academics and authors responded to it positively?
- How often does it appear to be cited by others?
- Don't forget: Approach sources in an unbiased way. A piece of research can be useful, even if you don't agree with it.

Truthfulness and integrity

As we will come to consider in Chapter 3 (Knowledge and truth in research), 'truth' is a tricky term to get your head around. 'Integrity' might be slightly easier – we might also consider it to mean 'accuracy' or 'reliability'. To consider the integrity of a source, it is important to consider whether it is being objective or not. An objective source is one that presents all sides of an argument in a balanced way. It is based on facts, rather than opinions. Subjective information is the analysis of facts and is often opinion. It is based on the viewpoint from which the author sees the world. We know that marketing materials and news articles might be influenced by a particular view. For instance, newspapers are considered to either lean towards the left or the right politically. This influences the way that they report stories, particularly stories relating to government decisions or policy. A 2017 YouGov UK survey found that, in the UK, *The Guardian* is perceived by the public as the most left-wing newspaper, whilst the *Daily Mail* is perceived as the most right-wing (Smith, 2017).

Peer-reviewed journal articles might also be influenced by a particular view. They might be scientifically accurate but be biased because of how they fall within a particular discipline. A press release might also be accurate, but not as objective as if the same information was presented by a neutral third party. But think – what information truly is objective? Being subjective does not make information invalid, it just means you need to pay close attention to its purpose and intended audience. It might be the case that a piece of evidence appears 'balanced', but we need to be aware of hidden agendas and emotive language. We might also want to be aware of whether the information has been written or sponsored by someone who has a vested interest, and thus has a stake in 'selling' a particular point of view. For instance, a charity may be subjective in which findings it chooses to emphasise, because it wants to influence government policy. It may be more likely to use emotive language, referring to 'shocking', 'upsetting' or 'heart-breaking' statistics, in an attempt to elicit donations from the public.

One way to think about the distinction between a piece of information that is subjective in comparison to a piece of information that is objective is in the difference between a CV that you might give to a potential employer and the reference that a potential employer might request from your referee. Your CV is likely to be subjective because you have a vested interest in getting a job, which means you might carefully choose what you are telling them and how you present it, and (more importantly) what you are not telling them. By contrast, a reference is more likely to be based on factual information like the dates of your employment, the number of days you have been absent and any disciplinary warnings you may have received.

TRUTHFULNESS AND INTEGRITY CHECKLIST

- Is information presented in an objective way?
- Does the author have a vested interest in presenting a particular point of view?
- What is the purpose of the source?
- Who are the intended audience of the piece of information?

Timeliness of the information

Another crucial element we need to look at in order to assess the quality of a piece of information is its timeliness. It is important to look at the dates of pieces of research so that we can appreciate whether the political climate has changed since it was written – for instance questioning which government was in power at the time of writing, especially if the piece of research refers to legislation and policy. It might be a limitation of the piece of research if a policy or law has changed between the article being published and you reading it. Sometimes it can be hard to find the date of Internet sources. Think – if you cannot identify how old a source is, do you think you should be referring to it in your academic work? Aim to find another piece of information that does have a date. For PDF documents, sometimes if you look at the 'Properties' of the document, it will tell you the date there. And remember, even information that is not particularly old might be out of date, if new research or statistics have been published in the meantime.

TIMELINESS OF THE INFORMATION CHECKLIST

- How old is the piece of information?
- Has relevant context (e.g. policy and legislation) changed since it was written?
- Don't forget: Always try to cite information that has a date of publication.

Style

Looking at a source to see if it is presented well and whether it looks professional can be a good first clue as to whether we should consider using it. However, remember the saying 'Don't judge a book by its cover'. Even if a source is presented well, that does not mean for certain that the information contained within it is accurate, reliable or relevant. Sometimes a source might have information that is incorrect or misleading, even if that source is presented well with clear information and appropriate language. This does not just go for written sources of information, the same is true for documentaries too. For instance, there is a well-respected BBC current affairs programme called *Panorama*, which features investigative reports and pieces of research carried out by BBC journalists. In 1957 *Panorama* did an April Fools episode, in which esteemed journalist Richard Dimbleby presented a piece about spaghetti farms and the annual 'spaghetti harvest' (BBC News, 2008). As in the 1950s not that many people were familiar with eating spaghetti, this fooled lots of people. Even though the documentary was presented well, it wasn't presenting information that was correct!

STYLE CHECKLIST

- Does the information look professionally presented?
- Can you see any spelling or grammar mistakes?
- Is it using appropriate language?

Provenance of the author

Finding out about the credentials of the author of a source can help you to identify the quality and worth of it. Moore et al. (2010: 60) presents 'three cascading areas of inquiry' to help us identify what are the best sources of information to be using. The first of these areas is the expertise (that is, provenance) of the author. They suggest that once we know who has written the piece of research, we can find out whether the author is considered an expert in their field and what else they have written. Often within peer-reviewed journal articles there will be a brief biography about the author or authors. This may also help you to identify whether they are writing from a particular perspective. We know that the field of Early Childhood Studies is informed by a range of disciplines, including education, health, psychology and sociology. Kehily (2009: 7) considers how different disciplines use different methods to study children and childhoods. For instance, she suggests that whilst both sociology and psychology have had a great impact on our understanding of childhood, those looking at children from a psychological perspective may be more likely to study the child as an individual, whereas sociologists are more interested in children as part of a social group.

Another means to assess provenance is to find out who else has referred to an author – again, you can use Google Scholar to identify who has cited a piece of research – and also what other things an author has published. It is important to consider how something has been published – if it is a peer-reviewed journal article then this means other academics have decided that the article is suitable to be published in the journal, like an extra verification check. On the other hand, anybody can create a website, so it is much harder to authenticate whether something you read on a website is true, particularly for entries on websites like Wikipedia, which anybody is able to edit.

PROVENANCE OF THE AUTHOR CHECKLIST

- Is the author well known in their field?
- What is the author's discipline? How might that impact on the perspective they take?
- Can you find other things that they have published?
- Who else has cited their sources of information?
- Don't forget: Looking at where the information was published can act as an extra verification check.

Relevance of the information presented

If you have decided that what you are reading is presented well, the information is timely and you believe the author has provenance, but if it is not relevant to the area you are wishing to explore, then you might as well stop reading. Think about whether the text is connected to your area of interest and whether it meets your need for information.

Guidance from the University of Leeds (2015) offers three points for consideration that might help us to weigh up the relevance of a source of information. First, a reader should think about the level of the information that is presented, to ensure that it is not too simplistic or too detailed for the reader's needs. Also, you need to consider the emphasis of a piece of information. For instance, you might be interested in exploring child poverty in the UK, so an article on poverty generally in the UK might not meet your needs. The third criterion the University of Leeds guidance (2015) mentions with regards to relevance is geographic location. If you are reading research that has come from another country or area, it might not be relevant for you to read. For instance, if you are interested in what happens when children start school in the UK, reading a study conducted in Germany or France might not be relevant to you.

RELEVANCE OF THE INFORMATION PRESENTED CHECKLIST

- Is the information presented in a sufficient level of detail?
- Does the source have an appropriate emphasis on the topic you are exploring?
- Where was the information published, or the research conducted? Remember: the geographic location could be a limitation of the source if it does not reflect the context you are writing about.

TIME TO CONSIDER

Choose a topic relating to early childhood that interests you. It could be something like child poverty, promoting reading, children's mental health or the commercialisation of childhoods. Find a source of information about the topic from (a) a newspaper article, (b) a peer-reviewed journal article and (c) a charity report or government report. How could you critique these three sources in line with the markers of quality outlined above? Remember, 'to critique' doesn't mean 'to criticise', but rather to evaluate the pros and cons of something. Drawing up a table like that in Table 2.2 might help you:

Table 2.2 Using markers of quality to critique a source of information

Source Reference:	
Marker of Quality	**Critique**
Resonance	
Truthfulness and integrity	
Timeliness of the information	
Style	
Provenance of the author	
Relevance of the information presented	

DEMONSTRATING YOUR CRITICAL THINKING

It is very important to use markers of quality to decide whether to read and refer to pieces of research in your work, but it is also very important that you show in your writing that you are thinking critically about the sources of information that you are using. In your university assignments, you want to show that you do not take what you read at face value, or take it as gospel. Think about how in your academic work you can refer to the markers of good quality that you have identified in a source, to show to your reader that they can trust the information you are using as evidence for the points that you are making. Similarly, do not be afraid to tell your reader what the markers of poor quality of a source might be, so that you show an awareness of the limitations of knowledge. For instance, this might be when you think that a piece of research is slightly dated or where the study needs to be considered in relation to its geographic relevance. In these cases, if you can find another piece of evidence, which was written more recently or is more geographically relevant for your context, which makes a comparable point or has similar findings, take opportunities to make links between the sources of information.

RESEARCH IN FOCUS

Television advertising food products to children

In 2008, Batada et al. (2008) found in their study of Saturday morning television broadcast in Washington, DC, in the USA, that 49% of the advertisements were for food, and 91% of those food advertisements were for food that was high in fat, added sugars or sodium (HFSS) or had low nutritional value. You might think that this was significant and could have implications for children's health. Yet, Batada et al.'s (2008) study is now quite dated and relates to television programming in the USA – we cannot assume that children in other areas of the world will be watching as many unhealthy food advertisements. However, a similar study was conducted in the UK that examined the content of 18,888 advertisements which were broadcast on the most popular 14 television channels for children and family viewing. The researchers found that only 12.8% of the advertisements were for food, although 'the majority of food advertisements on UK television channels popular with children in 2008 were for energy-dense, HFSS foods' (Boyland et al., 2011: 459). Thus, even though Batada et al.'s (2008) study lacks geographic relevance for a reader interested in children's experiences outside of the USA, similar findings about children's access to unhealthy food advertisements have been found elsewhere, and more recently, for instance in Boyland et al.'s (2011) piece of research.

TIME TO CONSIDER

Go back to the three sources of information that you critiqued in relation to their markers of quality. Think about how you could draw attention to how you have questioned what you have read within your academic work. Good ways to start sentences might include:

- A strength of this study is ... because ...
- One limitation of this study, however, is ...
- A weakness of this piece of research is ... because ...
- The findings of this study are supported by ...
- These findings are consistent with ...
- These findings are refuted by ...

CASE STUDY

Nick: a primary school teacher

Nick has been asked by his head teacher to deliver a Brain Gym® session every morning before lessons begin. He knows a little about the programme, which is based on the idea that there are particular physical movements that stimulate brain activity and can lead to benefits in terms of areas like concentration, memory and academic attainment. Essentially, his head teacher wants him to spend some time getting his pupils to do something like a mini-workout, to help their brains make connections. However, Nick doesn't want to take at face value that Brain Gym® will be effective for young learners – he wants to think critically about the evidence surrounding it.

He looks at the Brain Gym® website (Educational Kinesiology Foundation, 2016). He finds that the website is well presented, but he struggles to find any links to pieces of academic research that show evidence of a link between the programme's movements and its benefits on the website. He does, however, find some testimonials from parents and professionals about how Brain Gym® techniques have had a positive impact academically, socially, physically and professionally. However, he knows that the information that the website choses to publish is likely to be subjective, because the programme is a commercial venture and the website owners may have a vested interest in selling products and workshops.

Then he investigates whether any peer-reviewed journal articles have been published about Brain Gym®. He finds two in particular that look useful, by Hyatt (2007) and Spaulding et al. (2010). Both are published by academics working at universities in the USA within the field of education. Both include extensive links to literature about the theoretical foundations that Brain Gym® claims to be based on. Both find that there are many pieces of evidence that appear to contradict the assertions that the programme makes. They both then critique the same four pieces of research that appear to find the programme effective, but highlight flaws in how the studies were conducted and the details given when the studies were written up. Hyatt (2007: 112) says that this means that the studies fail to support the Brain Gym®'s assertions and Spaulding et al. (2010) concludes that there is no empirical (that is, verifiable) data to support the claims that Brain Gym® are making.

Hyatt (2007: 123) argues that teachers need to critically review programmes that they might be considering implementing in their classrooms, so that they select programmes that have sound evidence to support them. This is echoed by Spaulding et al. (2010: 28), who suggest that both educators and parents must become 'critical consumers' of programmes like Brain Gym® by looking at the research that supports programmes, because there are other interventions that do have high-quality evidence to support them. Nick decides to set out to investigate other programmes instead, to see whether he can find an alternative programme that is supported by research, which he can then suggest to his head teacher.

FINAL REFLECTION

There are many reasons why it is important to think critically about pieces of research and many ways that we can do this. In this chapter, you have thought about what these ways might be and how you can go about showing that you are thinking critically in your academic writing. Through Nick's case study, we have also thought about the important implications of not taking given information at face value.

KEY POINTS

- It is important that you think critically about the sources of information that you read and refer to. This is something you might do more naturally in non-academic contexts, but you need to get into the habit of doing it in relation to everything you hear, read or see. Doing this will help you to identify and question assumptions that are made in pieces of information, or that you might hold yourself.
- You can use a variety of markers of quality to help you to think critically. These include looking at the resonance, truthfulness, timeliness, style and relevance of a source, as well as the provenance of the author.
- It is also important that you take opportunities to show that you are thinking critically in your academic work by noting markers of poor or good quality, so that your reader knows that you are not taking what you read at face value.

FURTHER READING

Bennett, T. (2013) *Teacher Proof.* Abingdon: Routledge.

A very interesting and accessible book that introduces why teachers need to think critically about the research that is presented to them as evidence for why they need to educate children using certain techniques.

Goldacre, B. (2009) *Bad Science.* London: HarperCollins.

Goldacre critiques and shares examples of the limitations of popular scientific beliefs, pieces of research and programmes, including, in particular, interesting chapters on Brain Gym® and the research linking MMR vaccinations with a diagnosis of autism.

3

KNOWLEDGE AND TRUTH IN RESEARCH

INTRODUCTION

Knowledge and truth are complex concepts.
This chapter will ...

- Develop your understanding of what knowledge is, how it is constructed and how its nature is subjective and never value-free.
- Ask you to reflect on how practitioners' definitions of truth will influence how they engage with research about young children and their families.

HOW DO WE KNOW WHAT IS TRUE?

In 2016 the Oxford Dictionaries word of the year was announced as being *post-truth*. It was defined as 'relating to or denoting circumstances in which objective facts are less influential in shaping public opinion than appeals to emotion and personal belief'. Some of us were surprised with this choice because we were still grappling with a definition of *truth* never mind its successor. Have you ever got into an argument with someone when you were both convinced that you were right and you both thought you knew the truth? In the 1980s there was a song whose chorus went '... This much is true ... I know this much is true', but how can we really know what is true especially if there are certain things we cannot agree on? We see a good example of this dilemma woven through the media every time there is an election or a referendum about an important issue. Have you voted and how did you decide who to vote for? How did you determine who was telling the truth? In this chapter, we will think about why truth is a difficult concept to unpick. We cannot really consider truth without also thinking about the parallel concept of knowledge and how we make constant decisions about which knowledge we can accept as the truth. We only have to consider the various historical truths below to see how knowledge is constantly evolving:

- In the 19th century a myth was circulated, which became subsequently embedded in modern consciousness, that in the middle ages explorers believed the earth was flat (Russell, 1997).
- The saying 'spare the rod and spoil the child' was used to justify the use of corporal punishment by parents wanting to raise 'considerate, law-abiding adults' (Eron, 1997: 309). Present day consensus however would suggest the opposite: that hitting children can encourage them to be violent themselves (BBC News, 2015).
- It was common practice at one time to put babies to sleep on their tummies. Now however we 'know' differently and put babies to sleep on their backs to keep them safe and healthy (The Lullaby Trust, 2017).

In 1946, Spock published the first edition of his *Common Sense Book of Baby and Child Care* to advise parents on the best way to look after and bring up their children. It has now been updated nine times and the common sense is continually changing and evolving concerning the best care for children. Some of his 'common sense' recommendations that have changed include:

- the benefit to young children two years and over of a vegan diet (7th edition, published in 1998)
- the danger of children choking on their own vomit if they are placed to sleep on their back (2nd edition, published in 1957)
- the benefits of circumcision for male babies (1st edition, published in 1946).

The two key concepts of knowledge and truth are closely entwined so it would be a useful exercise to unpick what we mean by these words and what others might mean by them. Let us first turn our attention to the idea of truth and how not having a shared understanding of what this means could be problematic for us as students and practitioners working with young children. Before we go any further, try to come up with your own definition of truth. Complete the following two sentences:

- 'Truth is ...'
- 'When I say something is true, I mean ...'

It would be good to do this with a peer so that you can compare your own personal definitions. Put these definitions to one side then you can come back to them at the end of the chapter. You may still agree with them at that point or you may want to modify them. In Table 3.1 you can see how various writers have defined truth. Do you agree with all of them? If there is one definition you prefer, consider why this might be.

Table 3.1 Some different definitions of truth

What is truth?
'Truth is defined as the accurate representation of an independently existing reality' (Smith and Hodkinson, 2008: 413).
'Absolute truth can never be found' (Creswell, 2014: 7).
'Truth, or meaning, comes into existence in and out of our engagement with the realities in our world' (Crotty, 1998: 8).
'Declaring something as a "truth" gives it authority and power. To see this truth as natural and neutral is to simply accept things as they are (MacNaughton, 2005) and leaves the power relations within that unchallenged' (Tayler and Price, 2016: 23).

You may be wondering what the purpose of this exercise is and why how we define truth matters. If we are telling you something is true then it is important to examine any power relationship between us. If we are your teacher, or a politician or claiming to be an expert in a certain area, then it could be very important for you to know what we mean by the word truth. A common phrase used by people nowadays is the idea of being 'economical with the truth'. Perhaps one place this is seen clearly is in children's school reports. If teacher A writes 'Ben is developing his ability to concentrate' teacher B knows that Ben cannot sit still for two minutes without disrupting the class. Teacher A may have told the truth but, by being 'economical' with it, they have not painted a truthful picture of Ben's behaviour in class for everyone, including his parents.

We can see from this that truth is a contested term. It is not a neutral word that is value-free and what we consider the truth may be very different to what you consider the truth. Let us return to our discussion of choosing how to vote in an election. Regardless of which candidate you are drawn to, it is hard to avoid thinking that election campaigns have become messy, and at times, nasty and highly personal competitions with each side accusing the other of non-truthful behaviours. What is very apparent is the conviction that many voters have; they are convinced that their candidate is the holder of the truth. There are highly complex influences on their thinking, which highlights the fact that our understanding of truth is influenced by the interaction of many different factors including our gender, social class, ethnic background, sexuality, where we live, our life experiences ... the list could go on and on. In this way we can return to Crotty's definition of truth in Table 3.1 and see here a clear example of how the supporters' understanding of truth is informed by their 'engagement with the realities in [their] world' (1998: 8).

Throughout the book we will be considering both key and minor pieces of research with a focus on young children so it is important that we have an understanding of the context of truth within which the researchers were working. We also need to know how they have arrived at the 'truths' revealed in their findings.

The illustration above demonstrates how, in an election, voters' own background influences their understanding of truth. The same can be argued for a researcher like Bowlby (1907–90), with his influential work on attachment theory and the repercussions of children being separated from their primary caregiver – in this context, the mother (Bowlby, 1952).

RESEARCH IN FOCUS

Bowlby and attachment theory

John Bowlby was a child psychiatrist who was interested in the impact of parent–child separation. He believed that a child's attachment to their primary caregiver had a biological basis and was crucial for optimal development. One of his research studies included a sample of 88 children who had been referred to the clinic where he worked; 44 of these had a referral for stealing. As part of the research, their parents were interviewed about events in the child's life as a baby. Bowlby found that more than half of this second group had been separated from their mother for longer than six months in the first years of their life. Bowlby's seminal work on the importance of a key attachment figure in a young child's life has greatly influenced early childhood practice. One example of this is the key person approach. At the time of its publication, however, his work was used to suggest that children needed a 'stay at home mother'. We have to be aware that Bowlby was working in the context of the post-World War II years when there was pressure for women to return to the home to free up employment for returning male troops. This may not have been Bowlby's personal belief (Bruce, 2011: 177) but it would have been difficult for him not to be influenced by the common discourse of that period in history. In addition to understanding how the historical context has affected the researcher's understanding of truth we also need to know what methods the researcher has used to arrive at the truth of their research. For example, Ainsworth's famous research on attachment theory (1964), the ethics of which will be explored elsewhere in Chapter 9 (The ethics of research), was based on the researcher's 'truth' that it was okay to cause children distress by separating them from their mother and placing them with a stranger as an experiment. It is only by questioning the 'truths' of these key pieces of research that we can make informed decisions as practitioners about how far they should impact on our practice.

We can see then that we could contest the idea that there is an ultimate truth and suggest that truth is something which is context-bound. However, just to confuse the issue even more, others would argue fiercely that of course there are certain things that must be true – such as whether the earth is flat or spherical. The important thing for us as students and practitioners, working with young children and families, is to be able to weigh up the mishmash of our reading and of our experiences so that we can come to a working definition of truth that will enable us to collaborate effectively with colleagues to impact on outcomes for young children.

TIME TO CONSIDER 

Think about all the different interconnecting factors that influence your thinking about what is true. Try to ask yourself the important 'So What?' question. How do these factors impact on your thinking? Use Table 3.2 to help you structure your thoughts; we have completed the first one for you.

Table 3.2 The different factors that impact on our understanding of truth and what that impact might be

Factor	So What?	Example
Gender	I may have been socialised into believing that men and women have different practices.	When Alice's car broke down, just as she was leaving for work one morning, she walked through the door of her first seminar of the day thinking 'I really wish there was a guy in this seminar so he could give me some advice on my car ...' She realised as soon as she thought it how ludicrous a thought it was!
Social class		
Ethnic background		
Sexuality		
Where you live		
Your life experiences		
Faith background		
Any other?		

HOW CAN WE DEFINE KNOWLEDGE?

We have already asked you to consider how you would define truth but what about the concept of knowledge? How would you define this idea? There is no denying that it is a difficult concept, so allow yourself to be baffled by the content of this section of the chapter – we really hope we are going to get you thinking! The most important thing is that you are having to think about the idea of knowledge at a deeper, not a taken-for-granted, level. Below are two statements that others have made about knowledge; take some time to read and reflect on their thoughts.

1. 'Effective learning is not just a matter of innate intelligence. We must not fall into what de Bono calls the "intelligence trap" (de Bono, 1992), and Boorstin (1985) calls "the illusion of knowledge", which is that the greatest obstacle to discovery lies in what people already believe they know or can do. They may become trapped in what they already know, and not open to new learning' (Fisher, 1998: 2).
2. 'Any idea or problem or body of knowledge can be presented in a form simple enough so that any particular learner can understand it in a recognisable form' (Bruner, 1968: 44).

Do any of these ideas resonate with you? You may be able to think of occasions when what you already thought you knew stopped you from learning more, as Fisher suggests (1998). This quotation always makes us think of children being placed in ability groups at primary school; those in the Eagle group just 'know' that they have more 'knowledge' than those in the Penguin group and vice versa.

Let us return now to Spock's idea of 'common sense' (1946). At times knowledge can be confused with common sense; how would you explain the difference between these two ideas? Let us look at the example of four-year-old Ben. He has just started school and is finding it difficult to sit and listen to the teacher at carpet time. 'Common sense' might say: 'He just needs to practise – the more he does it the better he will become. Perhaps he should have practised more in nursery so that he was ready for school', but 'knowledge' might cite: 'Sitting still may be the hardest physical action for them [a young child] to achieve' (Cooper and Harlow, 2018: 115). 'Knowledge' might add: 'He needs to be outside moving, jumping and climbing so that he can gain control over his movements and then he will be ready to perform this more difficult and complex physical task.' We can see a clear difference between knowledge and common sense in this specific context. Common sense is easily arrived at, does not take a lot of thought, is the easiest solution and perhaps, some would argue, intuitive. On the other hand, knowledge demonstrates a more expert understanding informed by reading, research and perhaps practical experience. It is also a product of having to think at a deeper level about problematic issues and perhaps recognise that we may be guilty of making the 'paradigmatic assumptions' (Brookfield, 2015) we talked about in Chapter 2 (Beginning to think critically about research). What a practitioner believes to be true about Ben will inform their practice and how they advise parents to support him in his learning and development; what a researcher of early childhood believes to be true about Ben will influence the way they carry out research on his development. It will also impact on what they choose to research. Our own personal values will shape what we hold as common sense, the value we give to the idea of common sense, and what we believe to be knowledge. Research writers will often use the term 'epistemology' to explore the idea of what is considered to be valid knowledge. For now, ponder on the three 'common sense' statements below:

- 'Little boys need male role models in the early years'
- 'The earlier children start school the more they will learn'
- 'Children need to live with a mother and father'

Some of these statements you may agree with whilst others you may vehemently reject. The important issue here is to understand why you have arrived at these decisions and how they highlight the values you hold. Dalrymple (2013: 47) argues that it is impossible to know what is true knowledge because people have been discussing this idea for more than 2,000 years. He states that it was originally Plato who raised this question and if there was a clear answer then surely we would have found it by now! He suggests then that this state of affairs could lead us to conclude that the answer is *relativism*.

The central idea behind relativism is that there is no absolute truth (*realism*) because all truth is relative. To help us understand this idea better we love to share this wonderful metaphor with students, which is offered by Braun and Clarke (2013: 28). They suggest we imagine we are looking through different kinds of windows to consider the different approaches to knowledge. Read the three descriptions and consider which best fits your own perspective on knowledge and truth:

Through the window 1

'*Realism* would be akin to looking at a view through a perfect glass window in your house. The information you access from this perfect glass window corresponds exactly to what really is outside – if you go outside, the path and the garden you have seen would be there; you can walk along the path, smell the roses, and thus verify the truth of what you have viewed. Your window has given you a way to determine the reality that exists beyond it, a way to measure what is there.' (Braun and Clarke, 2013: 28)

Through the window 2

'*Relativism* is better captured by the idea of prisoners looking at a view from their prison cells. Prisoners housed in different cells will see different views of the world outside the prison, but there is no way of prioritising one prisoner's view as more real than another's. Moreover, although the views appear real, they could be a projection or a hologram. A prisoner has no way to ascertain the truth of the information they have about what is outside the prison. It is impossible to step outside to determine if their view corresponds to the real landscape outside.' (Braun and Clarke, 2013: 28)

Through the window 3

'*Critical realism* would be like looking at a view where the only way to see it is through a prism, so what is seen is nuanced by the shape of the prism (the prism is culture, history, etc.). If you could just get rid of that prism you'd be able to see what lies behind it (the truth), but you can never get beyond.' (Braun and Clarke, 2013: 28)

We have seen in this section that, just as truth is a slippery term hard to pin down and hard to find agreement over, so too is the idea of knowledge. Our definition of knowledge will also be influenced by many factors. For some, the idea of 'common sense' is a positive word that means doing the right thing.

Having 'common sense' can mean not only being owners of appropriate knowledge but also being able to act on it; that is why we often say 'use your common sense!' For others, thinking in a common sense way is a negative. It hints at an inability or unwillingness to think critically. Using 'common sense' could be the opposite of really thinking about an issue and instead just accepting the first, easiest and most available response.

TIME TO CONSIDER

Think about something you do in your everyday life that is based on a common sense notion that has been 'handed down' to you. This might be something as simple as how to dress for certain occasions, whether eating breakfast is important or hair washing rules and rituals. Now do a little 'research' around this common sense idea either online or by consulting with peers. Can you find anything that contradicts what you have thought about this activity until now?

HOW DO OUR DEFINITIONS OF KNOWLEDGE AND TRUTH INFLUENCE HOW WE VIEW RESEARCH ABOUT CHILDREN AND THEIR FAMILIES?

Through this chapter, we have considered the important concepts of knowledge and truth. Let us now think about why this matters when we are looking at research about children and their families. As students of early childhood and as practitioners working with young children and their families, we will hold many different beliefs about them that will influence how we engage with research that focuses on them. Remember at the beginning of this chapter we asked you to come up with your own working definition of knowledge? Return to it now and see if it has changed in any way. As authors, we had a go at this exercise and came up with these two complementary strands to knowledge:

[1] Everything we think might be true, organised and compartmentalised for us to draw on as necessary when we need to understand an issue.
[2] Everything out there that we do not yet know that might help us to understand an issue.

You might have come up with similar definitions to ours or you may have different ideas; there are no right answers here but it is useful to know why we have arrived at a certain definition. If we look at ours, we can see that it is heavily influenced by our researcher identity; the verbs we have used (organised, compartmentalised) reflect what we have to do on a daily basis as part of our work. What about you? What has influenced your definition?

Alexander et al. (2012) decided to look at how undergraduate students defined knowledge and truth by carrying out a piece of research. They were researching in the context of the USA and they had a sample of 161 students. You can read for yourself about how the students participated and how the findings were analysed (see further reading at the end of this chapter). The researchers believed this was an important area to explore; their rationale was that information in a variety of forms bombards students on a daily basis: 'Such information comes at lightning speed from any number of avenues (e.g., telephones, computers, television, or radio) and greatly influences how people function in everyday life' (Alexander et al., 2012: 1).

Thanks to the Internet, it is certainly true that we have access to a wealth of information, more than at any other time in history. We need to be able to weigh up this information and consider how it might add to our knowledge. As we discussed in the previous chapter, when you carry out a search on the Internet, either for your own personal use or for university work, you need to be able to assess the value of what you find out. For example, as we write it is a cold November morning. People are deciding to put the heating on for the first time this autumn. However, there is some disagreement about the optimal temperature. Someone says 'I'll ask Google!' Google offers many sources where we can find out the information we need. Thankfully, there appears to be consensus but we do double check who is behind these sources. Remember what we said in Chapter 2 (Beginning to think critically about research) concerning hidden agendas and vested interests. People will make money out of our need to keep warm so could encourage us to have the temperature as high as possible. As we have discussed in Chapter 2 we need to be able to look at these sources critically.

In the same manner, when looking for information on issues that concern children and families we need to be able to look at sources critically and consider how they might add to our knowledge. We need to question what assertions of truth are being offered and if there is any evidence given to support these assertions. Finally, we need to ask ourselves whether what we have found out has impacted at all on the way we view young children and their families. For example, if we read a piece of research on risk taking in young children (Little et al., 2011) it might enable us to see young children as more capable and competent than we previously imagined. The next time you are asked to read a piece of research as part of your studies instead of just thinking 'what can I learn from this' try to approach the reading in a different way. Consider what you are bringing to the reading in terms of your own values and beliefs and how this influences your understanding of the content. You will encounter a great deal of reading of research on children and their families throughout your undergraduate degree; sometimes it will be contradictory and you are going to have to critically assess it and make a value judgement about its worth. At the same time, be wary of ruling out research if it contradicts values that you hold to be true; allow yourself to be challenged and your values to be questioned.

TIME TO CONSIDER

Can you think about how your views on children have changed since beginning your studies? For example, have you changed your views on such issues as school starting age, play, poverty or gender? What has led you to redefine what you believe about these issues? It could be a piece of research that you have read or a discussion with peers; it may even be what you have learnt in lectures. Why did this particular source have such an impact on your views?

CASE STUDY

Geri: an early years practitioner working with 3- to 4-year-olds

Geri has worked in her early childhood setting for 18 months. She loves her job and has already learnt a great deal about how to engage young children. She is proud of the impact she can see she is having on their development. Recently though she has become concerned that one of her key children, Ted, is finding it difficult to hold a pencil. She knows in a few months' time he will be starting school and she needs to ensure he is 'ready for school' (DfE, 2017a: 9). She had been embarrassed last year at a transition meeting when one of the Reception teachers was complaining that the children arrived from nursery totally unprepared. Geri took this as a personal affront but it did make her think about both her practice and the practice that was happening in school. Furthermore, she wants Ted to have the best possible chance of completing a successful transition into school. Geri decides the 'common sense approach' is to make sure Ted practises writing every day. She sees some simple colourful handwriting books at the supermarket that she thinks he will love. Ted, however, is less than enthusiastic. He would rather be outdoors with his friends and also complains that holding a pencil is making his hand tired. Geri does not want him to see writing as something negative but she is not sure of what to do. At lunchtime she discusses with her colleagues if they have any suggestions for a way forward. One of them mentions an article he has read which suggests that using clay can help children develop strength in their fingers; the article suggests it would be much better to let Ted play with a big lump of soggy clay to let his fine motor skills develop. Geri decides to give this a go, knowing how much Ted likes to 'get messy'. The activity is a great success with both Ted and the other children. Most of them are drawn to playing in it every day and Geri continues her reading of research articles to discover other resources and strategies that will support the children's fine motor skills.

TIME TO CONSIDER

See if you can find a research article that focuses on developing the fine motor skills of young children and challenges the common sense assumption that the best way to learn how to hold a pencil is to practise holding a pencil.

FINAL REFLECTION 

In this chapter you have been challenged to consider the simple word 'true' that probably you use every day at some point without even thinking of its meaning or implications. Begin now to have this word at the forefront of your mind when you are reading – yes even this book! – and continue to ask yourself 'but how does the author know that is true?' This is not to develop a cynical nature but rather a healthy scepticism that will help you develop the ability to think critically about your studies. Think about this chapter and how it has added to your knowledge; now that you have been challenged to examine your own definitions of knowledge and truth consider how this will impact on the work you do, or propose to do, with children and their families.

KEY POINTS 

- Truth is a value-laden term and we cannot take for granted that we all share the same definition of it.
- Knowledge, too, is a highly contested term and what we consider to be knowledge will impact on our practices as professionals.
- We can add to our knowledge to inform our practice through reading and research but it is always important to question what we read and find out.

FURTHER READING 

Alexander, P.A., Winters, F., Loughlin, S.M. and Grossnickle, E. (2012) 'Students' conceptions of knowledge, information, and truth', *Learning and Instruction*, 22(1): 1–15.

This is the article we mentioned earlier in the chapter. It is a piece of research that examined students' understanding of the terms *knowledge*, *information* and *truth*. You might find it a tricky read, but do persevere.

Hedges, H. and Cullen, J. (2005) 'Subject knowledge in early childhood curriculum and pedagogy: beliefs and practices', *Contemporary Issues in Early Childhood*, 6(1): 66–79.

Hedges and Cullen's research is set in the New Zealand context. They explore with early years practitioners, parents and children concepts of appropriate subject knowledge. Note how the authors state their research is 'located within a postmodern view of knowledge ... Rather than one "truth", the views of people are sought. Complexity, diversity, context and multiple perspectives are recognised' (p. 68).

4

THE LANGUAGE OF RESEARCH

INTRODUCTION

Learning about research is a bit like studying a new language; you first need to pick up some key words and then you learn how they fit together to make sentences. Initially it is just a case of familiarising yourself with these terms by learning what they mean and how to say them. It may involve you repeating others' ideas; eventually though you will be able to use these key terms confidently, applying them to construct original ideas of your own.

This chapter will ...

- Introduce you to some of the key terminology that is used in research.
- Establish the idea that the social science research community has its own shared vocabulary and a particular way of discussing research so that all community members have a mutual understanding.
- Examine the notion that such communities can be both inclusive and exclusive, linking this discussion to claims of gatekeeping.

WHAT IS THE KEY TERMINOLOGY USED IN BOTH SCIENTIFIC AND SOCIAL SCIENCE RESEARCH?

There are three key ideas we want to consider in this first section of the chapter as we introduce you to research terminology. Firstly many of the terms we meet in a research context will be words we use in our everyday conversations and we will discuss how this might be problematic for us. Next we will discuss how there is a 'borrowing' of words from scientific research which is apparent in social science research and we will ponder on whether this 'borrowing' is always appropriate. Finally we will consider why it is important to begin to engage with this specialist language as early childhood students even if we may be a few years away from undertaking our own research.

Most of us will have learned a language, such as French, at secondary school. Perhaps you remember those words which were called 'faux-amis' (false friends) because we thought we knew what they meant but actually they meant something different! For example '*joli*' means pretty not jolly and '*passer un examen*' means to take an exam and not, unfortunately, to pass an exam. We have to be very clear what words mean when we learn a new language and it is just the same with the language of research. In this context familiar everyday words can take on a different meaning. Look at Table 4.1; it includes some key research terminology. You will not need to know and understand all this vocabulary at this stage, nevertheless we think that if you begin to get to grips with it now then it will help you understand the landscape of research and therefore read other people's work with a more critical eye. You will need to check your understanding of some of these words; some of them may be used in different ways to that with which you are familiar. For those that you don't know, where could you start to find out what they mean?

Pat Thomson is a professor of education at the University of Nottingham. She writes a useful blog for postgraduate students engaged in academic writing and research but some of her blog entries are beneficial for undergraduates too. We particularly like this entry from 13th April 2015 and often share this metaphor with our students as well:

> Getting into a new area or mode of thinking is actually a bit like getting to know a new physical location. When you arrive in a new city you don't expect to know how to get around straight away. You don't expect to know a new place in the way you know your own home environment. You understand that you have to make several trips before you have a sense of what is where, and how to get from one place to another without looking at a map for general directions and/or reassurance. (Thomson, 2015)

We think this is a really helpful metaphor to help us understand the world of research and in particular the specific language it uses. At the moment some of you are new arrivals and some of you are on a second visit but still newcomers to the location. As Thomson suggests:

> You have to explore a bit. You have to get a sense of what is where – the histories of debate, the lines of argument, the language used, the kind of questions that are asked, the topics that are pursued, perhaps even the style of writing that is generally used in the field. (Thomson, 2015)

Let's look at some of the words on your 'location map'. We have listed a collection in Table 4.1. Can you sort them into those you are familiar with and those that you have never come across before?

Table 4.1 Some of the key vocabulary used in research

analysis	paradigm
case study	participants
design	qualitative
discussion	quantitative
epistemology	questionnaire
ethics	reliability
findings	results
interview	sample
methodology	survey
methods	triangulation
observation	trustworthiness
ontology	validity

We are not going to discuss all of these words at this point but they will be mentioned at times throughout the book. Some of these terms have been 'borrowed' from scientific research and therefore are not always appropriate to use in social science research which is concerned with people's behaviours. We will discuss in more detail the differences between these two kinds of research in Chapter 10 (How research is designed). Thomas argues that the disciplines of the social sciences suffer from low self-esteem and therefore feel they have to use the language of scientific research to justify their position in the academic world (Thomas, 2013: 118). This is particularly true of qualitative research (remember we introduced this idea in Chapter 1), which relies on words to paint a picture of a social situation or phenomenon. Because sometimes qualitative research has been accused of being woolly and having little substance (Attride-Stirling, 2001), Thomas argues that qualitative researchers borrow the language of science to give their research more status.

One good example of this is the term triangulation, which you can see we have included in Table 4.1. One definition of triangulation in social science research is 'Comparing different data and different methods to see whether they corroborate one another' (Silverman, 2014: 91). But some would argue that because qualitative data is context-bound and open to interpretation from the researcher it cannot be used in a 'corroborating role' and that it is more about 'complementarity, and nothing at all to do with mutual validation' (Gorard, 2004: 45).

Braun and Clarke (2013) offer us another superb illustration of this idea when they suggest that the researcher is like a sculptor standing before a piece of marble which is their data. There are two of us writing this book and we often work on pieces of research together. We have a little joke about what different things we might make out of our 'marble'; one of us a little cherub, the other a fearsome dragon. There are many factors that will impact on how we analyse our data (work out what our data mean), including our own personal researcher identity which we will discuss more fully in Chapter 12 (Your research journey has begun).

Beginning to learn key vocabulary at this stage can help you in your studies even though you are not yet at the point of undertaking research yourself. By acquiring the language of research, and knowing how to use it, you are demonstrating that you belong to the research community. Being confident with the appropriate terminology will support your critical reading of others' research and will also mean that by the time you come to carry out your own research you will not be grappling with this new terminology but rather will have a confident working grasp of it. It's a bit like trying to learn Spanish a few weeks before you go on holiday compared to diligently attending the Spanish conversation classes on offer every week without really knowing when and where you are going to apply your learning.

To conclude this section, we have seen that the terminology of research is not necessarily a list of words that you are unfamiliar with; rather it is a way of using, in a specific way, words that have been mostly accepted into our everyday talk. If we are discussing research we cannot use this vocabulary in a vague manner; we must employ it in ways laid down by the research community. Do you remember in Chapter 1 (Introduction to research in early childhood) we got you to think about what the term 'research' meant? From our many years of marking first year university essays, we have noticed that a phrase often used by students is 'From my research into this issue I have discovered ...'. Often what they really mean by this is that they have been up all day and night in the library reading the books off the module book list or even asking Google! While this is all very well and good, it is not the definition of a piece of research. Research is something that has been carried out in a systematic way with a consideration of both ethics (see Chapter 9 for a full discussion of this) and the gap in knowledge it is trying to address, as we discussed in Chapter 1.

TIME TO CONSIDER

This would be an excellent time to begin to build up your own glossary of research terminology. You will be tempted to use a dictionary to help you define words; this is acceptable as a starting point but don't forget our discussion about how words in research can be used in a different way. It will be much better for you if you can look for definitions in some of the research literature. Your university library will have a wide selection of books on research, including eBooks that you can access online. We have suggested some sources in the further reading section at the end of the chapter. Keep your glossary in an electronic format so that it is a dynamic document that you can regularly update as your understanding of research grows. Table 4.2 gives an example of how you might set out your glossary. We have done the first one for you as an example.

Table 4.2 How to set out an effective glossary

Term (in alphabetical order)	**Definition in my own words** (This could be constantly changing as you develop your knowledge and understanding of research)	**Examples from the research literature** (Don't forget to reference properly and to add to the bibliography you are building up in your studies)
Analysis (of data)	When the researcher works out what the data mean	'Analysis is about taking things apart ... After the taking apart, the deconstruction, it is about a process of careful inspection, to see the relationship of one thing with another: how are they connected?' (Thomas, 2013: 273) Thomas, G. (2013) *How to do your research project.* London: Sage.

WHY IS IT IMPORTANT THAT THE SOCIAL SCIENCE RESEARCH COMMUNITY HAS ITS OWN SHARED VOCABULARY?

Has it ever happened to you that you have had a conversation with someone when neither of you has a clue about what the other is trying to say? We have found that often this can be a generational thing, when the exasperated teenager and their exasperated parent can look at each other and exclaim: 'What are you going on about?!' Sometimes it is because one or the other is using a vocabulary that is unfamiliar to their listener. Having a vocabulary in common prevents the risk of confusion and misunderstanding. We can look at shared vocabularies in the context of research into early childhood and see how they can aid both the reader and writer. To have an agreed lexicon to draw on also supports the novice researcher as they grapple with new subject knowledge, new ways of thinking and seek access to a new community.

Shared vocabularies save time and ambiguity. Lave and Wenger (1991) coined the term 'Communities of Practice' to describe groups of people who come together with a shared aim and a mutual purpose. It is possible to belong to several communities of practice; you could describe your fellow students on your early childhood degree as such a community or your colleagues in the workplace. Think also about any clubs or societies you belong to; they too are potential communities of practice. What is certain is that you will have practices in common and a shared vocabulary which might not always be understandable to those outside that specific community. We remember for example when we first began to work in Higher Education. Although we had been through Higher Education ourselves we had never worked within a community of university tutors before and often we just could not understand what they were saying. At first we thought it was because they were much more intelligent but then we grew to realise that they were talking in a kind of code and if we learnt the code then not only would we understand but we could also participate in the discussion. Seen through the lens of Lave and Wenger (1991) we were newcomers, participating on the edges of this community. Those who had been totally encultured into the university environment, because of the length of time they had worked there, were 'old timers' (Lave and Wenger, 1991) who were fluent in this code. They did not always realise that they were not being inclusive by failing to take into account those who were unfamiliar with the shared code. You may be feeling the same as you hover on the periphery of the community of practice that is social science research. As students of early childhood you are the newcomers into this community and you will come across lots of 'old timers'; they will be tutors, postgraduate students and writers of research books. At times you will think they are speaking in a kind of secret language. It can be frustrating because just when you think you have understood what a specific term means you find another example which contradicts the definition you have arrived at. This is a bit like Piaget's idea of schema (2002), which he described as 'Cognitive structures [which] contain within them elements of "perception", "memories", "concepts", and operations' (1971: 139) to explain how children organise their learning and build on previous knowledge. We continue to do this as adults (Donaldson and Graham, 1999) and so understanding could be shaken when we meet an example that does not fit the schema we have built up, requiring us to rethink what we know.

As you familiarise yourself with this specialist vocabulary you will begin to look at other people's research in a different way and think critically about their findings. Let us consider, for example, the term 'sample' here. This word is frequently used both in research and everyday speech. When you are considering the trustworthiness of a piece of research you will need to know the detail behind how and why the participants were selected. If a group of researchers decide to find out about children's perceptions of suitable jobs for men and women they will need to make their sample explicit. This means they will need to say:

- how many children were asked
- how old the children were
- what the gender balance was
- how the children were recruited; did they go through school or directly to parents
- what kind of socio-economic, geographical and cultural area the children came from.

You can see from this level of detail that if an undergraduate dissertation contains the sentence 'My sample included 6 children – 3 boys and 3 girls' then they are demonstrating only that they understand the word sample as used in everyday life; they would need to add much more detail to demonstrate that they understood what it meant in the context of research. Another key word beloved by the research books and pondered over by both students and academic scholars is the term *paradigm*. Unlike sample, this is not a term you are likely to have used before if you are new to research. However it is a very important term when we want to consider what claims a piece of research is trying to make. Bogdan and Biklen offer a definition of paradigm as 'a loose collection of logically related assumptions, concepts, or propositions that orient thinking and research' (1998: 22). If we link this to the gender research already mentioned, the researchers in this context would need to make it clear within which paradigm their research is located and what assumptions they are making. They would need to let the reader know if they were claiming that there is a clear answer to the research question 'What are young children's perceptions of suitable jobs for men and women?' Or, as mentioned in Chapter 1, they must state clearly if they believe that their research was offering one interpretation of what young children might think. As you are reading peer-reviewed journal articles, see if you can work out what claims the writers are making by looking at their choice of language.

Learning the correct terminology is like becoming an apprentice of research. Just like an apprentice, your learning is not a one-off occurrence but something that you will return to again and again to refine and understand at a different and ever-deeper level. We have already shown how we can use the lens of Piaget (2002) to understand this and here it would also be appropriate to reference Bruner's spiral curriculum (1960) which supports an understanding of learning as a system 'where there is an iterative revisiting of topics ... [It] is not simply a repetition of a topic taught. It also requires the deepening of it, with each successive encounter building on the previous one' (Harden and Stamper, 1999: 141). As you return again and again to research terminology through your engagement with reading you will be developing a research toolkit which will help you move from the periphery of the communities of practice towards the centre.

This shared vocabulary becomes a kind of shorthand which reduces opportunities for ambiguity and misunderstandings to occur. It also supports the reader in more easily examining and unpicking the asserted truths behind a particular piece of research. The apprentice researcher is also 'scaffolded' if there are laid-down ways of proceeding and specific words to use; this transparency in turn could address issues of gatekeeping, which we will talk about in the next section.

TIME TO CONSIDER

Have a look at three recent research articles from a journal you have found useful in your studies so far. You could consider:

Childhood

Journal of Early Childhood Research

Contemporary Issues in Early Childhood

(Continued)

(Continued)

These are all available as electronic journals and should be accessible through your university library search engine. Look back at Table 4.1 and see if you can find any of these words in your three articles. You can use the CTRL+F search function to help you do this efficiently. Are they used in the same way in each article? Are any of the key words not used? Why might this be so?

WHEN CAN RESEARCH LANGUAGE BECOME A BARRIER?

We have discussed how supportive a shared language can be but it is also important to recognise that language can be used to exclude. We hinted at this when we were talking about communities of practice above (Lave and Wenger, 1991) and use the term 'gatekeeping' here to describe the barrier that language can become. 'Gatekeeping' is a term that sums up who is or is not allowed into the research community. A research apprentice needs to work hard to learn both the correct practices and the specific language required. Even so, they can encounter obstacles in the form of language used by those already established in the research community. Unwittingly, they may also use language to create a barrier themselves.

Imagine you are standing in front of a huge wrought-iron gate. You want to get to whatever is on the other side of it but it is padlocked. The good news is that someone has the correct key and they are standing by the gate ready to let you in; the bad news is they will only let you in if you ask them in the right way. You can cry, get cross, be frustrated but they will still not let you in – unless you say the right words. Do you ever feel like this as a student desperate to do well, wanting those higher grades? The term 'gatekeeping' was coined by Lewin (1943) to describe the power relationship that can exist in many areas of life between those who hold knowledge and those trying to access it.

In this context we are using 'gatekeeping' to describe the relationship between the 'old timers' of the research community and those on the periphery (Lave and Wenger, 1991) who want to demonstrate that they belong. Think, for example, of a university session you have attended or an article you have struggled to read. You may have come away understanding very little and even questioning your own ability. One of the authors of this book remembers attending her first postgraduate session at university. The lecturer was a renowned academic with numerous publications. As desperately as she tried to keep up with what he was saying, it seemed to be impossible. He 'salt and peppered' his talk with numerous writers whose names she had never heard of and terminology she certainly couldn't spell. She left the session debating whether she had bitten off more than she could chew. Tutors and writers may not deliberately 'gatekeep' but it does undermine a student's confidence when this happens. Thankfully this student decided to persevere and complete her studies. Sometimes now one of her students will quite rightly challenge her when she makes the assumption that they have a shared vocabulary and does not take into account their 'newcomer' versus 'old timer' status.

Gatekeeping is carried out by those who have the power to let others into a certain area of society. In this context we could say it is carried out by those who have the power and authority to let others into the research community. When you embark on your own research as an undergraduate then your tutors will act as gatekeepers when they mark your work; they will look for evidence which shows you can use the terminology appropriately as they decide whether to 'let you in'. They are accountable to the university, to the external examiners and to the discipline of early childhood in ensuring they only invite in those who meet the appropriate criteria. However a supportive tutor will be aware of how language can be used to exclude.

For some groups the use of specific language may be a bigger barrier than it is for others; all in the research community, whether 'newcomer' or 'old timer', need to be mindful of this. This could be because these individuals are from a vulnerable group or because they have had previous problematic encounters with the education system. If language is used in a non-inclusive way then it can also exclude participants and erect a barrier between the research and those who might benefit from it; this is a criticism that Pring (2006: 158) makes when he highlights that educational research when written up is often 'inaccessible in esoteric journals and in opaque language,' so that it never becomes something that informs practice. This distancing between research and practice can begin with the research design if issues such as use of language and dissemination of findings are not taken into account. Another example is when the language used in interviews and questionnaires is inappropriate and alienates the participant by any academic or researcher tendency to use jargon or literature-informed terminology. Morrison (2013) talks about 10 lessons for effective practice when interviewing children, including 'Use the language, genre and register of the children, including humour' (p. 334). Finally, the use of language needed to fulfil ethics committee criteria can alienate would-be participants and discourage them from taking part, as we will discuss in Chapter 9 (The ethics of research).

TIME TO CONSIDER

Jerusha would like to carry out some research in the early years setting where she works. She compiles a participant information sheet to hand out to the staff there. What advice would you give her as her tutor? Think about how accessible (or not) she has made the language and whether there are any parts that need rewriting.

Dear colleague,

It is requested that you take part in a qualitative research study. Please read the information in this letter carefully so that you understand why the research is being undertaken. This information is not confidential so you are allowed to consult with others. You may also ask the researcher if anything is not clear.

(Continued)

(Continued)

The researcher wants to carry out semi-formal interviews about practitioners' perceptions of the role of the adult in an early years setting. She requires a sample of 10 practitioners who hold a variety of qualifications. Recent research has demonstrated that practitioners are not confident in their role as the 'More Knowledgeable Other' (MKO) (Vygotsky, 1978) within a play-based curriculum.

You have been highlighted as a participant because of your work with young children. There is no obligation to participate; please make sure you are aware of your rights and also engage with the BERA guidelines. However, before taking part you are required to give informed consent by signing the attached consent form.

All interviews will be recorded and both the transcripts and the recordings will be stored confidentially. If you are harmed in any way then there could be grounds for legal action.

Yours faithfully,

CASE STUDY

Joel: an early years practitioner working in a baby room

Joel works in a baby room and competently uses observation to track children's learning and development. He generally writes a narrative description of what he sees his key children doing and then uses his growing knowledge of child development and Development Matters (Early Education, 2012) to reflect on the children's learning and suggest next steps. In his university sessions on early childhood research he is initially confused by the differences that are apparent in using the word 'observation' in research design. His peers suggest some useful textbooks to him and he soon can confidently discuss some different approaches to observations in research. For example, he reads in Edward (2010) that observations can be:

- 'anecdotal – that is, rich descriptions of a specific and informative event
- event sequenced – that is, noting when a particular behaviour occurs
- time sequenced – that is, collecting information at regular intervals' (p. 168).

When he has the chance to collect some data for a small research study into how children use the outdoor area he decides to try using all three approaches.

TIME TO CONSIDER

Think about the different kinds of information Joel will collect by collecting data in these three ways. What different evidence will he obtain and what sort of questions will he be able to answer?

FINAL REFLECTION

In this chapter you have been introduced to some terminology that you may not have come across before. There could be other words that you are very familiar with but you find that in research they carry a different meaning. We have shown how it can be very helpful to have this shared vocabulary almost as a shorthand between all in the early childhood community, including students. However this still doesn't mean there is no ambiguity as various research writers contest the meaning of certain key words and question their suitability in social science research.

KEY POINTS

- Research has its own vocabulary; some of it is generic, some more relevant to scientific research or social science research. However the suitability of a generic vocabulary for all areas of research is not something that all writers can agree on.
- Having a shared vocabulary reduces the risk of ambiguity and helps the reader to engage critically with a piece of research. It means they know what to look for and what questions to ask.
- We have to be mindful as researchers, or would-be researchers, that we do not allow language to become a barrier that excludes others.

FURTHER READING

Roberts-Holmes, G. (2018) *Doing Your Early Years Research Project: A Step by Step Guide*, 4th edn. London: Sage.

Roberts-Holmes' book will be really useful for you, particularly as you begin to compile your glossary. Have a look at his in this fourth edition of his very popular book.

Fenwick, S. (2005) 'Is the language of research the real barrier?', *Journal of Nursing* Administration, 35(12): 517–18.

This article is written in the form of a letter to the editor of the journal. The writer explains why practitioners (in this case nurses) would not be eager to engage with researchers. She claims: 'Some nurses just want to flee when approached about research for fear of being tagged as ignorant because they have difficulty with interpreting much of what is written in research articles' (p. 518). It is a clear illustration of how language can be a barrier in research.

5

APPROACHES TO RESEARCH ABOUT CHILDREN

INTRODUCTION

Often you might hear of researchers doing research 'about' children or 'on' children. We need to think carefully about whether this is always an appropriate thing to do.

This chapter will ...

- Consider what we mean by research 'about' children, what views of children inform the approach, how it has historically been conducted and how it is conducted in the present day.
- Introduce to you what we mean by the difference between research 'about' children and research 'with' children.
- Look at how, historically, children have been viewed as passive, vulnerable and incompetent, and how this perspective of them has informed the way in which research has been conducted on them as subjects rather than as participants.
- Explore how key theorists in child development have carried out research on children and how that has informed our knowledge of how children learn. Sometimes this has had the implications of unethical practice (see Chapter 9).
- Consider how approaches to research about children have developed and how it is typically conducted in the 21st century both within the UK and internationally. These ideas will be built upon in Chapter 7 (Longitudinal research approaches) and Chapter 8 (Cross-national research approaches).

So far in this book, we have considered what is meant by the idea of research with young children in quite a general way and how you might think critically about it. You have also considered how different people might define knowledge and truth in research in different ways, as well as the importance of considering the language of research. Within these chapters, we have thought about the concept of research in quite a broad way, however now we are going to begin to break this down and make a distinction between research 'about' and research 'with' children. We are defining research 'about' children as studies that are conducted where children are seen as 'objects' or 'subjects' of research (Penn, 2008: 142). In this situation, they might not be aware that they are being studied. Even if they are aware, and have given their consent, a great power imbalance may exist between the researcher and the researched, due to the adult-led nature of the study. In this category, we are also including studies that aim to inform our knowledge of children's lives, but may not have child participants. Conversely, we are defining research 'with' children as research that takes a more child-led approach, not only to data collection, but also ideally in research design and dissemination too. This chapter is going to focus on research 'about' children, and the following chapter (Chapter 6) will explore research 'with' children.

You have already begun to consider pieces of research 'about' children in this book. For instance, Chapter 1 introduced the EPPE Project (Sylva et al., 2010), which is a large-scale longitudinal study aiming to identify the characteristics of the most effective early years settings in England, in terms of supporting children's academic and pro-social outcomes. Some of the data collection methods of the study included observations on children in their early years settings, interviews with children's parents and setting practitioners, and analyses of children's results in nationally administered assessments. We consider this to be a piece of research 'about' children because although it is studying children's outcomes, both whilst they were in ECEC settings and also now they have begun compulsory schooling, it focuses on data from adults. For example, data has been gathered through interviews with adults close to the child and observations of children that adults have interpreted, and through research methods that children do not have power to inform (for instance, the analysis of children's SATs test results).

HOW HAVE THE WAYS THAT CHILDREN ARE VIEWED IN RESEARCH CHANGED?

Whether we do research 'about' or 'with' children is influenced by how we view them. Think back to Chapter 3 (Knowledge and truth in research). We know that people have different ideas of what counts as 'knowledge' about young children and their families, and people have different ideas about what is 'true' in relation to children. We have considered how the truths that researchers hold about children have an impact on how they choose to conduct their studies and what kind of knowledge they think they can reach.

You may already be familiar with how views of children have changed over time. For instance, you may know the old saying 'children must be seen and not heard'. If you apply this truth about children to the research that you conduct on them, this could lead to pieces of research that do not seek to discover the child's voice, or keeps them on the periphery of investigations into their lives. Views of children like this are often seen to fall into the 'traditional paradigm of childhood', which was particularly prevalent until approximately the 1980s (James and Prout, 1997). Jones (2010) argues that this way of viewing children sees them as incomplete, passive, invisible, vulnerable and incompetent. This was due to the fact that childhood was seen as 'preparation for adulthood' (Gabriel, 2010: 142), and children needed to be transformed into competent adults. However, in the 1980s the view of children as passive beings began to change in the UK, and people began to believe that children should be seen in the present as who they currently are, rather than who they would become.

This historic view has had a major impact on the way in which children have been seen in research. Just imagine how two people might conduct a piece of research differently if one of them holds a truth that children are passive and incompetent, whilst the other views them as active and powerful. When childhoods are viewed in a traditional way, children are seen as 'objects' of research (Penn, 2008: 140). They have experiences that adults, taking a protective role over them due to their vulnerable status, can control and influence in order to measure the impact of these experiences. When they are seen in this way, they will not have been asked for consent and may not be aware that a piece of research is being conducted (2008: 142). A second way of viewing children in research is as 'subjects' (Christensen and Prout, 2002: 481). This approach adopts a slightly more modern perspective of children, because in these cases children do know that the research is taking place, and are seen as competent and worthy to be asked for their informed consent. However, they are likely to be consenting to pieces of research that are adult-led and adult-designed. Finally, when researchers take the more modern view of children, they are more likely to be seen as 'active contributors who can be creative partners with adults' in research (Penn, 2008: 140). Here they might be considered 'participants', rather than 'objects' or 'subjects'. Although there are an increasing number of studies that do see children in this way, as the traditional view was dominant in the Western world for many centuries (Westwood, 2014), this has had a key influence in the design of many pieces of research that took place throughout the 20th century, and still has a big impact on the truths people hold today in the 21st century.

We can see how, if we believe the truth that children are passive, vulnerable and incompetent, we may lean towards viewing children as 'unknowing objects of research' (Penn, 2008: 142). With this truth, we see no need to gain their permission to study them, and see no worth in actively listening to their views, opinions or perspectives to answer our research question. Similarly, if we view children as 'aware subjects', we might acknowledge their competency to a slightly higher degree, but still perhaps not value their ability to have worthwhile opinions or input into data collection methods or project design.

TIME TO CONSIDER

Think about the truths that you hold about children and their families. How might that impact on the kind of research that you wish to read about, or the types of research that you think might give you the best access to knowledge?

HOW HAS RESEARCH 'ABOUT' CHILDREN TYPICALLY BEEN CONDUCTED?

You may be familiar with theories about how children develop. We argue that many child development theorists in the 20th century conducted research 'about' children, which has informed the beliefs we hold about how children develop and acquire new knowledge. It has also informed the practices that take place in early childhood settings.

RESEARCH IN FOCUS

Piaget and the four sequential stages of development

The Swiss psychologist Piaget constructed the idea that children work through four sequential stages in their development, as their ways of processing information and understanding the world around them changes while they develop the ability to think. Piaget conducted experiments in which he interviewed children, but his interview technique has been described as 'too subjective and value-laden' (Slee and Shute, 2003: 66) due to the language he used. For instance, in one of his experiments Piaget sought to assess children's conservation of number, which is the concept that an amount of objects remains the same irrespective of how it is displayed (Piaget, 1954, cited in Doherty and Hughes, 2014). The experiment begins by laying out two rows of the same amount of counters, equal in length, containing the same number. He asks the child 'are there the same number of counters in each row?' After the child had responded, he says 'watch this' and alters the spacing of one of the rows to make it longer, and repeats the question again. Piaget argued that between the ages of five and seven, children shift their thinking to understand that the rows of differing lengths still contain an equal number of objects – so whilst a child of five would say that rows of differing lengths contained a different amount of counters, a child of seven would respond that there were the same number.

CRITIQUES OF PIAGET

Margaret Donaldson spent a year working in Piaget's research institute in Geneva and then returned to her home of Scotland and investigated whether his findings could be replicated. She argued that children are not considering the researcher's second question in isolation, but they may believe that the statement to 'watch this' may mean that this is relevant to what happens afterwards, and thus the language used by the researcher is incredibly influential (Donaldson, 1978: 63). In experiments conducted with McGarrigle, Donaldson instead used a 'Naughty Teddy' to accidentally disrupt the length of one of two rows of toys, which meant that the child was not then interpreting the answer to the second question of length based upon a previous action of the researcher (McGarrigle and Donaldson, 1974). In this experiment, younger children were more likely to show conservation of number and display knowledge that lines of differing lengths can have the same amount of objects.

Piaget's experiments match with one of the ways that Penn (2008: 143) says research about children had traditionally been conducted – through 'artificial laboratory tests with complicated methods that young children often failed, and asking standard questions instead of questions about the child's own experiences'. The standard questioning that Piaget's interview schedule used confused the children and contributed to the responses they gave, which is why the children in McGarrigle and Donaldson's (1974) experiments were more likely to demonstrate an awareness of number conservation. Lindon (2012: 70) explains well what might explain the different responses between Piaget's and Donaldson's experiments: 'It is very possible that when an adult makes a change and then asks a question about whether it's still the same, children are misdirected into thinking that something must have happened. Otherwise, why would an adult ask that kind of question?'

Donaldson (1978) also criticised Piaget and Inhelder's (1967, cited in Doherty and Hughes, 2014) three mountains experiments, because, as Penn (2008) explains, rather than focusing on children's own experiences, it asked standard questions that the children could not relate to. In this experiment, a child was sitting at a table with a 3D model of three mountains, and asked to choose from photographs what a doll, who was moved to sit at other seats around the table, would be able to see. Piaget argued that this was evidence of children's egocentrism, which means that children think only from their own perspective, which he said lasted until a child was between five and seven years old. Yet Donaldson (1978) argues that in similar experiments by Hughes, for instance one in which children were asked to hide a boy doll from the view of two policeman dolls within a 3D model, 90% of 30 children aged from three-and-a-half to five could do it successfully. Donaldson (1978: 24) suggests that this is because the experiment made sense to the children and, although she acknowledged that children were unlikely to have had the personal experience of avoiding a policeman, they may understand the concept of hiding. This is, thus, evidence of the limitations of research 'about' children that are conducted in artificial laboratory environments and do not take children's own experiences into account. Yet, although we could argue that Piaget's standardised tests and experiments were not child-centred approaches to conducting research, Woodhead and Faulkner (2008: 27) note that Piaget was child-centred due to his aim to promote respect for children and their ways of thinking. And his theories have certainly informed child-centred educational practices in England. For instance, Piaget's ideas influenced 20th century policy such as 1967's Plowden Report, which reviewed primary and nursery education (Penn, 2008: 43), as well as practices in ECEC settings in the 21st century (David et al., 2003).

RESEARCH IN FOCUS 

Bandura and the Bobo doll experiment

Bandura is a psychologist in the United States who has been conducting research with child participants since the 1950s. One of his most famous experiments is the Bobo doll experiment (Bandura et al., 1961), in which children were individually taken to an experiment room that contained a small play area for the children to engage in arts and craft activities, and were accompanied by an adult model who played nearby in the same room either in a non-aggressive manner with some construction toys, or in an aggressive manner towards a Bobo doll (a weighted large inflatable doll) by punching, kicking it and saying comments like 'Sock him in the nose ...' and 'Kick him ...' . Children were not explicitly told to watch or observe the model and did not have the opportunity to join in. However, afterwards the child was taken to another experimental room, which contained both aggressive toys (like a Bobo doll, and two toy guns) and non-aggressive toys (like dolls and small world toys). The researchers found that children were more likely to choose the aggressive toys and display violence in this room if they had observed the model behaving aggressively.

Conducting an experiment in an artificial environment means that researchers can standardise what happens by controlling variables, like precisely how long the children in the Bobo doll experiment were able to witness the model and which toys the children had access to afterwards. This also means that it is easy for a study to be replicated. Penn (2008: 143) believes that another common way of doing research on children traditionally has been through 'standardised tests of "representative" children'. It could be argued that the Bobo doll experiment was a standardised test, but the extent to which the children were representative is questionable – they were typically white and from middle-class backgrounds (Cullen, 2011: 131). In addition, Woodhead and Faulkner (2008: 10) note that one key issue in conducting psychological research on children is how appropriate it is to use 'experimental design and laboratory measurement' as ways to consider children's lives. For instance, in children's everyday lives, it is unusual for them to be playing in a room with a stranger for a short period of time. It is perhaps much more likely they would copy the behaviours of adults they see more regularly and have a relationship with, like their parents, family members or teachers. Woodhead and Faulkner (2008) also suggest that a key issue in this type of research is the unspoken power relationship between researcher and participant (which we will talk about more in Chapter 9) when psychological testing, controlled interventions and systematic observations are taking place. Both issues are, again, common features of research 'about' children, which may be explained by the way that children are viewed when researchers take this approach.

Woodhead and Faulkner (2008) also consider how this kind of psychological research may bring ethical dilemmas; Messenger-Davies (2008: 82) expresses concerns about research that encourages young children to behave aggressively, as in Bandura's experiment. Bandura and his research team cannot be sure what the long-lasting impact of their experiments will be on their child participants. In a similar way, other studies that have taken a research-'about'-children approach may be critiqued not only due to their use of experiments and laboratory testing, but also due to major ethical concerns. For instance, following work by Pavlov, in 1920 the 'founder of behaviourism' (Lindon, 2012: 63) John Watson, and his colleague Rosalie Rayner conducted an experiment over a period of a month with an 11-month-old boy called Albert. Albert had spent almost his whole life in hospital as his mother was a wet nurse there. The researchers conditioned him to be scared of a toy fluffy white rat by striking a metal bar with a hammer behind the baby's head when he reached out for it. Albert's fearful response to the rat later transferred to other similar objects, like a fur coat, Santa Claus mask and toy rabbit, and he would whimper or cry when faced with them. The researchers had planned to later conduct experiments to attempt to remove the conditioned response, however Albert left the hospital before this could take place. Thus, even though Watson and Rayner themselves believed that they 'could do [Albert] relatively little harm by carrying out such experiments' (1920: 2), they did believe that his responses to white, fluffy objects were likely to continue unless an accidental way to change his conditioned response was discovered at home. Woodhead and Faulkner (2008: 23) describe the experiment as 'ethically untenable'. It is improbable that such a study would be granted ethical approval today, yet it illustrates the way in which children have been seen, and therefore treated, as objects and subjects in research. Table 5.1 highlights some further positives and negatives of conducting research on children in controlled environments.

You might have come across a famous piece of research carried out in a controlled environment known as the 'still face experiment', conducted by Tronick et al. (1978, cited in Maguire-Fong, 2015). You can find video clips

Table 5.1 Conducting research on children in controlled environments: positives and negatives

Positives	Negatives
• Researchers can standardise what happens by controlling variables • It is easier for the study to be replicated	• Not as representative of children's typical experiences • May be a larger power imbalance between the researcher and the participant • Can be more ethically problematic

that replicate the experiment online. Have a think about this experiment and what the positives and negatives of conducting the research in a controlled environment might be.

TIME TO CONSIDER

Think about what you know about theorists in the 20th century, and then consider how practices in early childhood settings might have been informed by them. What might be the impact of the bulk of what we know about children having been informed by this approach?

WHAT RESEARCH 'ABOUT' CHILDREN IS CONDUCTED NOW?

Despite the fact that views of children are changing, there are still many pieces of research that are conducted that align with a view of children as passive, incompetent and incomplete. We will be considering some of these studies in more detail, for instance some longitudinal studies about children in Chapter 7, and some pieces of cross-national research in Chapter 8. Some of the pieces of research conducted 'about' children are carried out by researchers who are not within the discipline of Early Childhood Studies, but instead may come from other disciplines, like health, education or psychology. We considered in Chapter 2 (and will consider in Chapter 10) how different disciplines use different methods to study children and childhoods (Kehily, 2009: 7), for instance that psychologists may use different methods to sociologists. Researchers holding different professional values may subscribe to different 'truths' about children, and different approaches to what counts as knowledge. As an example, Hogan (2005) suggests that developmental psychologists have traditionally seen children as 'research objects' and assume that children are context-free, predictable and irrelevant. Consequently, they may choose to approach answering a research question in a different way to that of an early years practitioner.

Viewing children as irrelevant makes the assumption that they are uninformed, passive, dependent and unreliable, and thus reports by adults about children are seen as having more worth than reports by children themselves (Hogan, 2005: 25). Doing research by using adults' perspectives is another way that Penn (2008: 143) says that research about children has typically taken place. More specifically, she states that it has been conducted by carrying out surveys not with children, but with their parents or teachers instead. One reason for this might be when researchers are viewing children as inherently vulnerable but seek to consider an area that is considered sensitive, for instance matters that are 'considered to be threatening, or to contain elements of risk' (Smith, 2011: 18). Sensitive areas may include those relating to topics like child abuse or neglect, domestic violence, parental separation or children's ill-health. For example,

Cossar et al. (2013) note that it is rare that children's views of their experiences of child protection are explored, particularly when those children are living at home rather than in care. Similarly, Penny and Rice (2012) argue that there is very limited research with child participants around childhood bereavement, as the majority of research focuses on adults reflecting on childhood experiences, or adult participants sharing information about children's lives. It can be hard to conduct research that focuses on sensitive topics because of a variety of reasons – firstly, it can be tricky to gain ethical approval (which will be considered in more detail in Chapter 9), and even if the research is seen as ethically sound to proceed, it can be difficult to recruit participants to take part, or convince gatekeepers to allow access to child participants (Smith, 2011). For example, Cossar et al. (2013) sought to recruit child participants to research their experiences of child protection, which the researchers themselves acknowledge is a sensitive area. Twenty-three of the 46 parents who were approached as gatekeepers to their child's assent said they did not want their children to participate. However, paradoxically, viewing children as vulnerable and thus denying them the opportunity to share their perspective on sensitive topics may in fact make them more vulnerable, if researchers are limited in their ability to suggest recommendations to practice and realise benefits to children because they don't know children's perspectives. Powell and Smith (2009: 129) argue that the risks for children of not participating in research on sensitive topics that seek to gather children's views may be more harmful than the risks of taking part, because they will not be able to benefit from advantages of participation like 'education, therapy and empowerment [or] the possibility of access to resources'.

It is certainly possible to gather children's perspectives in research 'about' children, but the adult-led nature of the research design perhaps means it is less likely that children will feel a sense of empowerment through taking part, and perhaps benefits to children are less likely to be realised. It is also more likely that children may feel less able to share their true perspectives with the researcher, because the child participants may feel a greater power-imbalance with the researcher than if a more child-centred, research 'with' children approach is taken. One example of a valuable study that seeks to explore children's perspectives through adult-designed research is The Children's Society's annual *The Good Childhood Report*, which aims to gather UK children's perspectives on their lives, and measure their levels of objective and subjective well-being. The Children's Society has been carrying out well-being surveys on children since 2007, and by 2016, when their fifth annual report was published, had gathered the perspectives of over 60,000 children across the UK (The Children's Society, 2016). A main finding from the 2016 report was that 14% of girls said they were unhappy with their lives as a whole, in comparison to 11% of boys. Knowing information like this, and the reasons why children and young people are unhappy, means that the charity is better equipped to know how to support children and young people. Having this information can be valuable for others too – for instance the report was referred to in a debate on children's well-being and mental health in schools in the UK Parliament in

January 2017, as evidence for why provision needs to be developed (House of Commons, 2017).

Yet others seek to conduct research about children's levels of well-being without asking children directly about their life or their experiences, but instead conduct observations so that adults can judge children's levels of perceived well-being and involvement. One tool for determining this has been developed by Ferre Laevers (2005), who has created two five-point scales, one to assess a child's level of well-being and one for their level of involvement. These scales have been used by researchers, such as Mackinder (2017), who used the involvement scale to assess through observation how involved children were in forest school experiences, and Declercq et al. (2011), who used both scales to identify that there were big disparities in levels of well-being and involvement across ECEC settings in a province of South Africa. The well-being and involvement scales are often promoted for use in ECEC settings to help practitioners identify how involved and content young children seem in their early years environments. However, carrying out observations on children in this way certainly supports a view of the child as passive and incompetent at sharing their perspective, and means that adult voices often do continue to dominate, even when the research topic is children's feelings and views.

TIME TO CONSIDER

Reflect on how research 'about' children has historically been conducted and how it is often conducted now. Draw up a list of what you think the advantages and the disadvantages are of gathering information and creating knowledge about young children in this way.

CASE STUDY

Jean visits her great-granddaughter in hospital

Jean is going to visit her two-year-old great-granddaughter, Ava, who has been admitted to hospital for a short stay. She thinks back to her own experiences of being a child patient in a hospital in the 1940s. She remembers feeling scared and anxious because her parents were not permitted to stay with her in the unfamiliar environment, which made her feel very unsettled and distressed. In contrast, when she arrives at the hospital, she finds that Ava has been accompanied by one of her parents for her whole stay. She seems content and cheerful.

Jean decides to find out why hospital practices have changed. In the time between her and Ava's hospital admissions, beliefs about what child patients need have transformed rapidly. Up until the 1960s, the prevalent view was that child patients were the same as adult patients: that they were 'small bodies that were ill, but cried a lot at the outset' (Lindon, 2012: 74), but they could not suffer long-term harm from parental separation, due to beliefs that children had relatively short memory spans. However, one influential figure in changing understandings, and therefore practices, was James Robertson (cited in Lindon, 2012), and later his wife Joyce. They made films in hospitals which evidenced the emotional distress of the children in the hospital. Robertson, who was working for Bowlby, known for his theory of maternal deprivation, recognised that this distress was more caused by parental separation than by medical interventions or procedures. The films were broadcast on national television, and contributed to the Ministry of Health publishing the Platt Report in 1959, which stated within it: 'Parents should be encouraged to visit children of all ages as much as possible' (1959: 168). Initially this was met with resistance from medical professionals, but Robertson's films inspired a group of parents in Battersea to form Mother Care for Children in Hospital, which aimed to persuade hospitals to follow the recommendations in the Platt Report. The group still exists today, as a charity called Action for Sick Children. Jean reflects on the implications that Robertson's (1958) research about children has had for changing government policy, inspiring community action and ultimately improving children's well-being during hospital stays. She wonders what research might currently be being conducted that will shape children's medical experiences in the future.

FINAL REFLECTION

This chapter has considered that research 'about' children has been the traditional way that researchers have found out about children's lives and through which theorists have developed theories of how children develop and learn. Research 'about' children is more likely to view children as subjects or objects in research than as participants, have an adult-led focus to research design and need careful ethical consideration. We do not want you to think that this type of research does not have a place in answering questions we may have about early childhood, but we do want you to recognise that it is not the only valuable way to discover new knowledge.

KEY POINTS

- Throughout the 20th century, a research-'about'-children approach has dominated how children's lives have been investigated. This is slowly changing as a research-'with'-children approach becomes more widely established and accepted.
- The research-'about'-children approach may have been informed by a traditional paradigm of children, which saw children as incomplete, incompetent and passive. This may have influenced how theorists in the 20th century, like Bandura and Piaget, developed their ideas about how children learn.
- There are still many pieces of research in the 21st century that take a research-'about'-children approach. They tend to be adult-led and adult-designed, but may be more likely than previous research to recognise children's perspectives.

FURTHER READING 

Hogan, D. (2005) 'Researching "the child" in developmental psychology', in S. Greene, and D. Hogan (eds), *Researching Children's Experience: Approaches and Methods*. London: Sage. pp. 22–41.

Hogan's chapter focusing on researching children in developmental psychology is worth a read to consider the assumptions that are made of children by developmental psychologists, how these assumptions have informed research practices and the challenges that their research approaches can face.

Woodhead, M. and Faulkner, D. (2008) 'Subjects, objects or participants? Dilemmas of psychological research with children', in P. Christiansen and A. James (eds), *Research with Children: Perspectives and Practices*. London: Falmer Press. pp. 10–39.

Woodhead and Faulkner's (2008) chapter about conducting research on children from a psychological point of view is interesting for the links between the discipline of Early Childhood Studies and the discipline of Psychology. Think about how psychologists might be informed by different 'truths' about children than early years practitioners, because of the knowledge base of their discipline.

6

APPROACHES TO RESEARCH WITH CHILDREN

INTRODUCTION

Having read the previous chapter, you may have decided that approaches to research 'about' children do not particularly fit with your way of viewing childhood. This is a key chapter and will consider the importance of doing research 'with' children and how children may be seen as active participants in research.

This chapter will ...

- Reflect upon how shifting perspectives of children have informed an increasing number of studies focused on participatory approaches with young children, including babies.
- Consider what the possibilities may be of such approaches and why it is important to listen to children's voices when conducting research in early childhood.
- Stress how research must be planned with child participants as willing and consenting partners in the research, regardless of their age.

WHAT VIEW OF CHILDREN UNDERPINS RESEARCH 'WITH' CHILDREN?

Within the last chapter, we thought about how traditionally the most common way to conduct research in relation to children's lives was by doing research 'about' them. We thought about the ways in which Penn (2008) says that research 'about' children has typically been conducted, and looked at what Woodhead and Faulkner (2008: 31) considered to be some of the key issues of doing psychological research in this way. The previous chapter considered that this was because the dominant way of viewing children has traditionally been as passive, incompetent and incomplete, which reinforced views of children as 'objects' or 'subjects' in research (Penn, 2008: 143). However, James and Prout (1997: 8) suggest that an emergent paradigm of childhood is developing which aims to give children a voice, and recognises that children are not 'passive subjects', but must be seen as active agents in their own social lives, or 'social actors' as Christensen and Prout (2002) say.

As a result, there is a growing amount of respect for children's perspectives and recognition of their voice, alongside a more widespread view that children are capable and competent. This means that research 'with' children is growing in popularity, and 'the notion of the child as subject (or object) is gradually being replaced by the notion of child as participant' (Woodhead and Faulkner, 2008: 31). We know you might be a little confused by this, because children may still be called 'participants' in research publications, even when they are actually being treated as objects or subjects in research. For this reason, we think that the term 'active participant' better encapsulates the shift in thinking to seeing children as social actors or active agents in their own lives.

When we view a child as an active participant, we consider their rights more than if we view them simply as an object. This means that we are more likely to ask for their informed consent to involve them as research participants, thus ensuring that the research that we are carrying out is more likely to be ethically sound. It also means that, because we are seeing them as competent and able to make and inform decisions, there is a higher probability we will take into account 'children's own views about good and useful research' (Penn, 2008: 142). This contrasts with pieces of research about children that have typically been conducted, for instance through surveys of adults, tests of 'representative' children and laboratory experiments. Pieces of research 'with' children ask for their views, consider their contexts (for instance the political or social context that may impact on them as individuals) and also make an effort to understand children's beliefs and behaviours to determine the rationale behind what they think.

It would be easy to believe that all research that purports to be conducted 'with' children sees children as equal partners in the research process, however this is simplistic thinking. Kellert (2005) argues that sometimes research with children as participants often has been done and still is done in a tokenistic way, where adults maintain control of the research and its focus, and thus there are still unequal power-relations. In some of these instances, children are described as 'co-researchers', which perhaps gives a construction of children as capable of contributing to, rather than taking control of, research studies. Kellert argues that instead of thinking about children as co-researchers, we should think about them as 'active researchers', which will empower them, give them agency and promote their self-development. However, she suggests that there is a lack of studies with children as active researchers, where adults take a supporting role rather than a management role in the project design, execution and dissemination. As an aside, it is important to note that Kellert's study on children as active researchers is now relatively old, and we know from Chapter 2 (Beginning to think critically about research) that we need to consider the timeliness of a source of information when thinking about how accurate it is. Later in this chapter we will consider how, although there is still a relative scarcity of children as active researchers, more studies have been published since Kellert's claim in 2005.

THE UNITED NATIONS CONVENTION ON THE RIGHTS OF THE CHILD

One of the reasons for the shift in perspective to seeing children both as participants in research and as researchers in their own right is due to the introduction of the United Nations Convention on the Rights of the Child (UNCRC) in 1989, which has shaped both national and international policy and legislation. The UNCRC was ratified in the UK in 1991, and has now been ratified in all UN member states except the United States of America (Unicef, 2017a), which means that it is seen as the 'leading global agreement' that all children have fundamental human rights, regardless of their gender, race, religion, language or any other characteristic (Kaufman and Rizzini, 2009:422). The articles in the UNCRC are often divided into three categories – those that offer provision, those that offer protection and those that offer participation (Penn, 2008; Kanyal, 2014). The groups of rights that are most relevant for considering the change in views about children are the articles that seek to ensure children's participation. For instance, Article 13 outlines that children have the freedom to express themselves and have access to information, and Article 12 states that children have a right to express their views and wishes and have these considered and taken seriously.

Evidence of a shift in acknowledging children's participatory rights has been growing in frequency over the last ten years. For instance, in 2010 the UK's Labour government produced a report that explained how implementation of the UNCRC was underpinned by legislation in England (HM Government, 2010). In the report, the government referred to Article 12 when explaining how children's voices are taken into account when writing policies that impact upon them. For instance, they referred to how they had consulted with children when deciding how to develop children's play provision within the government's 2008 report *The Play Strategy*, which outlined a new vision for children's play (DCSF, 2008a). They commissioned a market-research company called Sherbert Research to ask children what they think about play, what they would like from new play areas and what would make current play areas better (DCSF, 2008b). They also asked parents what they thought of their children's play. Findings of the report included that children often said that playing outside was their favourite type of playing, for instance because they said it gave opportunities for them to take risks and have a sense of freedom. Meanwhile parents said they had concerns about their children playing outside, because of reasons like 'stranger danger' and bullying. The research findings informed the government's strategy about how provision for children to play should be improved, for instance by publishing guidance on how to tackle bullying that takes place outside of schools and guidance about 'proportionate risk management' (DCFS, 2008a: 8) to support exciting play areas being developed. This shows how an awareness of the UNCRC has led to research being conducted that seeks to consider children's perspectives, with the intention of informing policy and provision.

When pieces of research are conducted, it is not always explicitly mentioned that children are afforded participation as a result of the UNCRC. Sometimes the reader might have to assume that the way in which children have been seen in the study has been impacted by the researcher's recognition and respect for the Convention – in particular in relation to Article 12 (that children have the right to communicate their views and have them taken seriously) and Article 13 (that children have the right for freedom of expression). However, there are times where researchers do specifically draw upon the UNCRC to justify their research decisions in how they involve children.

RESEARCH IN FOCUS

Using a UNCRC-informed approach

Lundy et al. (2011) sought to carry out a piece of research that used a UNCRC-informed approach with children as co-researchers to explore children's views of after-school clubs. They argued that 'when an explicit UNCRC-informed approach is applied to research, involving children as co-researchers, irrespective of age, takes on added significance and becomes, at the very least, a matter of principle' (Lundy et al., 2011: 718). They firmly kept Article 12 in mind when planning and conducting the research, and developed a model that shows how there are four concepts that support the UNCRC's participation rights – space, voice, audience and influence. That means that when children are involved in research, they must be supported to share their perspectives, in a place that is somewhere that is safe and meets their needs, and the information that they share needs to be listened to and acted on. Firstly, the researchers sought to build children's capacity to share their views through a variety of exercises, and when children had developed this, the researchers engaged the children in developing research questions, deciding what methods to use, interpreting the data and also disseminating it.

Whether researchers who do research 'with' children overtly acknowledge the role that the UNCRC has played in their research design or not, it certainly informs how research with children as participants is conducted. Similarly, it influences how children are seen and treated in early years settings more generally. If you have worked or volunteered in an ECEC setting in England, you may be familiar with the Early Years Foundation Stage (EYFS) (DfE, 2017a), which is the framework for ECEC provision for children from birth to five. You may argue that the EYFS does afford children the opportunities to express their views and wishes and have them listened to, in line with Articles 12 and 13. This is important to remember, as it means that if you are reading pieces of research that have been written by early years practitioners, the view they hold about children may naturally be reinforced by the curriculum framework that they work with on a daily basis.

TIME TO CONSIDER

The Early Years Foundation Stage (DfE, 2017a) is based upon four principles, including the first principle that 'Every child is a unique child, who is constantly learning and can be resilient, capable, confident and self-assured' (2017a: 6). What might this suggest about how research in early years settings should be conducted?

WHY IS RESEARCH 'WITH' CHILDREN IMPORTANT?

As we have already considered, research 'with' children is important because children have the right to participate in their lives as a result of the articles within the UNCRC. However, this is only one of many reasons why it is important to conduct research 'with' children. This section will consider why it is also important because it:

- supports children's empowerment;
- leads researchers to have a better idea of children's lives;
- provides perspectives about childhoods that adults are not able or willing to provide;
- suggests ideas to inform project design, which may lead to richer data collection;
- facilitates access to child participants who otherwise may not be involved.

As researchers who conduct research with children should always be putting the children first, it is appropriate to start by considering why this type of research approach is important for children. We already know that the rights that children have to participate are one reason why it is important to involve children in research and evaluation. Supporting children to participate allows them to develop new skills and feel empowered, particularly if child participants have an equal say to the adult researchers throughout the research process (Save the Children, 2000). The implications for empowering them through research may lead children to be empowered in other areas of their lives too. For instance, it may increase the extent to which they participate in their societies and communities and also how much they feel they are able to contribute to making decisions about areas that are relevant to them (Punch, 2002).

However, the reasons for involving children as participants in research are beneficial for researchers as well as children. This is because not only does it mean that researchers are adhering to the UNCRC, but they are also likely to get a deeper level of knowledge about what is important to children and what they think in comparison to the information they would gain about children's perspectives if it was filtered through the voices of adult participants, like parents or teachers. However, you might think that because adult participants like parents or teachers were previously children and school pupils themselves, it is not necessary to talk to children directly, because we can talk to adults about their childhood experiences. This is different to research that seeks to explore the perspectives of other vulnerable groups, such as people with SEN, when the researchers may not have had first-hand experiences of living with a special educational need or a disability. The idea of children as a vulnerable group is something you will consider more in Chapter 9 (The ethics of research). Yet, Kellert (2005) suggests that, despite the fact that some might argue that because all adults have been children at some stage and they can thus empathise with children's perspectives, since they have become adults they have acquired 'adult filters' (2005: 8), which means they no longer see things in the same way as children. She argues that children see and interpret the world through different eyes to adults and have different concerns. This means that children ask different research questions and collect different data. In this way, children therefore can generate new knowledge and information, which adults would be unable to do.

Linked to this, we know that adults will be basing their knowledge on their own childhood experiences, rather than the context of contemporary childhoods. Think about the adults that you interacted with growing up, in your home or in your primary school. It is probable that you will be able to identify or imagine differences between those adults' childhood experiences and your own. Thus, if we were to ask adults about childhoods, they may naturally reflect on childhoods of former generations, and may apply principles of previous childhoods to those of children today (Kellert, 2005).

There is one more reason why we can't rely on adults to give us children's perspectives retrospectively. You may be familiar with the idea of socialisation theories, which is where, throughout childhood, children are socialised into understanding the norms of their society and community through the interactions and relationships that they have with the people around them. That means that, over time, older children and adults may become socialised to say what they think they 'ought' to say, rather than what they really think. In comparison, we know that children can be almost too good at being honest about what they really think – you might have had a conversation with a child when you thought they were perhaps being too brutally honest about, for instance, somebody's appearance (often, unfortunately in earshot of the person whose appearance is being critiqued by the small child). So, as well as children seeing the world differently to adults because of their lack of adult-filters, they may also express their views of the world differently to adults, because they haven't yet developed a tactful nature, an understanding to avoid hurting others' feelings or have been socialised to think that certain topics or opinions ought not be expressed. This may be particularly beneficial if the purpose of the research is to evaluate programmes that children access.

You have already considered in this book how research can be useful to evaluate policies and programmes for children and see if they can be improved (OECD, 2012a). Save the Children (2000) note that in relation to research that seeks to evaluate services for children, gaining their perspectives can be important not only in terms of what they say in their evaluations of the service, but also what aspects they decide should be evaluated – in essence, choosing what information should be collected and how it should be analysed. For instance, Roberts et al. (1995) have written about some research they were carrying out about children and accidents. Although their research is now quite dated and focuses on older children as participants, they share an honest reflection on the limitations of their research design, until they sought the views of their teenage participants about their interview schedule. They say:

> Teenagers had little to say about the kind of events we [the researchers] had thought of as accidents. Nor did they respond well to the notion of safety or safe-keeping. In the end we asked them what our opening question should be. 'Ask us about our scars', they replied. So we did, and it resulted in animated and detailed information about a number of accident events. (Roberts et al., 1995: 34)

Essentially, this reflection shows that when children are included in the project design, the data that is collected can be a lot richer, more detailed and useful to the researchers. It might also better reflect an accurate picture of children's lives than can be gathered through research-'about'-children approaches. Bronfenbrenner (1979: 19, cited in Woodhead and Faulkner, 2008: 22) stated that conducting experiments with children in artificial laboratory environments demonstrates 'the strange behaviour of children in strange situations with strange adults for the briefest possible periods of time'. When children are viewed as competent and have the opportunity to develop skills and capacity to co-research, it is perhaps likely that the situations that those children are in will feel less unfamiliar to them than a laboratory, with adults that they have built up more of a relationship with (for instance perhaps their teacher or early years practitioner that they already know), over a longer period of time. Thus, the findings of the study may be likely to show a more reliable, accurate picture of children's capabilities, competencies and views.

Finally, an often overlooked reason why research with children as co-researchers is important is because child researchers may have access to the voices of other children that would be unobtainable to other adults (Kellert, 2005). This means a wider range of children's voices are able to be considered. The perspectives of other children that are gathered by child researchers may also be likely to reflect children's more genuine views and feelings; there might not be such an unequal power-relationship as between an adult researcher and child participant, so the child participants may feel more relaxed and comfortable throughout the research process. When adults conduct group interviews with children, a strength can be that children can 'help each other with the answers, remind each other to talk about the details, and keep the answers truthful' (Einarsdottir, 2007: 200). All of these benefits will arguably be apparent when children are themselves the interviewers. However, there are dangers to children interviewing other children and these should not be overlooked. There is a risk that children will over-identify with their participants, and thus assume that they know more about their participants than is really the case, losing their '"enquiring outsider" stance' (Alderson, 2001: 140).

Table 6.1 Benefits of researching with children

- Supporting children to participate allows them to develop new skills and feel empowered in other aspects of their lives.
- It maintains adherence to the UNCRC.
- Children can generate new knowledge and information, which adults would be unable to do.
- Children express their views differently to adults because they have not yet been socialised to say what they 'ought' or 'ought not' to say.
- Involving children in the research design can lead to richer data collection and a more accurate picture of their perspectives.
- Children may have access to the views of other children which would not be obtainable by adults.

TIME TO CONSIDER

Using Table 6.1, reflect upon what you know about why research 'with' children is important, decide what is the most important reason for you, and why. Now consider what the challenges might be of conducting research using this approach. We will come back to the difficulties of research 'with' children in the next section.

HOW CAN RESEARCH 'WITH' CHILDREN BE CONDUCTED?

If you now agree that there are many reasons why it is important to conduct research 'with' children, let us consider the variety of ways and methods that can be used to do it. In this section we will look at methods that have been developed by Clark and Moss (2011; Clark, 2017), Pascal and Bertram (2009) and Sherbert Research (2017), and how these methods have been used to gather children's perspectives so that researchers can find out more about their lives and opinions.

The Mosaic Approach (Clark and Moss, 2011)

Clark and Moss's Mosaic Approach (2011; Clark, 2017) is probably one of the most famous approaches to research 'with' children within early childhood. It was originally developed for practitioner researchers in ECEC settings to co-research with children aged three and four to find ways to listen to their voices. It has since been expanded to facilitate participation for children who speak English as an additional language, children aged under two, and for parents and practitioners. Clark and Moss (2011: 1) state that the approach is inspired by the pedagogical documentation of Reggio Emilia, which is significant because it shows how it is underpinned by an awareness that children are competent in Malguzzi's 'hundred languages of children' (Edwards et al., 1998: 3) and supports their view of children as experts in their own lives, skilful communicators, rights holders and as meaning makers (Clark and Moss, 2005: 5). It is described as a framework for listening that is 'multi-method, participatory, reflexive, adaptable, focused on children's lived experiences [and] embedded into practice' (Clark and Moss, 2011: 7) and is comprised of three stages. The first stage is about gathering information using the techniques in Table 6.2. You can see from this table how the research approach is multi-modal, for instance through how it considers the child's perspective through using a variety of techniques, as well as adults' perspectives too. Secondly, once all the pieces of documentation have been gathered, they are drawn together to bring together a clearer idea of what is important to children in early years settings, which can help make a 'living picture' (Clark and Moss, 2011: 42) of a child. Finally, the third stage is about 'deciding on continuity and change' (2011: 13) and intends to encourage practitioners to make a link between listening to children's perspectives and taking action to respond to what children said.

Table 6.2 Some of the methods used by Clark and Moss (2011; Clark, 2017) for gathering children's perspectives

Observations	Researchers can observe children and this may give an understanding of some aspects of their lives, although this is only the perspective of the adult who is observing
Child conferencing	Researchers can talk to young children about their early years setting in a type of interview, either individually or with other children. This can be useful to gather children's perspectives on (in particular) people, places and activities. It can be repeated with the same children over time with the same questions, so that children can reflect upon their previous answers and consider whether their views have changed

(Continued)

Table 6.2 (Continued)

Taking photographs	Researchers can give cameras to children to share their visual perspectives on their early years setting, which may provide more in-depth information into what they value or where they choose to spend time. These photographs are then used as starting points for discussions with the children that have taken the photos about the content of the photos. Clark and Moss also used this method to ask three- and four-year-olds to take photos on behalf of babies, as a type of 'children about children' (2011: 25) research approach
Tours	Researchers can ask children to lead tours for them, where children decide where to take the adult researcher, and how the tour is documented (for instance through audio-recording, photographs or drawings). This can be a way for adults to see what children are interested in in a more child-led, natural way than in an unfamiliar interview room
Mapping	Researchers can work with children to create maps that incorporate photographs that were taken during the tour, which can help researchers see what children prioritise and also which people, as well as places, are important to the children in their setting
Role play	Researchers can use small world play toys that are similar to the resources available in the setting to talk to children about their setting and, with older children, to help them 'tell their own narratives about life in the nursery' (2011: 33)
Parents' perspectives	Researchers can also gather parents' perspectives through, for instance, conducting interviews with them, so that they can share their opinion on their children and their experiences. This is especially important for children who are non-verbal
Practitioners' perspectives	Researchers can also interview practitioners for their opinions on the children in their settings and what they enjoy. Alternatively, they could also gather practitioners' perspectives through using methods such as cameras, video recorders or diaries
Researchers' perspectives	It is important within the Mosaic Approach for researchers to reflect upon their own perspectives, for instance through photographs, observation notes and field notes

Opening Windows (Pascal and Bertram, 2009)

The Mosaic Approach is one of the most commonly employed approaches to research within early childhood settings, but it isn't the only multi-method technique that is used to gather children's perspectives. For instance, Pascal and Bertram (2009) argue that if children are going to be seen in light of their rights within the UNCRC, the research that is conducted with them needs to take a participatory and inclusive form. They cite the Mosaic Approach as one approach that does this, and echo Clark and Moss's (2011) sentiments that it is important that researchers listen to children because it is not possible to fully understand or infer their perspective otherwise. They have developed a programme called *Opening Windows*, which provides training materials to help practitioners and researchers encourage interaction and dialogue between themselves, children and parents. The programme equips researchers and practitioners to use 'a menu of strategies to create and sustain democratic encounters with children' (2009: 258), including the following methods:

- video-stimulated dialogue
- cultural circles
- critical incident analysis
- story telling and naming your world
- wishing trees
- listening posts
- map making
- guided tours
- focused observations
- photography and film making (Pascal and Bertram, 2009: 258)

TIME TO CONSIDER

Take a moment to look at these techniques, and how you can draw parallels between these methods and the ones within the Mosaic Approach. What do you think the strength might be that there are so many different ways in which they both seek to gather children's perspectives?

One strength might be that because we know that children and their lives are diverse, we need a diverse range of methods to find out their views. For instance, Rabiee et al. (2005) argue that, traditionally, perspectives of children with disabilities have been gathered through talking to adults rather than the children themselves, which 'says more about unsuitability of research and consultation methods and adults not knowing how to relate to them than about the limitations on the part of informants' (2005: 387). Methods developed by Clark and Moss (2011; Clark, 2017) and Pascal and Bertram (2009) could support and provide extra scaffolding for children with disabilities to express their views.

Finally, it is important to acknowledge that it's not just academics who might be conducting research (either 'about' or 'with' children) – it might be the case that organisations commission other people, like market-research companies, to conduct research on their behalf. Earlier in this chapter we introduced Sherbert Research (2017), who are a market research agency that conducts qualitative research with children from preschool age and above. In 2014, they were commissioned by Ofcom (2014) to look at how children understand and manage online risks and decide what sources of information to trust online. To do this, they carried out three types of data collection methods. They used 'friendship triad' discussion groups, individual 'accompanied surfs' and finally, 'filmed, unmoderated sessions', which is where a friendship group are given a set of discussion topics, and then left alone whilst their conversation is video-taped (Ofcom, 2014: 3). The advantage of discussions where adults are absent is that it allows children to give more honest responses to the discussion themes, although it does mean that there is not an adult to mediate if the conversation digresses.

RESEARCH IN FOCUS

Researching the BBC's children's brands

In 2013, Sherbert Research was commissioned by the BBC Trust to consider what parents and children thought about the BBC's children's brands, CBeebies and CBBC (Karet, 2013). They recognised that, as the target audiences for CBeebies and CBBC are different (CBeebies is aimed at children up to six, whilst CBBC is targeted at children from six to twelve), the ways in which they gathered the children's opinions and views needed to differ depending on their age and stage of development. For children between 18 months and four years old, researchers held 'coffee mornings', where three parents with their three children met a researcher in one of their homes, and the researchers observed the children watching television, playing on the Internet and playing generally, and also spoke to the parents at the same time. For children from six to twelve, researchers used 'bedroom hangouts'. This is where children in 'friendship quads' met a researcher without their parents or carers present in one of their bedrooms. A strength of this method is that children are put at ease, feel confident to share their views because they are with their friends, and the researchers can see their home context and have a better idea of what the children's lives are like (Karet, 2013: 9).

DIFFICULTIES OF CONDUCTING RESEARCH WITH CHILDREN

However, although research 'with' children is important to do, it is not always easy to conduct. Bradbury-Jones and Taylor (2015) acknowledge that there are difficulties in engaging with children as co-researchers, and outline six challenges that may exist, and then offers a counter-challenge and a solution for each one. For instance, Challenge #4 is that 'remuneration is complex'. Take a moment to reflect upon if you had considered whether you would expect a child to be paid to take part in a research project. Then reflect upon whether you yourself would expect to be paid to recompense you for your time if you were an adult participant in a study. Bradbury-Jones and Taylor (2015) present several counter-challenges for this difficulty, for instance citing Alderson and Morrow (2011: 68) that children deserve 'ethically fair returns' in return for participating in research projects, particularly because children are often giving up their own free time to participate (Bergström et al., 2010). Their solution is that children must be compensated in an appropriate, context-specific way, but in a way that is not tokenistic, authoritarian or patronising. In relation to the Mosaic Approach specifically, Clark and Moss (2011) also believe that there are challenges to listening to children. For instance, despite the fact that earlier we considered how participating in research may empower children (Punch, 2002), Clark and Moss (2011) question whether it may be the case that if we have more information about a child and thus they are more 'visible' (2011: 54), then they might also be more easily controlled, so people will have more power over them. Yet conversely, the researchers do suggest that it is possible that using the approach may make children more confident and help them to develop new skills.

Often students who are undertaking a dissertation encounter other practical barriers of conducting research with children. For instance, it can be more time-consuming to work with children as co-researchers to design and conduct a piece of research, which may make it impractical. As you will consider in Chapter 9 (The ethics of research), it can be trickier to gain ethical approval because of seeking to recruit participants who are considered vulnerable. Finally, some students have difficulty gaining access to child participants. They need to think about the feasibility of approaching nurseries or schools and the likelihood they will be given permission to conduct research in their setting whilst still in the initial stages of planning their research.

TIME TO CONSIDER

You have now considered both what the advantages are of doing research 'with' children, but also what some of the disadvantages or challenges might be. Draw up a table of what you think the advantages and the disadvantages are of gathering information and creating knowledge about young children using research 'with' children approaches.

CASE STUDY

Xander: the deputy manager in a 0–5 setting

Xander wants to develop the experiences on offer in his early years setting and is wondering how he can involve the children in informing this small piece of research. He decides to read a study by someone who has used the Mosaic Approach, to see whether he thinks it will work for him. He finds a study written by Waller (2014), who used the technique to find out more about children's outdoor play in early years settings. What was a particular focus of Waller's (2014) data collection method was the use of digital cameras, which were used by the researchers, practitioners and children themselves to capture instances of outdoor play. In one of the settings in which Waller conducted his research, he incorporated a 'reactive method', which Corsaro (2015: 51) describes as when a researcher sits down near to where children are playing and waits until the children choose to

(Continued)

(Continued)

interact with them, rather than (as he says adults typically do) entering a play space and taking the lead on interacting with children. In Waller's research, that meant that 'children could decide to carry on playing, or to record an aspect of their play or space with the camera, or ask an adult to record it for them' (2014: 162). These images were then used to reflect upon children's experiences outdoors.

This is intriguing to Xander. However, he is also conscious that he doesn't wish to exclude the perspectives of the babies in the setting. He reads a chapter by Sumsion et al. (2011), who adapted the Mosaic Approach by adding the use of a 'baby-cam' (a small camera with audio-recording equipment that was attached to a baby's headband) to find out more about young children's 'lived-experiences' in their early years settings. Xander reflects upon the 'technical, methodological, and ethical challenges' (Sumsion et al., 2011: 119) of gathering data in this way, including that the children are unlikely to have an awareness or understanding of the research, and the risk to their privacy. However, he agrees with the authors that these challenges are outweighed by the benefits the method can offer in gaining more knowledge about very young children's views of their ECEC settings.

Xander reflects upon how digital methods that are informed by the Mosaic Approach could be used to build up a picture of children's experiences in his workplace. He plans to discuss the pieces of research with his colleagues at a staff meeting, to consider what they think the benefits and challenges might be of introducing digital cameras for older children in the setting and a 'baby-cam' for younger children as a way of gathering more information about what they do whilst they are at the nursery. He plans to follow this by explaining the methods to the children themselves and asking them what they would think about using cameras to take photographs and record what they do at nursery, to see whether they are likely to be willing to take part.

TIME TO CONSIDER

Imagine you want to involve children as co-researchers in a research project that seeks to explore children's perspectives of owning pets. Reflect upon the ways that research with children is currently conducted, and reflect upon how you could involve children in designing, directing and disseminating the piece of research.

FINAL REFLECTION

In this chapter we have considered various ways that research 'with' children can be conducted, which is increasingly replacing traditional research 'about' children approaches, particularly within early childhood and in ECEC settings. It can be an incredibly valuable and important thing to do, not only for the opportunities that it gives to create new knowledge, but because of the benefits it can offer for child participants too. Children's well-being must be placed at the forefront of decisions about research designs and delivery.

KEY POINTS 

- As the way in which children are viewed generally is changing, so are the ways that they are seen in research. Children are being seen as increasingly competent and with the right to participate, which reflects an increase in research that values their voice and contribution.
- It is important to conduct research with children for many reasons, including because it will help give researchers a clearer perspective on children's experiences and views, and because it acknowledges their rights within the UNCRC.
- There are a variety of ways that children can be involved as active participants or co-researchers. Typically, methods may be more innovative than are used in research 'about' children, and the diversity of methods reflects the diversity in children, their competencies and capabilities.

FURTHER READING 

Lundy, L., McEvoy, L. and Byrne, B. (2011) 'Working with young children as co-researchers: an approach informed by the United Nations Convention on the Rights of the Child', *Early Education and Development*, 22(5): 714–36.

This journal article breaks down really clearly how children can be involved in all stages of the research process, and how children's capacity to engage can be developed.

Clark, A. and Moss, P. (2011) *Listening to Young Children: The Mosaic Approach.* London: National Children's Bureau.

Clark, A. (2017) *Listening to Young Children: A Guide to Understanding and Using the Mosaic Approach*, 3rd edn. London: National Children's Bureau/Jessica Kingsley.

Have a look at the original book by Clark and Moss, and the most recent expanded edition, for a much more detailed consideration of the Mosaic Approach, including case study examples of each method and how the pieces of the mosaic can be brought together for particular children.

7

LONGITUDINAL RESEARCH APPROACHES

INTRODUCTION

Now you have considered research 'about' children and research 'with' children, let's move on to the role that longitudinal research has played in building up the knowledge we hold about young children and their lives. This method of tracking children over time can be an effective way to find out more about the impact of their experiences.

This chapter will ...

- Share examples of several pieces of longitudinal research on children, such as the EPPE Project (Sylva et al., 2004) and the Millennium Cohort Study (MCS) (Institute of Education, 2011), the National Evaluation of Sure Start (NESS Team, 2012), the Making of Modern Motherhood study (Thomson et al., 2008) and the Perry Preschool Project (Schweinhart, 2016).
- Consider some of the strengths and limitations of collecting information about children in this way and build your ability to critique this type of research design.
- Think about some ethical dilemmas of conducting longitudinal studies.

WHAT IS LONGITUDINAL RESEARCH?

In Chapter 1 you were introduced to the idea of longitudinal studies as one of the five main ways that the OECD (2012a) say that research in ECEC is commonly conducted. If you remember, we considered how longitudinal studies are pieces of research that are carried out about the same individual but at different times in their life. We looked at an example from the Millennium Cohort Study and how it can be used to identify links between children's development and their home environments.

Several organisations give useful definitions of longitudinal research. As a starting point, the UK Longitudinal Studies Centre (2017) describe it as 'a photograph album rather than a single snapshot. It tells a story of people's lives at a moment in time, but also over time, showing how individuals or families have changed'. This metaphor is echoed by Unicef (2017b), who suggest that longitudinal studies are 'more of a film strip than a single image'. They describe these types of studies as unique, because of the way that they can track the processes that impact on children's development, identify 'trends and trajectories' and help us to understand 'drivers and determinants' of children's outcomes. Identifying these trends may help researchers develop their knowledge in relation to a variety of issues and their causes, and their understanding of how effective policies and programmes may be over time (Economic and Social Research Council, 2011). The OECD's (2012d) definition is slightly more detailed but matches that of the UK Longitudinal Studies Centre and Unicef. They describe a longitudinal study as:

> A research study that involves repeated observations of the same variables during certain periods of time. Reiterative data, collected at different intervals on a representative national sample or on a population cohort of a certain type, that allow researchers to study – in depth and over time – important issues for children in contemporary society, such as quality parameters and their effects, or the relationship between family characteristics and children's health, educational or employment outcomes. (OECD, 2012d: 5)

A useful source of information about longitudinal studies has been written by the UK Longitudinal Studies Centre (2017), which was established in 1999 by the Economic and Social Research Council (ESRC). They describe how there are different types of longitudinal study, including individual surveys, household surveys and cohort studies. Cohort studies are the most common type of longitudinal studies to be carried out on children. They are when a sample of children of the same age are tracked to identify and assess their outcomes over time. Sometimes students get longitudinal studies, particularly cohort studies, confused with cross-sectional studies. Cross-sectional studies are, in comparison, when a selection of different people (for instance this may be children of different developmental stages) are assessed at one point in time to compare them (Knowland et al., 2015). Linking back to the photograph metaphor, it is like the difference between a school photographer coming into school on one day and you as a researcher looking at the photographs that have been taken of children in different years and comparing them (cross-sectional research) and you going around to somebody's house and seeing their annual school photograph from each year on display in their living room and looking at how they've changed as they've got older (longitudinal research). The strength of cross-sectional research is that it doesn't take years to collect the data, like longitudinal studies can, but a weakness is that there may be external variables and characteristics of the children that make them different to one another independent of their varying ages (for instance, their family structure or background). This means it is hard to compare like-for-like.

Longitudinal research has played an important role in influencing early childhood policies and we will consider several examples of this in the next section. Some of the main influences relate to child development and social mobility (ESRC, 2011). For example, the Allen Review (2011) was a report that sought to make recommendations to the UK Coalition government of 2010–15 about how to improve children's life chances through early intervention. It was informed by several longitudinal studies, including the Dunedin Study, that began tracking just over 1,000 children from Dunedin in New Zealand born in 1972–3 (Poulton et al., 2015) and the EPPE Project (Syvla et al., 2004). As a result of longitudinal data like this, researchers and policymakers are able to track children's development throughout their childhood and teenage years and consider the links between aspects of children's lives, such as their family background, educational attainment and later outcomes (ESRC, 2011). This means that it is possible to build up a greater understanding of social mobility, how to promote it, and the drivers of socio-economic inequality that stifle it.

It has been suggested that, despite the benefits of longitudinal studies, there are not enough longitudinal studies in early childhood that are of high quality, particularly when compared to other fields like medicine (Schweinhart, 2016). Linked to this, Schweinhart suggests that there are topics that are just as worthy as ECEC to explore, but do not attract longitudinal funding, like education and parenting programmes. He suggests it is assumed by policymakers that effective ECEC alone will be able to reduce inequality. This is why longitudinal research into what makes high-quality ECEC is invested in. However, in actual fact early education is only one facet of people's lives that needs to be high quality to combat the cycle of poverty.

TIME TO CONSIDER 

Reflect upon what you have learnt about the features of longitudinal studies. Try to write your own short definition. Now, take a moment to consider what you think some of the impacts might be of this type of research design on (a) children, (b) families and (c) their communities. Write a short summary of this.

HOW IS LONGITUDINAL RESEARCH TYPICALLY CONDUCTED?

The Effective Provision of Pre-School Education (EPPE) Project

You have already considered some longitudinal studies in the book which we will think about in more depth now. Firstly, we considered the EPPE Project (Sylva et al., 2004) back in Chapter 1. You will remember how the EPPE Project can be seen as a type of programme evaluation, which originally aimed to find out what makes effective early childhood education and care, and what the lasting effects of preschool might be on a child's development. The study began in 1997 by recruiting a sample of 3,000 three-year-old children, who attended a range of different types of early years settings, with some attending no early years setting at all. Data on the children was collected using methods such as observations, interviews with their parents and practitioners, standardised assessments and social/behavioural profiles completed by the child's early years setting (Sylva et al., 2004). Since then, the children's behavioural and academic outcomes have continued to be tracked, to identify whether there are any long-lasting impacts of attending an early years setting. Findings from the study are plentiful, but one of the key findings from when the children finished Key Stage 1 was that 'pre-school experience, compared to none, enhances all-round development in children' (Sylva et al., 2004: 4). The impacts on policy of the EPPE Project have been vast – including that the Labour government of 1997–2010 decided as a result of the findings in 2004 to offer free part-time early years education to every child the term after their third birthday (Melhuish, 2016: 7), and in 2012 the Coalition government extended free early years education to two-year-olds in disadvantaged families, following EPPE evidence that attending high-quality ECEC settings was beneficial for two-year-olds. The EPPE study also found that integrated centres (those that had integrated childcare, early education and sometimes other family support and family services) were a particularly beneficial type of ECEC setting for children's intellectual outcomes and social development. As a result, Melhuish (2016: 7) credits the EPPE Project, alongside the National Evaluation of Sure Start (NESS), with influencing the implementation of Sure Start Children's Centres (as opposed to Sure Start Local Programmes).

The National Evaluation of Sure Start (NESS)

The National Evaluation of Sure Start (NESS) is one of two large-scale longitudinal studies in the UK that Eisenstadt (2011) claims have been especially influential in bringing about changes to government policy – the other being the

EPPE Project. The NESS impact study carried out longitudinal research on 5,883 children when they were nine months, three, five and seven years old to evaluate the effectiveness of Sure Start Local Programmes (SSLP). SSLP were early intervention programmes aimed at integrating health, social care and education services for children from birth to four, where those implementing the programmes had a great deal of autonomy in deciding how they would be delivered. This aimed to ensure that families across areas were having their individual needs met and could have a say in the programme design, but this also led to huge variations in how SSLPs were organised. The NESS impact study originally showed that SSLPs were having a positive impact on deprived children who were attending, but not the most deprived. Subsequently, as a result of these findings, and the findings about integrated settings from the EPPE Project referred to above, the decision was made to transfer all SSLPs to Sure Start Children's Centres. Later longitudinal findings showed that attending a centre was beneficial for children, for instance in terms of their behavioural, emotional and personal development, and for their parents, for instance in terms of their parenting and the relationships they formed with their children. Because of this, the Labour government announced in 2003 that by 2010 there would be 3,500 children's centres. However, Melhuish states of this decision:

> While this policy decision was influenced by NESS results, it was not supported by the actual NESS evidence, and this illustrates how politicians will use evidence to suit their own goals rather than following the logic of the evidence itself. (Melhuish, 2016: 8)

This is important to remember, when considering not just longitudinal research, but research in general. Policymakers may misinterpret the findings ('results') of studies, or analysis ('evidence') of studies, or cherry-pick elements from research findings to support their own agendas ('suit their own goals'). Think back to two important things from Chapter 3 (Knowledge and truth in research). Firstly, remember how people, including politicians and policymakers, will hold their own truths about children, and secondly how when you read a piece of research, you need to think about the values and beliefs that you are bringing to the reading, and how that has an impact on how you understand it. The values and beliefs of the policymakers who decided to expand the provision of children's centres may have led them to read the NESS study through a different lens to Melhuish (2016).

The Study of Early Education and Development (SEED)

As well as providing evidence for how the NESS study and the EPPE Project have been significant in informing early education and care policy in the UK up until this point, Melhuish (2016) puts forward that the Study of Early Education and Development (SEED), a relatively new longitudinal piece of research, will be the driver of future early childhood policy. The study aims to interview families of 8,000 children in their homes when their children are two, three and four years old, and will follow these children until they finish Key Stage 1 (Department for Education, 2017b). Visits will also be made to 1,000 early years settings to carry out observations to assess the quality of those settings. In this way, the study draws parallels with the EPPE Project but, as Melhuish (2016) acknowledges, because so much has changed in policy and practice since the sample of participants in the EPPE Project attended their early childhood settings, a new study is necessary to consider what early education looks like in the UK currently. It is intended that the study will add to knowledge about the long-term benefits and impacts of early childhood education and care, and help inform government spending decisions by building understanding of the cost-benefits of investing in early childhood education. Take a moment to think about this. If you were to conduct a longitudinal study that aimed to assess the impact of childcare and early education, how would you go about it? Would you track children by interviewing families in their homes? Would you use observation rating scales of quality, like the researchers involved in this study are doing? Or would you use different techniques? Why?

However, it is not only government policy about education that has been influenced and is being influenced by longitudinal studies that are tracking children. It is health policies too. A report produced by the Institute of Education (2011) about the Millennium Cohort Study highlights how research about breastfeeding that used MCS data has been effective in influencing health policy both in the UK and internationally. Some MCS research has found that children who are breastfed are less likely to be admitted to hospital with diarrhoea and respiratory infections (Quigley et al., 2007). Other studies based on MCS data have found that the child participants who were breastfed were less likely to be overweight (Hawkins et al., 2009) and more likely to have higher cognitive scores at age three (Dearden et al., 2011). The Institute of Education (2011) note that MCS research has had an impact on health organisations within the UK, like the Department of Health and the National Institute for Health and Care Excellence (NICE) (2008), who refer to research by Quigley et al. (2007) in their guidance on maternal and child nutrition. However, they also note that the research has been used internationally, for instance it has informed the government's breastfeeding policy in South Africa, it has been cited by Unicef (2015b) in a report recommending the benefits of breastfeeding, and has been referred to by the World Health Organisation. This is significant because it shows that, although a limitation of longitudinal studies may be that researchers have to wait a long time to be able to collect, analyse and disseminate the data, their findings can have an impact both on a national and an international platform.

MCS findings have not only influenced policymakers, but have been identified as shaping thinking and opinions of the public too, particularly in relation to controversial topics like breastfeeding and parenting practices

(Johnson and Antill, 2011). The Institute of Education (2011) say that the MCS has attracted an 'exceptional amount of TV, radio and web coverage' (2011: 5), both within the UK and abroad. However, Johnson and Antill (2011) suggest that the media attention that some MCS press releases have generated may have drawn awareness to the Millennium Cohort Study but there is not clear evidence that this will play a role in shaping policy; although they do provide a case study from Wales that says that media coverage of the MCS has helped Welsh Ministers to understand the significance of the study (2011: 32). They also note that there are many instances where newspaper articles report MCS findings, but without naming the study explicitly, as is common in mass media reports. Think back to Chapter 2 (Beginning to think critically about research) and how we considered that newspaper articles are not considered to be scholarly sources of information, and thus you should try to avoid using them as references in your academic work and find journal articles instead. Johnson and Antill's (2011) point that the MCS is not always overtly named in newspaper reports is evidence of this – in your academic work you want to show how deep your level of knowledge and understanding is, and you can't do that if you are reading newspaper articles that are not clear in telling you where their information has come from.

TIME TO CONSIDER

Think about the specific areas that you are interested in that relate to children and families. If you could conduct a piece of longitudinal research, what would it be? Why?

WHAT ARE THE STRENGTHS AND LIMITATIONS OF LONGITUDINAL RESEARCH?

We have already thought in this chapter about what some of the strengths of conducting longitudinal research can be. For instance, in terms of evaluating policy, it can help in assessing changes over time and evaluating how the outcomes of interventions may alter as time goes on (OECD, 2012d). However, longitudinal research is not only beneficial for policy research, but can give an insight into societal changes in attitudes and behaviours too. These studies are more likely to use qualitative methods, which were briefly introduced to you in Chapter 1, and will be considered in more depth in Chapter 10 (How research is designed). Thomson et al. (2008) carried out a qualitative longitudinal study, called *The Making of Modern Motherhood*, which followed pregnant women in the UK through their journey of becoming first-time mothers by using interviews, case studies and questionnaires. Findings focused on topics such as the women's changing identities, what the concept of motherhood meant to them, how they 'practised' motherhood and the resources and advice they used to help them through their journey. The strength of this approach is that it allowed an in-depth picture to be built of the participants' views and experiences, which would be harder to gather in a study that did not track the same participants over time.

RESEARCH IN FOCUS

Corsaro and Molinari (2017)

Sociologists Corsaro and Molinari (2017) have also conducted qualitative longitudinal studies. They hold a belief that, when studying children's social worlds, it is imperative to do it longitudinally because of how children's relationship with their culture and society changes as time goes on. Their chapter shares the longitudinal ethnography about children's transition from preschool to school in a city in Northern Italy. Corsaro shares his experience as a field researcher in the preschool classroom and how his relationship with the children developed and his participation as a member of the class grew. This research illustrates that when we think of longitudinal studies, we do not have to envisage large-scale pieces of research that comprise of thousands of participants who are tracked for many years, like in the MCS, SEED or the EPPE Project. Instead, longitudinal research can be like Corsaro and Molinari's (2017) study, which took place in one classroom, over months rather than years. Both approaches will give a photo-album, rather than a snapshot, of the child participants' lives, which, as you will remember, is a key feature of longitudinal research (UK Longitudinal Studies Centre, 2017).

However, there are limitations to longitudinal studies too. One is that it takes time for patterns to emerge about the positive and negative impacts of children's experiences. This means that findings that can inform policy and practice come too late to positively impact on the participants themselves. This is the caveat that Eisenstadt (2011) puts on this type of research design. She argues that, even though 'Britain has led the world in longitudinal studies' and they have been incredibly significant in developing policy, their findings do not benefit the children involved in the study, and thus it is necessary to find some 'simple, real-time, non-intrusive and not terribly expensive' alternatives (2011: 155). Have a think about this. What do you think these alternatives could be?

In relation specifically to qualitative longitudinal studies, Thomson and Holland (2003) suggest that one difficulty can be in ensuring 'continuity of funding and personnel' (2003: 242). For instance, challenges can include maintaining a consistent researcher–participant relationship, to reduce the risk of participants dropping out and to increase the quality of the data that is collected. Whether longitudinal research is qualitative or quantitative, the cost of the studies can be great, and unlike studies that can be conducted over a short period of time, maintaining funding over years can be difficult, especially when it can take time for them to show that the research findings are worthwhile. Similarly, attrition rates or withdrawal rates of participants can be a challenge too. Recognising the importance of this, Thomson et al. (2008) attempted to minimise the number of participants who dropped out from their study by seeking to build up strong relationships between each participant and the researcher who conducted interviews with them.

Some people think that one limitation of longitudinal research is the ethical concern of those that use randomised controlled trials (RCTs). RCTs are a way of evaluating a policy or programme intervention by offering some people at random to receive the service, and then assessing their outcomes against a control group who don't take part in the programme (White et al., 2014).

RESEARCH IN FOCUS

The Perry Preschool Project

One very famous longitudinal study that used RCTs was the Perry Preschool Project (Schweinhart, 2005). This study began in 1962 in the United States with a sample of 123 'low-income African-American children who were assessed to be at high risk of school failure' (2005: 1). They were split into two groups – one of whom began to access a high-quality preschool programme, and another that did not. Researchers began to collect data on the children in relation to their education, employment, criminal activity, health and relationships, and have continued to track them into adulthood. By age five, 67% of the group attending the preschool programme had an IQ of 90 or above, in comparison to 28% of the non-programme group. Sixty-five per cent of the preschool attendees graduated regular high school, in contrast to 45% of the children that didn't attend. And by age 40, 36% of the preschool programme group had been arrested at least five times, in comparison to 55% of the non-programme group. The Perry Preschool Study has been used as evidence for the long-term impact of high-quality preschool experiences on children both in the UK and internationally.

Before we go any further, take a moment to reflect on what the implications might be of randomly selecting some children to access a high-quality programme, and then comparing those to a group that you do not give the service to. How would you feel if you grew up as one of the children who was in the control group of the Perry Preschool Project, now knowing how different your outcomes might have been if you had received the preschool provision that one of your friends or neighbours did? Do you think there may be ethical concerns? The ethical implications of doing RCTs are most significant when the control group is not receiving any type of intervention because there is the highest likelihood that this group will be disadvantaged (White et al., 2014: 7). It might also lead to conflict or disharmony between participants in the control group and those receiving the intervention.

Sammons et al. (2005) drew upon the methodology used in the Perry Preschool Project when justifying the research design of the EPPE Project. They argue, however, that using RCTs in research that seeks to explore the impact of preschool presents grave practical and, more importantly, ethical limitations. They say that in England, parents would not find it suitable that somebody randomly assigned their child to a type of preschool programme, especially as it is not compulsory for children to receive early years education in the UK. Another limitation is that although RCTs can help researchers identify the impact of an intervention, it is not always possible to apply findings to other contexts or other populations. It is relevant at this point to remember that although the EPPE Project recruited participants who received a range of preschool experiences, the researchers had not randomly allocated children to a type of service (or no service at all). Instead, they had monitored the experiences that the children would naturally have received.

However, in a report produced for the Cabinet Office, Haynes et al. (2012) state that it is a myth that RCTs are always unethical and say that sometimes there might be ethical advantages. They acknowledge that it would be unethical to provide an intervention to a randomised group of participants if we have the knowledge that the intervention is going to be beneficial. But if that evidence does not exist then it might be more ethical to trial it with a smaller group of people, in case there is no benefit (or even a harmful consequence). They cite the case of the phased introduction of Sure Start Local Programmes as an example of this. It can be argued that, because the researchers who conducted the Perry Preschool Project back in the 1960s might not have had the knowledge or evidence that preschool was going to have a positive long-term impact, there is not the same level of ethical concern as if a similar longitudinal study were to be conducted today, with the knowledge that we now hold.

TIME TO CONSIDER

Draw up a table of what you think are the advantages and the disadvantages of doing longitudinal research. Do you think the benefits outweigh the limitations? Why?

CASE STUDY

Pooja: a community outreach officer in a children's centre

Pooja works in a children's centre as a community outreach officer. Part of her role involves supporting children's home learning environments (HLE) by delivering the Bookstart Corner programme (Booktrust, 2017). She works with individual families who have a child aged between 12 and 30 months in their home to deliver four sessions that focus on books and rhymes. The families are given a small number of resources that promote stories and songs, like picture books, rhyme sheets, a finger puppet and an informational DVD for parents. She knows from her own professional experience that the programme can be effective in supporting the children's HLE, for instance she has anecdotal evidence from parents that they have begun taking their child to the local library following their four sessions. She has also read research which shows the positive impact of the Bookstart Corner programme on children's HLE. Families in one study reported that there was a significant increase in the number of books that the children owned and were bought following completion of the programme (Demack and Stevens, 2013). There was also an increase in the number of parents that read to their child every day. However, Pooja wants to know what longitudinal evidence exists that there are long-term benefits to a high-quality HLE for young children. She decides to look at two longitudinal pieces of research – the EPPE Project and the Millennium Cohort Study.

Firstly, she explores findings from the EPPE Project. She finds one peer-reviewed piece of research by Sammons et al. (2015) which says there are actually rather few studies that have assessed whether there is a link between high-quality HLE in the early years and academic outcomes when the child is older. However, the EPPE Project findings state that, even when children's individual and family characteristics are considered, 'the early years HLE continues to predict students' later educational success in secondary school demonstrating long-lasting positive effects on academic attainment at age 14 and 16' (Sammons et al., 2015: 194). Specifically, children in the highest HLE category in their earliest years had better grades in English, Maths and Science at age 14 than those in the lowest category, and at 16 they received better English and Maths GCSE results. The researchers suggest that there are implications for policy and practice, because it has been identified as worthwhile and beneficial to develop children's HLE to improve their later educational outcomes. Pooja also reads Frank Field's (2010) review of poverty and life chances in the UK, which draws on evidence from the EPPE Project to argue that a high quality HLE is a key driver of life chances throughout childhood. He thus recommends that increased funding should be offered to support good home learning environments as one way to attempt to break that cycle of poverty that currently exists for many families (Field, 2010: 7).

Secondly, she looks at the Millennium Cohort Study (MCS). She finds an impact evaluation conducted by the ESRC of the MCS that shows how MCS datasets have been used by researchers to investigate the importance of HLE and the role that these pieces of research have had in informing policy (Johnson and Antill, 2011). She reads that one analysis of MCS data has found that there were huge differences between the social, emotional and cognitive development of the poorest and the richest children at age three, and the gap widened when the children in the sample reached age five (Dearden et al., 2010). Linked to this, Dearden et al. (2010) found that poorer children typically have a lower-quality HLE, for instance they were read stories less frequently. Dearden et al. (2010) argue that policies focused on improving HLE may reduce educational inequalities, particularly if the policies are focused at children who are aged three, rather than five. This is interesting to Pooja, as she had wondered why the Bookstart Corner programme was targeted only at children up to the age of 30 months. However, Dearden et al. (2010) do not say that the differing levels of quality of HLE are solely responsible for differing levels of development, which is why Johnson and Antill (2011) suggest that the implications of

(Continued)

(Continued)

this for policy are that more funding is needed for early and *earlier* interventions, but not those that focus only on HLE.

Pooja reflects on the information she has read about the long-term impact that a high-quality HLE might have on some of the children who attend her centre. She now thinks about how she can share this research with the families she works with in a way that is accessible to them, so that they can see how sharing stories and rhymes with their babies and toddlers can be a way of investing in their children's future academic success.

TIME TO CONSIDER

Pooja considered the role that longitudinal research has played in informing practices and policies around supporting children's HLE. See if you can find out what longitudinal studies like the EPPE Project and the MCS says about the impact on children of growing up in poverty, and how these studies might have influenced child poverty policies.

FINAL REFLECTION

This chapter has explored what we mean by longitudinal studies and given some examples of them. There are certainly limitations to carrying out these types of studies, and we do not expect that these are a type of research design that you might be involved in conducting as an undergraduate student. However, it is very useful to know about longitudinal studies to see how research can be used to inform national policy and build up an understanding of trends in childhood over time.

KEY POINTS

- Longitudinal research is research that is gathered about the same participants over a prolonged period, for instance through assessments, interviews or questionnaires at intervals throughout their life.
- Longitudinal research may be conducted in qualitative or quantitative ways. Some of the most famous studies conducted in the UK that relate to children are the Millennium Cohort Study, the EPPE Project, the National Evaluation of Sure Start and the Making of Modern Motherhood.
- Longitudinal studies have both strengths and weaknesses as a type of research design. They can provide in-depth information about participants over a long period and assess the long-term impact of interventions. However, they can be very costly to conduct, and the drop-out rate can be problematic for researchers.

FURTHER READING 

Melhuish, E. (2016) 'Longitudinal research and early years policy development in the UK', *International Journal of Child Care and Education Policy*, 10(3). DOI 10.1186/s40723-016-0019-1.

Have a look at Melhuish's journal article about the EPPE Project, the NESS and the SEED study for a greater understanding of these three pieces of research and the impact they have had (or it is envisaged they will have) on early childhood policy.

Johnson, S. and Antill, M. (2011) *Impact Evaluation of the Millennium Cohort Study*. Available at: www.esrc.ac.uk/files/research/research-and-impact-evaluation/milennium-cohort-study-impact-evaluation/ (accessed 2 January 2018).

Johnson and Antill's report on the impact of the Millennium Cohort Study is a really interesting and accessible read.

8

CROSS-NATIONAL RESEARCH APPROACHES

INTRODUCTION

We have considered how one common way that we can find out information on children is through longitudinal studies and now we are going to consider how cross-national research approaches are often used as well.

This chapter will ...

- Explore how cross-national research in early childhood takes place, and why it is important for research to be conducted that explores how practices and provision differ across countries.
- Consider the role that cross-national research can play in informing national policy.
- Look at pieces of research conducted by Unicef and the OECD to consider the type of data and areas that are often explored in cross-national studies.
- Introduce you to the dangers of thinking ethnocentrically when exploring research that spans geographic regions.

WHAT ARE CROSS-NATIONAL RESEARCH APPROACHES?

You will remember that in Chapter 1 we referred to 'comparative, cross-national research' as one of the most common types of research designs that is used within ECEC (OECD, 2012a). Cross-national research is when researchers work across countries to collect data about children. Comparative, cross-national research is when the data from the various countries is compared, so that similarities and differences can be identified in what is happening in those countries, and what experiences the children are having. For instance, it might be used to compare rates of child poverty across nations to think about what strategies might be successful in alleviating it. Some argue, like Baistow (2000), that all cross-national research seeks to compare, whether 'comparative' is stated explicitly in the name or not. Cross-national research typically has a variety of aims, but these often include:

> Improving understanding of one's own country; improving understanding of other countries; testing a theory across diverse settings; examining translation processes across different contexts, examining the local reception of imported cultural forms; building abstract universally applicable theory; challenging claims to universality; evaluating scope and value of certain phenomena; identifying marginalised cultural forms; improving international understanding; and learning from the policy initiatives of others. (Livingstone, 2003: 479)

The OECD (2012a: 3) states that this type of research is useful because it 'identifies specific policies and practices from which people in other countries can draw inspiration'. That means it can help practitioners, policymakers and researchers identify the differences and similarities between early childhood practices in different parts of the world. For instance, they note in particular the disparities between how ECEC is funded in different countries, drawing from their 2006 publication *Starting Strong II*. In the last chapter, we looked at the Perry Preschool Project, which is often used (including by the OECD in 2006) as an argument as to why it is important to invest in early childhood education and care. Yet despite the evidence from the Perry Preschool Project about how great the returns on investing in high-quality preschool programmes can be, the OECD have historically identified big differences in how much countries spend on ECEC provision. For instance, they found in a survey in 2004 that 2% of Denmark's gross domestic product (GDP) was spent on ECEC services, in comparison to only 0.3% in Canada. Although we know that 2004 is a long time ago, at that point, the UK invested 0.5% of their GDP on ECEC services (OECD, 2006: 105). When differences are noted, this is significant for two reasons. It can help those who inform and enact policy to decide whether they might need to change their policies (and therefore practices) based upon what is happening in other countries. Another reason why cross-national research is important is because it can be useful for researchers to know what further issues in a particular country might warrant research. Do you remember how in Chapter 1 we thought about how research is important because it might lead to questions being asked about the way that we do things (Tisdall et al., 2009)? Cross-national research can help us think more critically about what is happening within our context, because we are comparing it to other parts of the world. It can also be a tool for others, who are less acquainted with our contexts and therefore perhaps more enquiring, to ask questions. Or, as Bertram and Pascal (2002: 32) say, these types of studies 'serve to make domestic practices visible to those who are outside the uncritical eye of tradition and make the familiar questionable'.

In Chapter 1 we said how research has allowed questions to be asked about whether it is appropriate for children in England to be starting compulsory formal schooling at the age of five, when research findings that identify benefits of starting formal schooling at age four or five are non-existent. The OECD (2015: 23) has compared the starting age of compulsory school across OECD countries and found that the average is six years old, with compulsory schooling starting at age three in Mexico, but not until seven in Finland and Sweden. We must acknowledge that the compulsory school start age is not always an accurate representation of when children start school in practice – we know that in reality in England the vast majority of children start school in the September after their fourth birthday, rather than the term after they turn five. However, having information about how policies and practices differ can be a way for policymakers and practitioners to think more critically about their own contexts, because they have a point of comparison to other parts of the world.

Can you think of any other reasons why cross-national research might be important to conduct? Rodd (2013) highlights how within early childhood, cross-national research can be used not only to compare children's outcomes, but to compare experiences of the people who work with young children too. She shares an example of a cross-national research collaboration called the *International Leadership Research Forum* (ILRF), whose members have worked together to focus on research on leadership in early childhood. Despite the challenges in bringing together cross-national collaborative research teams, like language barriers, misunderstanding of key terms (where consistency is particularly important when employing qualitative methodologies) and issues with trust and ownership of data, she describes how these partnerships can 'bridge and transcend national boundaries by comparing and contrasting what is learned from research in a particular country with what is known in other countries' (2013: 36). This type of research can be particularly desirable for researchers who value diversity, although the diversity of research teams and research contexts can come with its own challenges. Although there is a definite methodological strength to carrying out cross-national research due to the richness of data that can be collected with a large variety in participating countries and participants themselves, there are clearly complexities in collecting information in this way, too. One is that the societal norms that exist between countries differ, and thus it can be hard to extrapolate from findings what policies are working effectively and what 'best practice' should be across countries (Bertram and Pascal, 2002).

TIME TO CONSIDER

Imagine you, like Rodd (2013), are part of a cross-national collaborative research team which is exploring an area of early childhood. What area would you choose to explore? Why is it important to use a cross-national approach to find out the answer to your research questions?

HOW IS CROSS-NATIONAL RESEARCH TYPICALLY CONDUCTED?

There are several examples of cross-national research that are important for those interested in early childhood to consider. Two organisations that conduct a great deal of cross-national research are Unicef, an international organisation that works in 190 countries, and the OECD, a group of 35 member countries who work to monitor what is happening in those countries to support governments in moving forward with social, economic and environmental change. In this section, we will look at pieces of research produced by both of these organisations, as well as consider the work of other research teams.

Unicef have written a series of reports that demonstrate the differences in early childhood across countries of the world. One of these reports focuses on children's well-being in 'rich countries', which provides useful information on the differences between children's levels of objective well-being (Unicef, 2013). Through using a series of indicators, like each nation's infant mortality rate, the participation rate of children in ECEC and the teenage fertility rate, Unicef have ranked 29 of the richest countries in the world in relation to five dimensions of well-being–material well-being, health and safety, education, behaviours and risks, and housing and environment. They believe that international comparisons on child well-being are important, because the findings say to countries, 'this is how your performance in protecting children compares with the record of other nations at a similar level of development', whilst at the same time showing to those countries what it is possible for them to achieve (2013: 4). Essentially, it shows to the world how each country is doing at meeting the needs of their children on a global stage, which might provide impetus for them to change if they are not performing as they wish to be seen. You might be interested to look at Unicef's (2013) document, which shows how they rank the UK 16th out of 29 in terms of children's well-being. You might be surprised by how low this is, but actually this is a big improvement on a similar study that was conducted in 2007, when the UK ranked bottom out of 21 countries in terms of children's well-being (Unicef, 2007). What do you think might explain this? However, we do not want you to think that the sole purpose of cross-national research approaches is to construct 'league tables', which identify which countries are doing well and which countries are doing not so well in different aspects of ECEC. There are more important reasons for using cross-national approaches.

In the previous chapter, we considered how some researchers use a longitudinal approach to collecting data about children. In fact, longitudinal approaches and cross-national approaches are not mutually exclusive – some researchers conduct research that comprises both designs.

RESEARCH IN FOCUS

Young Lives

One example of a current cross-national longitudinal study is being conducted by Young Lives (2017a). They are tracking 12,000 children from four countries across the world (Ethiopia, India, Peru and Vietnam). Half of the children were born in 1994–5, and half of the children were born in 2001–2. The study aims to explore childhood poverty in developing countries, and uses a longitudinal approach to be able to assess how the impact of child poverty may change over time, and what the causes of child poverty might be. They suggest that although it might not always be possible to make direct comparisons between different countries, by gathering longitudinal data in more than one country it is possible to see whether the reasons for child poverty and the impact of it are typically the same or different across countries. Thus, it allows the researchers to identify whether it is possible to generalise the findings to other countries that fit the same socio-economic profile as the four that are being investigated (Young Lives, 2017b). They give the example of a finding that is consistent across the four countries, which is that some children who suffer malnutrition when they are very young do later make gains in their height growth, which is evidence for investment in children's nutrition not only when they are in their earliest years, but later in their childhoods as well. As they have provided evidence that this is the case across the four countries that are being studied, it means that there is a higher likelihood that it may be the case in other countries as well, and that the children's outcomes are not just unique to one geographic area or set of circumstances.

The UK Office of National Statistics (ONS) also considers some of the strengths of longitudinal cross-national research. The ONS is an organisation that collects and collates statistical information for the UK, including data from the Millennium Cohort Study and other UK birth cohort studies (prior to the Millennium Cohort Study other birth cohort studies began in the UK in 1946, 1958, 1970 and 1990) (Schuller et al., 2012). They say longitudinal studies within one country can identify what the impacts might be of differing experiences like schooling and healthcare. But a limitation is that they cannot identify what the impact is of social factors all together, which cross-national longitudinal studies allow for (2012: 7). However, again they acknowledge that it can be hard to compare cross-national data because of language barriers, or methodological differences like different sampling techniques. They say that one way to overcome these difficulties is to design longitudinal studies with cross-national comparison in mind, so that the data can be jointly analysed.

RESEARCH IN FOCUS

International Early Learning and Child Well-being Study (IELS)

As well as these existing studies, new pieces of large-scale cross-national research are continually being designed. One that is currently being developed is the International Early Learning and Child Well-being Study (IELS) (OECD, 2017b). It aims to assess the levels of five-year-old children's learning and development across three to six OECD countries, to identify what the factors are that lead to effective early learning. Four main benefits are proposed: that the findings will help contribute to higher quality ECEC environments, better levels of support for parents, greater understanding of what children need to support their early learning and, finally, identification of what types of ECEC settings are the most effective. Data will be collected through parent and practitioner questionnaires, which seek to explore children's literacy, numeracy, self-regulation, and social and emotional development. England's Department for Education (DfE) has indicated that England will be one of the countries that will take part, but many academics and practitioners have expressed concerns about the study. The early years organisations the Early Childhood Studies Degree Network (ECSDN), the Association for Professional Development in Early Years (TACTYC) and the Sector Endorsed Foundation Degree in Early Years (SEFDEY) have published a joint response that outlines their concerns about the study, including that the DfE has not made it clear how the data collected may negatively or positively impact on children, families and professionals (ECSDN, TACTYC and SEFCEY, 2017). That means it is not possible for participants to make an informed decision about whether to take part. They also express apprehension that there are limitations in the use of parental and teacher questionnaires to collect the data, which raises 'many concerns about methodological rigour, reliability, comparability and ethics' (2017: 1). Can you think of any other reasons why academics and practitioners might be reluctant for this piece of cross-national research to take place? Moss et al. (2017) also share their thoughts about the study and the implications it might have for children, parents and those working with them. One of these is that the IELS documentation does not acknowledge the criticisms placed on the methodology of the similar PISA study (which you will consider in more detail in the case study at the end of this chapter) about the dangers of overlooking the complexities of different contexts and cultures within cross-national research, and instead naively assuming that what works in one country can be transferred to work effectively in another.

TIME TO CONSIDER

Imagine you are a teacher of five-year-old children in England, and have been asked to fill in a questionnaire about each of your pupils' literacy, numeracy, self-regulation, and social and emotional development as part of the IELS study. How would you feel about it and why? Do you think that all of your fellow teachers would be accurate in the answers they give? Why? (Or why not?) Now imagine you are a parent of a five-year-old, and have been asked to fill in a similar questionnaire. How would you feel about that?

WHAT ARE THE DIFFICULTIES OF CROSS-NATIONAL RESEARCH?

We have already considered that there are important reasons for doing cross-national research, and identified some of the strengths that this type of research design can bring. We have also briefly considered some of the difficulties in conducting comparative research across countries, which this section is going to expand upon.

In Chapter 4 (The language of research) you thought about how language can act as a gatekeeper, which is why researchers need to think carefully when they are designing data collection methods like interview schedules or questionnaires, to make sure that they are inclusive and accessible to their participants. This is perhaps especially true in cross-national research, when data collection tools need to be translated in a variety of languages but the translation of each word needs to maintain the same meaning and connotations. Bhopal et al. (2004) note that translating questionnaires so that they can be used cross-culturally (that is, not necessarily to be used across nations, but across people who speak different languages) is an incredibly tricky task. Paid translators might use a very formal sounding translation of a term, when a more colloquial or informal phrase may be more suitable. Plus, 'people who speak different languages may interpret concepts, words, or phrases in different ways, and cultural differences may render some questions offensive, irrelevant, or inappropriate' (Bhopal et al., 2004: 1). As an example, recently both the authors of this book attended an international conference, with academics speaking from over fifty countries. The vast majority of presentations were in English, despite the fact that English was the first language for very few of the presenters. We noticed several speakers refer to 'normal children' when meaning 'children who do not have special education needs'. Although this made us feel uncomfortable with the insinuation that children with SEN are 'abnormal', we understood that this was something lost-in-translation by the speakers, rather than a value-judgement being placed on children with SEN.

Thus, a huge methodological challenge of conducting cross-national research can be how to maintain the consistency in the questions that are being asked of participants, when they are being asked in a variety of languages. Similarly, care needs to be taken when data from cross-national studies needs to be translated so that it is accessible to all the researchers involved in analysing the data. Later in this book, in Chapter 11 (Creative approaches to research), you will be introduced to a piece of research by two Norwegian academics, Haldar and Wærdahl (2009), who carried out cross-national research by analysing home–school diaries that had been distributed in China and Norway. However, the Chinese diaries were translated into English so that the researchers could compare them to their Norwegian data. Here, again, it is possible that the meaning of some of the diary entries may have translation inconsistencies.

Wilson (2001) also talks of the problems of translated data, in her case in relation to research relating to social policy, and how researchers are increasingly being asked to compare data across countries so that comparisons between social policies can take place. However, she argues that although within scientific research, words might have defined meanings and can be translated with ease, within the social sciences, those that translate information are 'likely to bring different cultural influences to their understanding of the meaning of the data' (Wilson, 2001: 321). You might think that the issue of mistranslation could be overcome by relying on numerical data, collected by government bodies or on behalf of governments, as this is less open to being misunderstood. However, the data that governments choose to collect will be informed by their own values and beliefs. Wilson gives the example of Finland, which does not differentiate between children growing up in households with one adult and those that grow up in a household with two adults. This might influence how researchers can compare data and policies about single-parent families, as the data may not exist in all the nations that you might expect. As another example, there are some nations that might put great importance on how many children are born out of wedlock. But governments across the world do not place the same significance on this, and thus cross-national comparisons might be hard to achieve.

This idea of differing values across countries and cultures links to the notion of ethnocentrism, which we need to understand if we are going to appreciate research that explores childhoods in different cultures and countries. Ethnocentrism is defined by Westwood (2014: 14) as 'the belief that one's own culture and way of behaving is the correct way; all others are judged by this standard'. Generally, ethnocentrism often leads to problems or issues from indigenous societies and cultures being interpreted in a 'Western' way, due to the relatively greater power of the generally wealthier Western world.

RESEARCH IN FOCUS

School readiness in Australia

Take, for instance, research carried out by Taylor (2011) in which she looked at how ready Aboriginal children in Western Australia were to start school. In Australia, in 2017 around 5% of children attending preschool programmes were Aboriginal and Torres Strait Islander children (Australia Bureau of Statistics, 2017). Traditionally there have been huge variations in the proportions of Indigenous students in schools – in a report from 2007 just less than half of schools had fewer than 5% of Indigenous pupils, whilst 25% had none and in 2% of schools more than 95% of the pupils were Indigenous (ARACY, 2007: 5). In Western Australia, pre-primary education has been compulsory for children in the academic year in which they turn five years old since 2013. When they first start pre-primary, children are assessed in literacy and numeracy (Government of Western Australia, 2017). However, Taylor proposes that the on-entry assessment does 'little but assess that which particular cultures, socio-economic circumstances and individual families have or have not instilled and reinforced' (2011: 145). By this, she means that the ways that children's school readiness is being assessed is through on-entry assessments that examine the children's cultural and personal life circumstances. She continues that 'with notions of normalcy uncritically embedded in structure, curriculum, pedagogy, assessment and resources, those children not reflecting a somewhat narrow view of the "normal" are in effect deemed deficit and from the outset construed as problems' (2011: 145). By this, she means that what is considered as 'normal' for pre-primary children to be able to achieve and do in terms of literacy and numeracy by the Western Australia Department of Education comes from an ethnocentric non-Indigenous belief, so when Indigenous pupils are assessed in the on-entry assessments, they are seen as 'problems' and 'deficits'. In terms of ethnocentrism, the Western Australia Department for Education are judging the Indigenous students on the standard of the non-Indigenous culture.

As a further example of ethnocentrism, Woodhead (1996) talks about the dangers of having a 'basic set of standards' for what is a quality environment for young children. For instance, one factor in a quality environment in an early years setting could be seen to be how much play space is available. Woodhead (1996) compared UK research from Smith and Connolly (1980) to that of Liddell and Kruger (1987) in South Africa. Smith and Connolly examined how space affected children's play and social behaviour. They found that a suitable amount of space per child was 1.5m^2 per child and if a child had less than this then their play and social behaviour was adversely affected. However, Liddell and Kruger (1987) conducted a study in an urban area of South Africa, when children in a nursery had between 0.56m^2 and 1.56m^2 per child, dependent on how many children were in attendance in the setting on each day. They found that when the children had the most amount of space, the children had higher levels of cooperative play and involvement. Comparing the two studies, we see the findings are similar – the more space available per child, the better the children played. However, children in South Africa were playing effectively in the amount of space per child where children in the UK seemed to display unwanted behaviour. Thus, if we were to consider Smith and Connolly's (1980) findings from a Western ethnocentric perspective of environment quality in early years settings, we may say that children need at least 1.5m^2 per child of space to play effectively. Likewise, we may judge early years settings in South Africa as substandard when they have less than 1.5m^2 per child to play. This shows the values of comparing findings across cultures, but the dangers of assuming the findings from one country will also hold true in another.

We know that, as you are a savvy student who has being paying attention to this book, you will be thinking critically about that last paragraph. We know you will be thinking, 'But wait a moment. Back in Chapter 2, they told us we need to think critically about the timeliness of sources of information. And now they are referring to research from the 1980s to justify their points!' If you are thinking that, then that's brilliant. We offer these pieces of research as examples of how we cannot generalize research findings from one country to another, and as a warning of the dangers of thinking ethnocentrically. We do not offer these pieces of research as evidence that these amounts of space are still considered ideal for children to have to ensure engaging and effective play opportunities. Instead, for that we recommend you look at more recent sources of information, like the OECD's (2012c) *Starting Strong III*. They refer to cross-cultural studies as evidence to show that more space in ECEC settings can lead to more opportunities for children to learn and play. Specifically, they cite Sheridan et al. (2009), who conducted a comparative study that explored the quality of preschools in Sweden and South Korea by using the Early Childhood Environment Rating Scale (ECERS) (Harms and Clifford, 1980). The Swedish preschools typically displayed higher levels of quality than their South Korean counterparts, and said that the limited physical space and the low priority placed on 'space in which to be alone' (Sheridan et al., 2009: 152) in the South Korean settings may be one reason that could explain this.

TIME TO CONSIDER

Now that you have considered both the strengths and the weaknesses of conducting cross-national research, draw up a table like the one below to see if the benefits outweigh the limitations:

Table 8.1 Strengths and limitations of conducting cross-national research

Strengths	Limitations
It can allow researchers to look with a more critical eye at their own context, because they are comparing it with another	Can be hard to ensure translation consistencies if the data collection methods or data needs to be in more than one language

CASE STUDY

Harry: a primary education student

Harry is currently doing a placement in an infant school in England. He has noticed that some of the children find mathematics really difficult and he is interested to know whether this is the case internationally. He has heard about the OECD's Programme for International Student Assessment (PISA), which seeks to compare 15-year-old children's abilities in core subjects like science, mathematics and reading across many countries of the world every three years (OECD, 2017c). He is familiar with it because he has heard about the OECD's proposed International Early Learning and Child Well-being Study, which has been dubbed the 'Baby PISA'

(Pence, 2017). Harry finds out that the 2012 PISA test focused on mathematics, so he decides to look in depth at the results of this study (OECD, 2014). Around 510,000 15-year-olds took part in the test, from 65 countries in the world. They were required to take a 2-hour assessment, and children in some countries additionally completed a 40-minute computer-based test too. Students and their head teachers also completed a background questionnaire, comprised of questions about their personal and schooling circumstances.

When Harry looks at the findings from the 2012 PISA, he sees that the UK ranks 26th of 65 countries in mathematics, and the mean score for pupils in the UK actually matches the mean score for the OECD average (OECD, 2014: 5). The area with the top score for mathematics is Shanghai-China, where pupils are described as having 'the equivalent of nearly three years of schooling, above the OECD average' (2014: 4). He wonders what might explain the difference between children's mathematical abilities in China and England.

Harry finds a cross-national piece of research conducted by Miao et al. (2015) that compared the teaching of mathematics in primary schools in China and in England, and thinks this will be perfect to consider why there might be differences in children's mathematical ability at the age of 15. Seven classes of nine- and ten-year-old children who were deemed to have 'average performance in mathematics' (2015: 394) and their teachers took part in the study (three classes from England and four from China) and data was collected on them using observations, questionnaires, interviews, focus groups and standardised tests. The researchers wanted to find out whether there was a link between how the teachers behaved and their pupils' performance in mathematics, and, if there was a link, how much of an influence the teachers' behaviour had. They found that the teachers in the Chinese classrooms were more likely to display what they considered to be effective teacher behaviours, which included whole-class interaction, promoting active learning and clarity of instruction. They found that whole-class lectures and interacting only with part of a class were ineffective as teaching techniques, which the English teachers did to varying degrees, but the Chinese teachers never did. Miao et al. (2015: 400) state that the findings should be a 'wake-up call to practitioners, policy-makers, educational improvement researchers and all other stakeholders of education in both countries and beyond', because of the implications that the findings have for how the teaching of mathematics could be developed and improved. Harry reflects on the extent to which the teaching practices he has observed in his placements feature characteristics that Miao et al. (2015) found effective.

However, Harry knows that he should not take the PISA results at face value, so he also tries to find some articles which will help him think critically about whether they are an accurate, reliable measure of children's levels of attainment. He finds that the OECD has been criticised by Goldstein (2004) for implying that it is possible to directly compare different educational systems through the use of a cross-national standardised test, when longitudinal data is necessary to do this, to account for differences in social and economic variables. It has also been critiqued for not attempting to account for different levels of difficulty in the test owing to its translation into different languages (Goldstein, 2004: 322), which Harry also knows can be a methodological limitation of cross-national research. Despite these criticisms, Harry reads that PISA has 'paved the way for significant

(Continued)

(Continued)

educational reforms' (Kanes et al., 2014), for instance in terms of putting a focus on research exploring pedagogic practice (Ertl, 2006). Harry believes this rationale could fit with the reason for Miao et al.'s (2015) study. Harry reflects on the PISA rankings; how cross-national research can be used both to develop teaching practices and what he has read about what effective teaching practices for mathematics can look like. He thinks about how he might trial changing his own teaching style as a result.

TIME TO CONSIDER

In 2015, the main focus of PISA was on science. Find the PISA report (OECD, 2016) and have a look at how nations compared in relation to their children's attainment in science. Have a look at how the UK ranked, and consider what lessons the UK might learn from what the findings tell us about what is good practice in relation to teaching science.

FINAL REFLECTION

There are many advantages that cross-national research can offer in giving researchers high-quality data, that can be important in promoting changes in policy and developing pedagogic practice. However, there are also huge difficulties in doing this type of research, which means that students should think particularly critically about the design of these pieces of research, so that any methodological issues are not overlooked.

KEY POINTS

- Cross-national research allows researchers to compare and contrast what is happening in more than one nation. That means that policymakers can see the effectiveness of approaches and programmes from different parts of the world, and reflect upon their own services as a result.
- There are a variety of well-known organisations who conduct cross-national research, including Unicef and the OECD. Some of these pieces of research, such as PISA and the proposed IELS, have attracted criticism on methodological and ethical grounds.
- The dangers of cross-national research should not be overlooked. In particular, researchers and those that cite research should take care not to think ethnocentrically when comparing their home country and culture to that of other nations.

FURTHER READING 

Tobin, J., Wu, D. and Davidson, D. (2001) *Preschool in Three Cultures.* New Haven, CT: Yale University.

Tobin, J., Hsueh, Y. and Karasawa, M. (2011) *Preschool in Three Cultures Revisited.* Chicago, IL: The University of Chicago Press.

These two fascinating books offer a comparative view of preschools in China, Japan and the USA.

Organisation for Economic Co-operation and Development (2015) *Starting Strong IV.* Paris: OECD Publishing.

Since 2001, the OECD have published a series of reports called *Starting Strong,* which offer a comparative analysis of policy in OECD countries. All of them are worth a read. The most recent report, *Starting Strong IV,* issued in 2015, is interesting to look at for a cross-national comparison of how ECEC practices in OECD countries differ, and how different countries take different approaches to monitoring what is happening in ECEC settings.

9

THE ETHICS OF RESEARCH

INTRODUCTION

Every day, whether at work or home, you will be making decisions about how to behave and conduct yourself in relation to other people. But how do you decide on appropriate courses of action and what has informed your moral code? Your cultural background, religious upbringing and parental values will all have contributed to an internal ethical 'checklist' you will use to decide how best to proceed.

This chapter will ...

- Develop your understanding of the use of ethical checklists in research.
- Consider the ways that participants must be protected especially if they are children or from vulnerable groups.
- Build on the discussion in Chapter 6 (Approaches to research with children) to emphasise how participants have much to contribute to the research process.
- Explore the contested nature of ethics and the impact of ethical considerations on all who are involved in research.
- Make links between theory and practice by considering some ethically controversial key pieces of research.
- Use the term 'reflexive researcher' (Warin, 2011) to describe how the ethical process in research is influenced both by the parallel checklists of statutory guidelines and the researcher's personal ethical code.

WHAT ARE ETHICS?

Ethics is a key term in research and one that you will come across many times. As such, it is important that you have a good understanding of what it means.

It is defined as 'the moral rules and principles that are culturally acceptable to a society in order for it to function' by Macpherson and Tyson (2008: 55). In the context of research we could say it is 'the moral rules and principles' followed by those who engage in research. In the previous chapter (Chapter 8, Cross-national research approaches) we considered how research can support our understanding of practices in other countries and cultures. However, regardless of which methods are most frequently adopted or the 'epistemological pluralism' (Strike, 2006) which describes specific cultural attitudes towards knowledge and truth, all research-active countries will have prescribed codes of ethics that must be adhered to whenever research is carried out. No matter how useful or interesting it might be, research unfortunately does have the potential to harm those who take part in it. When the research involves young children the harm may be much greater. This does not mean, however, that children should not be involved in research; instead we should be aware of what the issues might be and how children can participate yet at the same time be protected from harm (Randall et al., 2016).

Roberts-Holmes (2018: 57) reminds us that the Nuremberg Code (1949) has greatly influenced the way we view ethics in research today. It was created in the aftermath of the Second World War when the terrible experiments carried out on human participants by the Nazi regime were revealed. The code was addressed to those engaged in medical research, but it has subsequently come to influence ethics across a range of disciplines, for example educational research, by insisting on 'the voluntary consent of the research subject, the notion that unnecessary suffering should be avoided, and that risk to a subject must be justified by the potential benefits of the research' (Strike, 2006: 68).

In this chapter we will argue that regardless of ethical considerations in place, things can go wrong in research. Furthermore ethics in research can become problematic. At times this can be because of the many ways that words and ideas can be interpreted. Let us look at one example of this by considering the BERA (British Educational Research Association) guidelines. These are a set of principles for informing ethical research that most universities in the UK will subscribe to. They state: 'Researchers must recognise that participants may experience distress or discomfort in the research process ... They must desist immediately from any actions, ensuing from the research process, that cause emotional or other harm' (2011: 19). But the word 'harm' could be interpreted in many different ways and from many different perspectives. How can a researcher measure in particular the emotional harm that may subsequently arise because of participation in the research? Firstly, it may not be apparent, secondly it may arise after the event when the participant looks back on their contribution, and thirdly, as researchers we may measure harm in a very different way to you. Bearing these thoughts in mind the chapter will go on to consider how the participant can be protected through the research process. First let us consider how 'harm' in research can arise.

Ethics need to be given detailed consideration when designing any research project. The researcher needs to ensure that they follow Punch's advice and engage in 'principled deliberation about morally salient issues and acceptable courses of action' (2014: 37). Ethics need to be attended to at two different levels; one that we shall name *ethical compliance*, and one that we shall name *ethical values*. There is naturally some overlap between the two areas yet the researcher needs to be explicit about the distinction between ethical decisions they have made to ensure that the research follows established, laid-down procedures (ethical compliance) and ethical decisions taken that reflect their own personal researcher identity (ethical values).

WHAT IS ETHICAL COMPLIANCE?

Ethical compliance describes how recognised 'procedural requirements' (Punch, 2014: 36) are respected to ensure that the ethical content of the research meets the requirements of the wider research community; each piece of research allows the researcher to either join that community (for example, an undergraduate producing a third-year dissertation) or remain part of it (for example, an established researcher submitting a piece of work to a peer-reviewed journal). So, for example, if you were carrying out a piece of research as an undergraduate student you would need to ensure that the specific ethical procedures of your own university were followed closely. At this stage in your research career you would not necessarily need to submit your proposal to an ethics committee as you would be supported in your research by one specific tutor who will be your research supervisor. However, if this tutor was carrying out their own research then they would need to ensure that all necessary documentation was submitted to the university ethics committee. In both cases the would-be researcher would need to engage with recommendations, make adjustments and then resubmit updated documentation for approval. This documentation might include participant information sheets, consent forms, survey proformas and proposed interview questions. Specific university ethical guidance will be informed by discipline guidelines such as the British Educational Research Association (BERA) Guidelines (2011), the BPS (British Psychological Society) Code of Human Research Ethics (2014) or the EECERA (European Early Childhood Education Research Association) Ethical Code for Early Childhood Researchers (2014). In this way each specific piece of research carried out, at whatever level, needs to ensure that it would meet the approval of the wider research community. The ethical compliance checklist below shows the key issues the researcher will have to address.

ETHICAL COMPLIANCE CHECKLIST

I have considered ...

- if there is any risk to the participants.
- if the participants will be deceived in any way.
- how participant confidentiality will be maintained.
- how participants will give their consent.
- how the aims of the research will be shared with the participants.
- how the collected data will be stored securely.
- how long the collected data will be stored.
- how the collected data will be disposed of.
- what happens if participants change their mind.

However, completing this checklist is not a simple exercise; ethical procedures can be open to interpretation depending on the ethical values of the decision-makers.

ETHICAL VALUES

We use the term 'ethical values' here to describe how the researcher strives to ensure that their own 'philosophical principles' (Punch, 2014: 36) as a researcher are apparent in the research design. We talk about research design in more detail in Chapter 10 but for now let's understand it as the way a piece of research is put together. 'Ethical values' is a dynamic phrase that suggests that ethics should not just be considered at a certain stage, for example when designing the research or applying for ethical approval. Instead, it should be at the forefront of the researcher's mind through every stage of the research and should be revisited constantly. Table 9.1 sets out some of the ethical considerations at each stage of the research and how they might be addressed.

Table 9.1 Ethical considerations at different stages of the research

Stage of research	Ethical issue	How this might be addressed
Choosing an area to research	The choice of research focus may contribute to a discourse that reinforces negative stereotypes. For example, by researching 'Boys' underachievement in education' the discussion around boys as victims of a 'feminised' profession may be being reinforced	The researcher needs to always bear in mind the 'costs–benefits ratio' (Frankfort-Nachmias and Nachmias, 1992); if there would be more gains from researching this area than risks for carrying out such research then this would be a clear rationale
Formulating a research question	By formulating a question about a certain issue the researcher could be inviting a critique of certain sections of society	In the example of gender the research question needs to ensure that it encapsulates both male and female voices on the issue

Stage of research	Ethical issue	How this might be addressed
Searching the literature	The reflexive researcher will need to ensure that they are not led to ignore certain areas of the literature or previous research	In early childhood research it is good to be guided by special interest groups such as those of the European Early Childhood Education Research Association (EECERA)
Methodology adopted	The reflexive researcher needs to ensure they are adopting an appropriate methodology to allow participants to have a voice	Researcher needs to be aware that the language and terminology that they use when interacting with participants does not create a barrier to participation
Analysis of the data	The researcher's identity will have an impact on the findings	This is where it could be important for the researcher to have critical friends to talk through both their design and analysis
Trustworthiness of findings and any claims made	The claims that the researcher is making need to be trustworthy	The reflexive researcher needs to pay 'continuous, recursive ... and excruciating attention to being trustworthy' (Ely, 1991: 156) so that their findings are 'worth paying attention to' (Lincoln and Guba cited in Ely, 1991: 156)

IMPLICATIONS FOR DESIGNING ETHICAL RESEARCH

As admirable and necessary as it may be, considering the ethics so thoroughly could present the reflexive researcher with several problems. One of these may be to do with the part of their researcher identity that is informed by a professional background. Researchers with a professional background and not a pure academic one may discover that they have to be the translator of two very different languages as they move between documentation that meets the approval of the ethics committee and documentation for participants. They will need to satisfy both but may find it difficult to be happy themselves with a compromise in language, as we will see from Melitza's experience in the next paragraph.

CASE STUDY

Melitza: ethical implications when designing research

When Melitza carried out research into practitioner gendered practices for a postgraduate degree she used the term 'Learning Journey' on any practitioner/parental consent form. She used this as a shorthand term to describe the collection of annotated photographs that would be used as part of the interview. In so doing,

(Continued)

(Continued)

she was making use of a shorthand that both these groups of people – parents and practitioners – would understand. However those outside the professional area of early childhood, such as the people on the ethics committee, were not familiar with this term. This meant they asked for much more detail included on the form. This created two problems for Melitza. Firstly, it meant that she had to begin to discuss in much more detail how the photographs would be used. She was worried this might alarm parents and lead to them inferring that she was doing something outside normal everyday setting practice. Secondly, this added to the wordage of the documentation and therefore the reading and engagement that these two busy groups of people, parents and practitioners, were required to do. As a reflexive researcher Melitza did not consider this to be either respectful, helpful or particularly honest. It made her reflect on the whole process of gaining ethical approval and wonder if it would be more effective as a researcher to sit before the committee and be able to articulate and justify her ethical decisions before gaining approval.

As this illustrates, on the one hand, gaining ethical approval can be a lengthy and frustrating procedure, yet on the other hand, we can wonder how ethical approval was ever granted for certain projects. Take for example the case of Professor David Southall, who between 1986 and 1994 carried out research using hidden cameras to understand the causes of Sudden Infant Death Syndrome (SIDS).

RESEARCH IN FOCUS

David Southall

In Southall et al.'s case study (1997) covert methods, such as videoing participants, were used to research into potential links between child abuse and SIDS. The research took place in two UK hospitals and included a sample of 39 children aged between two months and four years; they were covertly filmed along with their parents. A control group of 46 children, who were believed to have breathing difficulties caused by genuine medical problems, were also monitored. The video data collected led to 33 prosecutions of parents for child cruelty. Some parents considered the research techniques to be unethical and accused the research team of creating an environment of heightened anxiety that impacted on their behaviours. Furthermore, others recognised themselves in the journal article write-up of the research although their consent had never been sought. Should Southall et al.'s participants have been asked for permission? Do you consider this to be an ethical piece of research? Coady (2010: 78) talks about the 'risk/benefit equation', claiming that 'the greater the benefit to be gained from a piece of research, the more risks are acceptable'. We have to consider whether the risks in Southall et al.'s research were acceptable and why.

TIME TO CONSIDER

No doubt you will have seen video clips that illustrate research into attachment theory and in particular 'The Strange Situation' (Ainsworth et al., 2015). In this research a mother briefly leaves her child in the company of a stranger. When she returns, the way that the child responds to the reunion is observed and recorded. If you want to remind yourself of the experiment, there are many clips you can access through Google for example. As you watch, reflect on the ethical implications using the questions below to scaffold your thinking:

i. Were the participants damaged in any way?
ii. Does it matter? Could there be any implications?
iii. Did all the participants give consent?

If we return to Coady's risk/benefit equation (2010), she suggests that: 'In research on attachment, the temporary upset shown by a baby separated from its mother would probably be acceptable, but only if the research was seen as providing new and significant data' (2010: 78). Watch a clip before deciding whether you agree or disagree with this statement.

Now watch the clip again and then complete Table 9.2, which considers the risk factors for all involved in this experiment:

Table 9.2 The risk factors for all the participants in 'The Strange Situation' experiment

What is the risk to ...?
the children?
the parents?
the wider family?
the professionals involved?

In our work with students we have found that considering the ethics of 'The Strange Situation' provokes a rich discussion with support for both sides of the argument. Some people have a strong affective reaction to seeing the child left, although they can see how important this kind of research has been. It is always interesting to consider whether you could offer an alternative method that would minimise the risk of distressing the child. Woodhead and Faulkner (2008) reflect on the contrasting ethically inappropriate situation of parents being upset if researchers encouraged children to run away from their parents in a zoo. Does that suddenly make you look at The Strange Situation experiment in a different way?

When we reflect on issues of ethics we must always ask questions about how power relationships work. By this we mean what are the power dynamics in all of the human relationships connected to the research and how are the participants being encouraged to have a voice? If you remember we began to think about this matter in Chapter 2 (Beginning to think critically about research). It may be a simple matter for researchers to complete an ethics checklist but the reflexive researcher will look far beyond the basic entry level requirements to consider what their own ethical values are and what this would look like in practice. In this way the researcher will never permit a situation where the participants become mere fodder. The next section will go on to explore in more detail how the reflexive researcher can consider the protection of their participants.

HOW CAN PARTICIPANTS BE PROTECTED IN RESEARCH?

Participants can be competent co-constructors of research (Silverman, 2016: 351) and the protection element is to ensure that both they and the researcher have the appropriate research environments, or as Silverman describes them, 'special social spaces' (2016: 351), to be able to contribute effectively. We need this effective contribution because social science research can help us understand how people and societies operate, offering us useful insights into the beliefs and experiences of groups of people. It can help us to change our practice so that these groups of people may benefit. For example, the Early Years Foundation Stage (DfE, 2017a) was informed by wider research, such as the EPPE (Sylva et al., 2004). It is now a statutory requirement in all early years' settings ensuring that young children receive developmentally appropriate education. However, ethics can be problematic, particularly in the three key areas of (i) *disrespectful methods*, (ii) *power imbalances* and (iii) *consent.*

Disrespectful methods

Roberts-Holmes (2018: 65) cites Alderson (2008) and what she perceives to be 'disrespectful ethical methods'. She is talking about these in relation to children but they could equally apply to older participants. What do you think 'disrespectful ethical methods' could be? Try to make a list before you go on to the activity below.

Table 9.3 considers some of the 'disrespectful ethical methods' as outlined by Alderson. It considers why we might label them so and suggests how they could be improved.

Power imbalances

Disrespect in research may occur when there is a power imbalance in the research relationships. For example, the researcher may appear as an authority figure whom the participant feels they are inferior to, or the researcher's

Table 9.3 How methods can be disrespectful and how this can be minimised

Disrespectful ethical method	Why?	Improve by ...
1. Talking down to children	Because there will be a power imbalance. Children may think they have to guess what is in the researcher's head rather than giving an authentic response	Ensure researcher uses methods that allow the children to share their knowledge and understanding
2. Making covert observations	Because the participant has not been given the opportunity to give their consent	Ensure participant has been informed about the research and been able to give their consent
3. Using deception	Because this could cause the participant emotional harm	Ensure each participant is clear about the research aims
4. Publishing results which reinforce stereotypes	Because this could also cause emotional harm or cause marginalised groups to be further marginalised	Ensure participant voice is included in the findings

eagerness to treat the participants respectfully may mean they fail to give power imbalances due consideration. Punch suggests this can happen when:

> Those who consider children to be 'essentially indistinguishable from adults' (James et al., 1998: 31) employ the same methods as those used with adults ... It is then the responsibility of the adult researcher not to draw attention to any adult–child distinctions by treating them in any way other than as mature, competent people (Alderson, 1995). However, such an approach may mean that the power imbalance between adult researchers and child subjects is not always adequately addressed (Morrow, 1999). (Punch, 2002: 322)

In this scenario the researcher has no malicious intent but rather has either not thought through participant needs adequately or is viewing their participants through a particular lens. A more problematic issue, in terms of the ethics of research, is when the researcher puts their own research needs above those of their participants so that participants come to be seen as 'research fodder'.

Abuse in research may thus occur if the researcher has not looked critically at the methods employed and considered whether they may be 'disrespectful' according to Alderson's list. At the same time, thoughtful consideration must be given to power imbalances between researcher and researched and how these will be addressed so that the participant never becomes mere 'research fodder'. Consideration must also be given to any necessary protection of participants and this is what we will discuss next.

Consent

If we remember our discussion of the Nuremberg Code earlier on in the chapter we will recall that participants should always give their consent to partake in research and if this is not obtained then they should not be included. But how would a researcher know if a participant had truly given their consent? A child may feel they have to say yes to an adult figure in authority such as a researcher; therefore when the reflexive researcher is looking to obtain consent they must be aware that giving consent is a continual process of 'ethics in practice' (Warin, 2011) not a one-off tick list event. This involves watching the participants' body language for any signs they may be giving that they are not comfortable participating even if they have been able to give their informed consent.

It can be tricky to ensure that participants have understood what they are consenting to; they may be unfamiliar with terminology and concepts articulated by the researcher. As Warin states, 'Even when working with adults "informed consent" is a much more complex business than it a first appears, since researchers have to make difficult decisions about the quantity, quality, and timing of information' (2011: 807). By sharing information about the research in a way that the participants can understand they are then able to give their consent. Flewitt (2005) describes her child participants who were only three years old. She felt confident that they demonstrated an adequate understanding of how the research might impact on them so that they were truly offering 'informed consent'. In her view they demonstrated this by asking questions about whether taking part would interfere with their play time; she also let them handle the video equipment she intended to use and thus felt they showed a good understanding of the data collection methods that would be employed. Another device she utilised effectively was to get the parents to explain the research to the children because she knew they were best placed to articulate it in a way their individual children would understand.

The 'reflexive researcher' (Warin, 2011) will give consideration to a number of areas to ensure that adequate protection is in place to protect their participants from any emotional harm. This will include a consideration of meaningful consent based on secure participant understanding and whether total anonymity can be assured. As Lewis suggests: 'In any study, it is important to give consideration to ways in which taking part may be harmful to sample members, and to take aversive action' (2003: 68). If the researcher proactively heeds this advice then they can ensure that their participants are properly protected.

In summary, this section of the chapter has argued that there are several reasons why participants may need protecting in research even with all the appropriate guidelines in place. These reasons include power relationships, affective impact or being unsure about consent issues. There is always the danger that participants' vulnerability may be abused in some way even though 'there is much scholarly disagreement over the appropriate meaning and application of this concept [vulnerability] in research ethics' (Bracken-Roche et al., 2017: 1). Of course if we only view our participants as those in need of protection this is quite a one-dimensional viewpoint which does not recognise the great contribution they can make, and it is this idea we will turn our attention to next.

HOW CAN PARTICIPANTS BE ALLOWED TO CONTRIBUTE?

In Chapter 6 we discussed in detail how research participants, and particularly children, can be active contributors in the research process. Roberts-Holmes (2018) suggests that as a society we have become increasingly aware of listening to children. For example, we have an early years curriculum (DfE, 2017a) that focuses on the interests of the individual child and the relationship shared with the practitioner. There are many other ways that children are encouraged to participate in society, such as being part of school councils for example, and as we have already discussed in Chapter 6 (Approaches to research with children), the United Nations Convention on the Rights of the Child (UN, 1989) is a key document that insists children are allowed a voice and opportunities to participate in decisions made about how they are regarded. When researchers work with children, however, there is always going to be an issue of where the power lies.

TIME TO CONSIDER

Look back at the information you explored concerning the 'Mosaic Approach' in Chapter 6. How might approaching research in this way effectively deal with power issues between the researcher and the researched?

Macpherson and Tyson (2008: 59) argue that 'One of the prime considerations for carrying out any type of research with children and young people is how we view them within the research.' How do you view children? Do you see them as vulnerable and needing protection in research or do you consider that they have something to contribute which is of equal value to adults? Reflect on Christensen and Prout's description of children as 'as active participants in the research process ... fellow human beings and ... active citizens' (2002: 481).

TIME TO CONSIDER

Do a simple Internet search to find a variety of ethical guidelines then compare and contrast these. Look for common threads and any major differences. For example you may look at:

- BERA (British Educational Research Association): www.bera.ac.uk/wp-content/uploads/2018/06/BERA-Ethical-Guidelines-for-Educational-Research_4thEdn_2018.pdf?noredirect=1
- BPS (British Psychological Society): www.bps.org.uk/system/files/Public%20files/code_of_human_research_ethics_dec_2014_inf180_web.pdf
- EECERA (Ethical Code for Early Childhood Researchers): www.eecera.org/custom/uploads/2016/07/EECERA-Ethical-Code.pdf

CASE STUDY

Tamsin: an ECS university lecturer

Tamsin, as part of a university teaching seminar with undergraduate students on children developing prosocial behaviour, decides she will use video clips from a recent reality TV series which looks at the social interactions of 4-year-olds. She enthusiastically discusses her session plans with her colleagues over coffee, happy to share the teaching and learning strategies she is using and delighted that she has a resource at her disposal that the students will relate well to and which will help them make clear links between theory and practice. However, far from sharing her enthusiasm, some of her colleagues begin to debate the ethics of filming young children in this way. They question how far the children were able to give consent, what were the parents' motives and what were the researchers' responsibilities in protecting the children. They also discuss how the clips are edited to portray certain children in certain lights and what the affective impact of this will be in the child's later life.

TIME TO CONSIDER

Consider some of the pieces of research we have looked at in other chapters (the EPPE Project, Mosaic Approach, MCS). Now you have a good understanding of ethics, critically reflect on the ethical approach taken in these pieces of research. Was it respectful or was it problematic in any way?

FINAL REFLECTION

We have argued in this chapter that the reflexive researcher should be continually making decisions about how to conduct research relationships with participants. They will have to draw on established guidelines but also on their own personal, ethical code to do this. It is a question of balancing the 'research scales' so that there is both protection and involvement of participants in equal measure.

KEY POINTS

- Ethics are a key component of any piece of research. Ethical approval must always be obtained before any research activity can be carried out.
- Even when ethical approval has been obtained, the reflexive researcher will consider if they have ensured that their participants are fully protected through the research process. For example, they will reflect on how to address any imbalances of power in the researcher–participant relationship.

- Wanting to protect participants does not mean that the reflexive researcher views them in a deficit way; rather the personal ethical values of the individual researcher may lead them to encourage their participants to become as involved in the research as possible.

FURTHER READING 

We learnt in Chapter 2 (Beginning to think critically about research) that using newspapers as an academic source is not advisable. However, it is of interest to see how academic ideas are portrayed in the media so we have suggested the two newspaper articles below. They discuss Professor Southall's research where parents and children were filmed in a hospital without their consent. The first reports on the controversy over the research and the second is Southall offering a rationale for his ethical practices 16 years later. See if you can find any other discussion of ethical issues in the media.

Morgan, B. (1997) 'Parents cast doubt on secret abuse study'. Available at: www.independent.co.uk/news/parents-cast-doubt-on-secret-abuse-study-1291580.html (accessed 4 July 2017).

Dyer, C. (2010) 'David Southall: I will not apologise for what I did.' Available at: www.theguardian.com/society/2010/may/05/david-southall-health (accessed 4 July 2017).

10

HOW RESEARCH IS DESIGNED

INTRODUCTION

Research can be designed in numerous different ways and there are countless issues that the would-be researcher needs to take into consideration at the planning stage.

This chapter will ...

- Explain some different approaches that may be chosen when constructing a research project.
- Consider how the specific characteristics of social science research and early childhood research informs these choices.
- Focus on approaches that use numbers and words as data and consider the benefits and limitations of these various practices.

METHODOLOGY: WHAT METHODOLOGICAL CHOICES DOES A RESEARCHER NEED TO MAKE?

In the previous chapter (Chapter 9, The ethics of research) we discussed how ethical considerations impact on how a researcher chooses to design their research so that they can ensure they can make valid claims whilst supporting their participants' contribution. Think about a visit to a restaurant that you recently made; you may have pored over the menu to make an informed choice about what to select. In the same way, researchers need to have engaged with the research literature in order to make considered choices about ways to proceed. In the restaurant your choices will be informed by personal preference, or perhaps calorific and nutritional value; the researcher's choices will also include personal preferences but in addition 'should be informed by an understanding of what is at stake in a specific project and in its execution' (Maggetti et al., 2012: 5). This chapter is all about researcher choices.

The decision-making process firstly involves what the researcher believes can be defined as truth and knowledge (see Chapter 3, Knowledge and truth in research, for our discussion of these key concepts) and what are the best ways to uncover this. They must also decide on what is the best kind of data to answer the research question they have opted for. Additional choices include what they will do with the data once collected and how they will present what they have found out in an accessible way. This latter point means they will also have to decide who they wish their intended audience to be. As the chapter proceeds we will help you understand some of the thought processes researchers have to go through as they consider all these factors.

Another metaphor to help us understand the process of research design is that of flat-pack, self-assembly furniture. We can look at the photograph of the completed furniture on the instruction booklet but this does not show you clearly all the components and all the processes that will need to be considered to achieve the finished piece. Rather, you need to open the brochure and follow the step-by-step guide. The brochure will (hopefully) tell you explicitly how the piece should be assembled just as the researcher should let the reader know transparently how the research was put together (the research methodology).

Methodology is one of the terms we came across in Chapter 4 (The language of research) and it is a key word in this chapter; before we go any further we should look to define it and consider why it is so important that the researcher makes this explicit when they write up their work. You may very well have come across the term 'methodology' before; perhaps to do with research or perhaps in other contexts. Before you read on, try to define it – what does the word mean to you? In the context of research it has a very specific meaning though you will see it defined in several different ways in research books. Often it is compared to the word 'methods' though it has to be said that sometimes the two terms can be used interchangeably. This is confusing for the reader new to research and irritating for those of us who have been wrestling with these terms for slightly longer. Altman (2013) attributes the term methodology to Plato who he suggested defined it as the 'pursuit of knowledge' (2013: 112); but as we know from Chapter 3, knowledge, like methodology, can be defined in several ways. Below is a definition from Braun and Clarke (2013) which we particularly like because it both sums up our own understanding and also sets out a clear difference between the two terms methodology and method. Braun and Clarke (2013) state:

> **Methodology** ... refers to the framework within which ... research is conducted. It consists of theories and practices for how we go about conducting research. It provides a package of assumptions about what counts as research ... and the sorts of claims you can make about data. It tells us which **methods** are appropriate for our research and which are not. **Methodology** can be understood as a theory of how research needs to proceed, to produce valid knowledge ... (Braun and Clarke, 2013: 31)

We can see here a clear distinction between the two terms methodology and methods; this is a difference we will explore fully so that by the end of the chapter you can use the terms confidently and accurately and therefore not interchangeably. Firstly though let us consider in more depth why it is so important to know about the researcher's methodological position. As readers of research we need to know the methodological position the researcher is adopting and how they are intending to 'pursue knowledge'. Do you remember we looked at the word *paradigm* in Chapter 4 (The language of research) and considered the definition of it as 'a loose collection of logically related assumptions, concepts, or propositions that orient thinking and research' (Bogdan and Biklen, 1998: 22)? It is only by knowing the researcher's choice of paradigm that we can know their approach to knowledge and truth (see Chapter 3) and therefore the claims their research can make. Mackenzie and Knipe (2006) describe how 'the research paradigm and methodology work together to form a research study'. The researcher makes assumptions about knowledge and how it can be pursued; these assumptions then inform their research design.

We have already stated, and will reiterate here, that it is important to know how the methodology is different to the term methods; the researcher's adopted methodology will inform the methods that are used. Mackenzie and Knipe (2006) claim they were 'surprised to discover that a large number of texts provided no definition for the terms methodology or method, some texts use the terms interchangeably and others use them as having different meanings' but in this chapter we are very clear about the differences and have set them out accordingly. Perhaps some of the confusion arises through differences of use in different academic disciplines. Here we are concerned with use in the social sciences and in particular in Early Childhood Studies.

Early Childhood Studies is a discipline that incorporates many other disciplines so it will naturally incorporate all these methodological influences. It also sits within the social sciences, so has this additional influence on how research can be carried out in this area (Ingleby, 2012). It would be good to clarify at this point what we mean when we talk about research within the social sciences and how this might differ from other forms of research.

When we are looking at the main differences between scientific research and social science research it is useful to consider how Punch unpicks the two words 'social' and 'science' to offer a helpful explanation:

> 'Social science' refers to the scientific study of human behaviour. 'Social' refers to people and their behaviour, and to the fact that so much of human behaviour occurs in a social context. 'Science' refers to the way that people and their behaviour are studied ... If the aim of (all) science is to build explanatory theory about its data, the aim of social science is to build explanatory theory about people and their behaviour. (Punch, 2014: 9)

RESEARCH IN FOCUS

Sustained Shared Thinking

The REPEY study (Researching Effective Pedagogy in the Early Years) (Siraj-Blatchford et al., 2002) developed theory around 'Sustained Shared Thinking' (SST) by gathering data through observations of what effective practitioners do when engaging with children (Siraj-Blatchford, 2009). SST is described as occurring 'when two or more individuals work together in an intellectual way to solve a problem, clarify a concept, evaluate an activity, extend a narrative etc. Both parties must contribute to the thinking and it must develop and extend the understanding' (Siraj-Blatchford et al., 2002: 8). Callanan et al. (2017) subsequently built on these findings using both interviews and observations to explore good practice in early childhood settings. Their findings once again pointed to the importance of 'high quality adult/child interactions' (2017: 23) and so continued to add to our knowledge of how we should be engaging with young children.

One of the rationales for introducing Early Childhood Studies degrees in 1997 was so that there would be a research basis for pursuing research with children, their families and communities from a much more holistic view than specific disciplines such as psychology or health had been able to do up to that point. One of the tensions had been that each discipline viewed the child in a different way; remember we discussed some different ways that children may be viewed in Chapter 5 (Approaches to research about children). This time we are going to develop our understanding of this by considering how a child might be viewed within the different disciplines that contribute to Early Childhood Studies.

Table 10.1 How different disciplines might view the child

Discipline	The child is viewed as ...
Law	one to be protected; a holder of legal rights
Health Studies	one to be kept healthy; one who can be measured and counted
Psychology	one who can be measured, counted and categorised
Education	one who can learn, achieve or fail
Gender Studies	one who has gender norms imposed on them
History	one who is a construct of the society they are living in
Social work	one who is a member of a family

The human participants included in social science research contribute additional layers of complexity. This is because there are always many variables to consider, such as how the participants are feeling and where and when the research is taking place. As Law suggests, the social sciences are often attempting to describe something 'complex, diffuse and messy' (2001: 2) so it is naïve to approach such research in a linear way.

GATHERING DATA

There are two key ways to gather data in social science research. The researcher can take an approach where they look to use numbers or they can adopt an approach that uses words. They may ask people open-ended questions or carry out narrative observations (words) or they may count responses in surveys and measure factors in observations (numbers). Often these two ways of proceeding can be defined as qualitative (words) or quantitative (numbers), though it would be too simplistic to state that this is always the case. Note the two definitions given below which ask you to remember Braun and Clarke's window metaphor (2013) from Chapter 3 (Knowledge and truth in research); read them and then consider what are the advantages and drawbacks of both approaches?

In *qualitative* research the researcher is looking through either the prison cell window or the window is obscured by the prism of their own experiences. They know that there is more than one reality which is constructed both by themselves as researcher and others who may be participants. This isn't a problem for them as they are interested in the 'complexity and diversity of human interactions' (Roberts-Holmes, 2018: 83).

In *quantitative* research the researcher is standing in front of the perfectly clear window looking at a view that they can go out and experience by counting how many flowers there are or by measuring the height of the trees. This researcher believes that 'the truth is "out there" waiting to be discovered' (Roberts-Holmes, 2018: 83).

Before designing a piece of research, the researcher will need to make some decisions about what they consider the nature of knowledge and truth to be – hence our earlier chapter (Chapter 3) on exploring the nature of these two important concepts. If they believe there is a truth to be discovered by measuring and counting then their design and data collection method will reflect this; if, however, they believe that there are a multitude of representations of reality or multiple truths then they will acknowledge that the 'truth' they are looking to discover in their research is contextual and therefore only one of various truths. In both cases it depends on whether the research is 'knowing in the quantitative paradigm' or 'knowing in the qualitative paradigm' (Cutcliffe and McKenna, 2002: 611).

Qualitative and quantitative methodologies both have their devotees and their critics; some would suggest that by focusing on the differences, or the 'paradigm wars', rather than the value of combining the two approaches can lead to 'unduly impoverished research' (Mackenzie and Knipe, 2006). This combination of both approaches is often referred to as mixed methods. We have already introduced you to the EPPE Project (Sylva et al., 2010) which is a good example of research using a variety of methods (both qualitative and quantitative). By combining the two methodological styles in this way, the strengths of both approaches (Punch, 2014: 303), such as the breadth of quantitative research and the depth of qualitative research, we can compensate for the weaknesses of both approaches such as the subjectivity of qualitative research and the way that quantitative research 'dismisses the experiences of the individual' (Carr, 1994: 718).

TIME TO CONSIDER 

Imagine one of your fellow students is considering some of the ideas and themes they have covered on the Early Childhood Studies programme so far and they are thinking ahead to ideas for their final dissertation. One has enjoyed investigating sibling relationships in their Child Development module and is thinking about exploring the idea of family with child participants. The other has really enjoyed their placement module and is interested in the idea that the setting staff seem to have difficulty in engaging effectively with parents who have English as an additional language. Consider the two areas they intend to research; what methodological advice could you give them and why?

METHODS: WHAT ARE THE DIFFERENCES IN APPROACHES USING NUMBERS AND WORDS AS DATA?

Just like the term methodology, methods will have a different definition depending on which research book or article you are reading. We like to compare methods to the metaphor of a recipe; if we wanted to replicate a piece of research we had read about we would want to know exactly what the researcher did as opposed to why they did it (methodology). We would need all the necessary details, such as how many participants were involved, how they were recruited, how they actually provided the data; in fact everything that involves 'the forms of data collection, analysis, and interpretation that researchers propose for their studies' (Creswell, 2014: 16). We must state though that by using the recipe metaphor we are not seeking to 'dumb down' the research process. We are aware that some might contest this 'simple cookbook' view of methods as too simplistic (Maggetti et al., 2012: 4) and an 'unrealistic, idealistic approach to real world research' (2012: 4). This ties perfectly with Law's idea of 'messy research' (2001: 2) and the problematic layers we have suggested are added once human participants are involved.

So although the metaphor of the recipe can be helpful in understanding methods we have to be careful that we do not forget that it is a 'messy recipe' and understand it is not a simple 'how to' list of instructions.

TIME TO CONSIDER

Find a peer-reviewed journal (for example, you could have a look at one you found for Chapter 4) and see if you can answer the following questions relating to the methods:

- How many participants were included? (*sample* size; see Chapter 4, The language of research)
- Do we know anything else about the sample? (how were they recruited; gender; age; geographical region etc.)
- What kind of *data* was obtained? (numerical; non-numerical; other)
- How was the data collected? (interviews; surveys; questionnaires; observation etc.)
- Over what length of time was the data collected?

If you knew all the answers to these questions then you could conceivably carry out the same piece of research replicating it as closely as possible. Whether your findings were the same though is an entirely different discussion. What do you think?

Let us look a bit more closely at the various ways, or methods, for collecting data. As we have already stated, the main two types of data that can be collected are numbers and words; we will look at other kinds of data in Chapter 11 (Creative approaches to research). These numbers and words can be collected in a variety of ways. Miles and Huberman (1994), when discussing these two types of data, explain that:

> Words are fatter than numbers and usually have multiple meanings. This makes them harder to move around and work with. Worse still, most words are meaningless unless you look backward or forward to other words ... Numbers are usually less ambiguous and can be processed more economically. Small wonder, then, that many researchers prefer working with numbers alone. (1994: 56)

As students you may often have been involved in providing numbers as data to be analysed; one example is module evaluations where you are required to circle numbers to indicate your satisfaction with various aspects of the module's teaching and learning strategies. Other ways of collecting numerical data include observations, as in Callanan et al.'s (2017) research we mentioned earlier on; here they used scales such as the Sustained Shared Thinking and Emotional Wellbeing scale (SSTEW). Questionnaires or interviews with closed questions can provide numerical data; these methods, however, can also be used to collect words or qualitative data.

You may also have provided words as qualitative data on module evaluation proformas. If all students have circled 1 for Excellent when asked about teaching strategies in a specific module this might make tutors happy but it would not give them any detail so that they knew specifically what it was about the techniques that the students had appreciated. Without this knowledge how could they replicate these teaching and learning strategies in further modules? This is why on module evaluations there is always room for students to give some more open feedback to support tutors' understanding of their quantitative responses or, as Watkins suggests, 'To get the complete picture' (2012: 153).

COMBINING QUALITATIVE AND QUANTITATIVE DATA

There are a variety of ways that numerical and non-numerical data can be collected and the researcher needs to select carefully to ensure they have the best possible chance of answering their research question. Sometimes it might be more appropriate to combine these two approaches into a 'third methodological movement' (Creswell and Plano Clark, 2011: 1), as we mentioned earlier on in the chapter. Let's return to a discussion of mixed methods now and explore it in a bit more depth. It is not without its difficulties; what if the two forms of data disagree with each other? It is useful though to combine two approaches to give us the breadth and depth we talked about above.

One effective marriage of two methods could be surveys (numerical) with interviews (non-numerical). If the interviewer used surveys in the first phase then they could pick up on anything interesting that arose and use these points to explore issues in much greater detail in semi-structured interviews. Interviews also fit well with other data collection processes. Another partnership could be observations (numerical) alongside interviews (non-numerical); then the researcher can see if the claims participants make about their experiences are actually observed in practice.

A predominantly quantitative approach with some opportunity for qualitative comments is taken by the NSS (National Student Survey). This is a survey that all students studying at English universities are asked to complete in their final year. It is a survey which may not necessarily build theory but which has certainly become a powerful tool to give students a voice in higher education. Academics do not always see it in a positive way though, with one describing the NSS as 'the sword of Damocles ... always hanging over our heads' (Sabri, 2013: 4). However it continues to be perceived as 'an unbiased source of information' (Cheng and Marsh, 2010: 707) and conclusions are drawn quantitatively both by specific universities about their specific programmes and the education media to compare similar programmes at other institutions in a hierarchical ladder of excellence. In this sense it is useful for programme leaders when looking to identify the strengths and areas of development for their programme and also for prospective students looking to choose the best programme and institution to suit their learning needs.

The data can offer mixed messages about the successes and areas for development for individual programmes. For example, students could highlight high satisfaction through their quantitative responses and then make highly critical comments in their qualitative responses. This could be for many reasons, including the fact that as qualitative responses are more time consuming for the participant then perhaps only those who have had a negative experience of the programme will take the time to make their voice heard. Such mixed messages may prompt those who lead programmes to question the reliability of the data and whether 'their activities and achievements are properly represented' (Ashby et al., 2011: 5). By adopting a predominantly quantitative approach to students' experiences 'there's no way of knowing what lies behind those percentages' (Sabri, 2013: 5). This has led many researchers interested in these matters to suggest that a more effective way to proceed from this data would be to now 'get underneath' it by exploring with small groups of students what they were actually trying to say through their responses in much the same way as Sabri has done in her research (2013). This may offer more opportunities to develop 'concrete enhancement strategies' (Cheng and Marsh, 2010: 695) to the programme.

This way of auditing what is happening in higher education is described as being the 'performativity culture' (Murray, 2012), which has become such a prominent part of the education landscape. Early childhood, regardless of its emphasis on play and the holistic development of the individual child, has also not been able to escape this 'tick box' way of working (Osgood, 2011: 51), where children, early years practitioners and early childhood settings are 'measured' in a quantitative way. This could have the above-cited impact on practitioners as it has on tutors in the higher education context leading them to feelings of anxiety and inadequacy. In fact, Kilderry (2015) did discover this level of anxiety in her research in the Australian early childhood context though other practitioners reported feeling either an increased confidence or an increased disregard with this way of working. Think about early childhood settings you have been in; do you recognize this 'performativity culture'? Can you think of examples when children, staff or the setting are measured? What is the impact of this?

TIME TO CONSIDER

In this section of the chapter we have focused on various methods that could be used in research. In Chapter 2 (Beginning to think critically about research) we quoted Goldacre (2009: 248) on subconscious bias. In his book *Bad Science* Goldacre considers one particular piece of research in a chapter entitled 'Why clever people believe stupid things' (2009: ch. 13). He describes an experiment where the participants are playing the role of 'teachers' using rewards and punishments to make children arrive on time for school. He describes how the participants are convinced that their use of the reward/punishment system impacts on the arrival times of the children over the 15 days the experiment takes place. Goldacre (2009: 247) states that this is in part due to the bad science that 'we see causal relationships where there are none' and the children were allocated entirely random times to arrive. Consider how you could develop this research to understand why children

(Continued)

(Continued)

might be late for school. There are lots of things that you would need to take into consideration: for example

- What would your research question be?
- Would you need words or numbers (or both!) to try to answer it?
- Who would you ask?
- What would the ethical considerations be?

WHAT ARE THE BENEFITS AND LIMITATIONS OF THESE VARIOUS METHODS?

Having described the various methods on offer let us now consider what their benefits and limitations might be. For example, if a researcher decided on interviewing their participants what might they have to be mindful of? Or what would be the benefits of choosing this approach? Table 10.2 suggests a variety

Table 10.2 Benefits and limitations of data collection

Method	Benefit	Limitation
Interviews	Gives the researcher an opportunity to gather more detailed information	Could be intimidating for a participant
Questionnaires	Gives the participants time to reflect carefully on their responses	Only confident writers will be happy to engage
Focus groups (usually to include participants who do not know each other)	Effective use of time; participants can prompt each other in their thinking and responses.	One or two participants may dominate so that diverse voices are not heard.
Group interviews (usually to include participants who know each other)	Can offer reliability and validity to the responses	Possibility of 'group think' where participants feel they have to go along with what the majority of the group say even if they disagree
Email exchanges	Informal therefore less threatening for participant	Informality may mean participants overshare (and then regret it)
Observations	Researcher can see what is happening without having to rely on participant accounts	Presence of researcher (or video camera) can impact on behaviours of participants
Field notes (notes a researcher makes whilst spending a length of time in a locality)	Researcher has time and opportunity to really reflect on what they observe	Researcher bias will impact on how they interpret what they see
Surveys	Can be time- and cost-effective; can reach a large sample	Can only capture a snapshot of the issue being researched

of methods which are often selected. We have deliberately not sorted them into quantitative and qualitative methods because they could be used in either approach though some are naturally used in a more quantitative way (surveys) and others are used in a more qualitative way (focus groups). We have listed some benefits and limitations to each approach in Table 10.2; can you think of any others?

We have discovered that no approach is without its limitations and the thoughtful researcher will make this explicit to their reader when they write up their report. Kumar (2014: 273) describes limitations as 'structural problems relating to methodological aspects of the study' and adds that they should always 'be communicated to readers'. The important factor here is that researchers make these limitations known; they have a duty to not pretend that research is straight forward but recognise instead that research is indeed a 'messy business' (Newby, 2014). We will see in the next chapter (Chapter 11, Creative approaches to research) that considering the limitations of research design can help researchers to think creatively about the methods they adopt.

TIME TO CONSIDER

See if you can find two more definitions of methodology and methods from two other sources. Can you find one you prefer?

CASE STUDY

Lettie: an EYITT university lecturer

Lettie is working with a group of students training to become early years teachers. In a module that focused on creativity and play she asked them to read and discuss an interesting article on sand play therapy (Zhou, 2009). This led on to a more general discussion of the benefits of sand play and good pedagogical practice. The students felt they had seen very little effective practice or indeed children totally immersed in play and learning when at the sand tray. As a group they discussed how they could find out what was really happening when the children were involved in this activity and what learning may be taking place. Lucy encourages her students to plan a small piece of research around how children use sand play. They all choose to approach it in different ways. Some students decide to do narrative observations, others to produce a checklist of certain behaviours. Still others decided to record every hour who is using the sand tray and what they are doing there. Not all students want to do observations; some decide they are going to either interview or ask practitioners to complete a simple questionnaire; yet others believe that talking to the children will provide them with the most useful data. When the students bring their data back to the university session they can see collecting data in various and contrasting ways has allowed them to build up a picture of what might be happening in sand play and how this knowledge could inform their practice.

TIME TO CONSIDER

Think about the kind of data the students will collect. What could they do with the data, and what sort of information will it give them? How could they use this information to improve practice in their own setting?

FINAL REFLECTION

Undertaking research is all about making choices and then making the choices explicit to your reader. The reader needs to know the researcher's methodological position and then how this has informed the methods they have chosen. All methods have their own limitations and it is important that the researcher recognises these.

KEY POINTS

- Methodology is informed by what the researcher thinks knowledge and truth is and how these can be accessed.
- Methods are the practical ways of gathering data. There are many different kinds of methods. Before deciding on which to use the researcher needs to consider which is the best way to answer their research question.
- Data can be gathered in the form of numbers (numerical data or quantitative approach) or words (non-numerical data or qualitative approach); sometimes researchers combine the two in a mixed methods approach.

FURTHER READING

Walker, J., Crawford, K. and Taylor, F. (2008) 'Listening to children: gaining a perspective of the experiences of poverty and social exclusion from children and young people of single-parent families', *Health and Social Care in the Community*, 16(4): 429–36.

This research article has a particularly clear methodology. As you read it bear in mind the questions we asked earlier and which are repeated here:

- How many participants were included? (sample size)
- Do we know anything else about the sample? (how were they recruited; gender; age; geographical region etc.)
- What kind of data was obtained? (numerical; non-numerical; other)
- How was the data collected? (interviews; surveys; questionnaires; observation etc.)
- Over what length of time was the data collected?

Mukherji, P. and Albon, D. (2018) *Research Methods in Early Childhood.* London: Sage.

This book is aimed at students who are beginning to carry out their own research. However, it will also really help you develop your growing understanding of how research is designed and give you lots of examples of what this looks like in practice.

11

CREATIVE APPROACHES TO RESEARCH

INTRODUCTION

When we think of being creative we might think about producing a piece of art or dance; however, creativity has its place within social science research generally and Early Childhood Studies research specifically.

This chapter will ...

- Help you develop your understanding of creative approaches to research.
- Build on the concept of creativity in research and consider such research ideas as using visual imagery, digital methods, photo elicitation and naturally occurring data.
- Encourage you to not merely accept the descriptions of creative research methods given but also critique them using your growing understanding of research design and its limitations.

WHAT DO WE MEAN BY CREATIVE APPROACHES TO RESEARCH?

When we talk about creative approaches in research we are thinking of methods that have moved away from more traditional approaches to encourage a different kind of participation from those involved. Kara (2015) suggests that when researchers from different disciplines come together then such methods can 'help them vault out of silos and leap over boundaries' (2015: 3). She further concludes that creative approaches will support those 'who want to break out of traditional disciplinary confines, or who need to do so because their research questions are too complex to be restricted by the traditional methods and techniques of a single discipline' (Kara, 2015: 3). This is particularly relevant when we look at the subject area of Early Childhood Studies; this discipline is a fusion of 'history, psychology, education, health, welfare, sociology, social policy, cultural studies, the law, and political and economic perspectives' (QAA, 2014) and so particularly needs a multi-disciplinary approach to research. One such approach could be the use of visual imagery which we will go on to explore in the next section.

TIME TO CONSIDER

Think about all the different disciplines that contribute to Early Childhood Studies. This is a strength of this area of study but it could bring its own tensions to research. Take a few moments to consider what you think these tensions might be. You might want to look back at the table you completed in the previous chapter on how research is designed (Table 10.1).

WHAT IS VISUAL IMAGERY AND WHY MIGHT IT BE A USEFUL RESEARCH STRATEGY IN ECEC?

In Chapter 10 (How research is designed) we looked at the differences between research using *numbers* and research using *words*. However, researchers do not need to limit themselves to these two methods. In our day-to-day lives we are surrounded by images so it would make sense to include them in research also. Pink explains that images are 'inextricably interwoven with our personal identities, narratives, lifestyles, cultures and societies, as well as with definitions of history, space and truth' (2006: 21), and so using visual imagery could help participants to share their ideas, thoughts and perceptions in several different ways. Prosser and Loxley (2010: 202) give us a clear rationale for the use of visual imagery in research, arguing that a move away from the traditional data collection vehicles of words and numbers is appropriate in a society that has become increasingly dominated by the visual and where 'what we see is as important, if not more so, than what we hear or read'. Think about 'what we see' then list as many different examples of types of visual data that participants could be asked to produce or that researchers could collect to analyse. Do this before you look at the next paragraph.

Did you list the following?

- Drawings
- Photographs
- Models
- Video clips
- Adverts
- Signs

You may have been able to think of many others; if you have, consider how they might be used in early childhood research. Table 11.1 offers suggestions of how they have been used previously, but can you think of others?

Table 11.1 How visual imagery has been used in previous research

Method	Example of research
Drawings	Ford (2011) asked children to produce drawings of their time spent in hospital in order to understand their 'experiences of surgery'
Photographs	Warin (2000) asked children to be photographed in gender-specific clothes, for example a pink frilly dress, to explore children's perceptions of gender
Models	Gauntlett (2007) asked adult participants from a variety of backgrounds to use Lego® to build a model to represent their identity. He also used photographs and audio recordings of people involved in the activity as part of his dataset
Video clips	Boyd (2014) asked practitioners to wear portable cameras during their setting sessions and then select clips to support a discussion of their interactions with young children
Adverts	LoDolce et al. (2013) analysed TV advertisements to find out how sugary breakfast cereals were 'sold' to children
Signs	Trinch and Snajdr (2017) analysed shop signs to consider how they might include or exclude different sections of the population

Each piece of research mentioned in the table would certainly provide some interesting and useful data but each would also have its own limitations; in Gauntlett's Lego®-based research (2007) the participants may have built models to show how they would like to be seen rather than who they think they really are. This is a key idea in research and one that was written about at length more than 50 years ago by an American sociologist called Erving Goffman (1922–82). He suggested that we are all social actors who are putting on a show for people who may be observing us. We can see that this might be an issue in creative research, especially when participants may choose what behaviours and beliefs they present to others who are observing or interacting with them. If the participants are 'putting on a performance' (Goffman, 1990) then how useful can the piece of research be in terms of what it adds to our knowledge? Go back to the examples of research mentioned in Table 11.1 and consider what other limitations or issues there might be. To help you do this we will now look at a further piece of research, which used visual methods.

RESEARCH IN FOCUS 

Hattingh and de Kock (2008): collages

Hattingh and de Kock (2008) were working with students training to be teachers in the context of South Africa. They wanted to find out what these students thought about the role of the teacher. Instead of simply asking them questions they invited

(Continued)

(Continued)

their participants to make individual collages to represent the role of the teacher. By engaging with this activity they hoped that the students would participate in 'deep reflection and inner exploration' and that some 'rich and thick data' would emerge. Why do you think the researchers thought they would get richer data this way? Is it because they thought they were using a strategy that the students would feel comfortable with?

Possibly the researchers believed this would be a successful method because this was an activity that was part of their university teaching sessions so they were not asking the students to do anything different or additional. They may have believed that the student responses to the activity would have been more spontaneous, authentic or honest than if they had been asked to produce something specifically for a piece of research. If we substituted the participants for young children, we would imagine that if we collected and analysed a selection of their drawings we would have very different data than if we asked them to draw something for a specific reason. Can you see anything problematic about this data collection method though?

SELECTING WHICH METHOD

There are always going to be issues when we choose data collection methods that we believe will allow our participants to give the most 'truthful' answer; you will remember of course our discussions around how we know what is true and how we can understand knowledge in Chapter 3 (Knowledge and truth in research). If a university tutor is asking a student to produce a piece of work that will also be used as data then both the tutor and the students are positioned in 'dual roles' (Shi, 2006). The tutor is both teacher and researcher whilst the student is both learner and participant (Shi, 2006). Shi worked as a tutor to student teachers and wanted to do some research on their uses of technology. The data was to be gathered as part of the teaching sessions and the collection was carefully planned so that students could both 'opt out of the research project anonymously but, at the same time, not … [be denied] … their access to learning opportunities' (2006: 205). In writing up the report of this research Shi describes the tensions for both researcher and participant, concluding that rather than benefiting from the research to explore and reflect on learning, many students complained about their sense of *being used* as research participants. Even if the students had been happy about the whole research experience there is also a power imbalance to be addressed. The tutor has the 'power' to award marks and grades therefore a student producing such a piece of work may have at the back of their mind that a piece of work equates a mark. If so they will then position their tutor as a 'marker' rather than a researcher. If this is the case then how can we argue that the students have produced an authentic response? If Hattingh and de Kock had wanted to consider this and how it may have limited their research then they could have acknowledged the power issues such as those we have discussed in Chapter 9 (The ethics of research) and looked at ways to include the students as more active participants; they could have asked the student participants what they believed was the best way of gathering their perceptions on the role of the teacher. Regardless of any limitations to this kind of research, however, using visual data can have many benefits and can be useful in particular research situations, as we will now go on to discuss.

When deciding which method to use in research, the researcher must never begin with a consideration of methods – this is a misunderstanding and mistake often made by those embarking on their dissertation in an undergraduate degree. Rather the researcher should always consider which methods will best help them answer their research question after of course considering the nature of the knowledge they believe they will be able to contribute to. They may consider visual data because, despite the issues highlighted above, this can be a non-threatening way to gather data from a diverse range of participants. It can offer diversity both in the outcomes and the opportunity for participants to demonstrate knowledge and understanding in different ways. Interviews or questionnaires may intimidate participants but gathering data in a creative way where there is no right answer could be said, in some respects, to deal with those issues of 'social power' acknowledged by Opie (2007). Children do not respond well to being 'over-questioned' (Fisher, 2016) but they may feel happy to produce a drawing or take a selection of photographs to record how they understand a certain issue. Meehan (2016) demonstrated this when she worked with student researchers to explore children's understanding of certain issues, such as friendships, poverty or homelessness. Prosser and Loxley (2010) use the metaphor of the bridge to describe how visual methodologies are 'less threatening than words/numbers-based methods' and they can 'build bridges between researchers and researched' even 'empowering' the participant. Can you think about how a child might be empowered by being asked to produce a drawing on their understanding of a particular concept such as friendship, poverty, or family? We will go on to look at the use of drawings as a data collection method next.

USING CHILDREN'S DRAWINGS IN RESEARCH

Using drawings is a particularly popular method with those researching with children and we considered this when we looked at the Mosaic Approach in Chapter 6 (Approaches to research with children). It allows participants to engage in a non-verbal way and to work at their own pace. Einarsdottir (2007) carried out longitudinal research in an ECEC setting using a variety of methods looking to find one that would be the most effective when working with young children. She found this to be a useful method stating: 'the children are active and creative while they draw. Most children are also familiar with the activity of drawing, they can change and add to the drawings as they choose, and drawings often take time so that a quick response is not demanded' (2007: 201). However, drawings could be limited in the information they provide for the researcher, particularly if you consider how the random mark marking of a two-year-old may be difficult to decipher compared to the more formal depictions of a four-year-old.

Nevertheless, Fargas-Malet et al. (2010) list a number of strengths in using drawing as a data gathering method when working with young children. They suggest that:

> Drawings can be used as a good ice-breaker, can help children relax and establish rapport, can act as prompts and as triggers for remembering or for eliciting discussion, and may help children organize their own narratives (Hill, 1997; Miles, 2000). This technique may also enable children to gain more control over the interview. (2010: 183)

As it is not a simple matter to analyse children's drawings, Fargas-Malet et al. (2010) suggest that it is important to also get the children to talk about what they have drawn so that any analysis is not just from the adults' perspective. Einarsdottir (2007) also emphasises the importance of this and draws on other writers (Punch, 2002; Clark, 2005; Veale, 2005) to support her assertion that 'Placing an emphasis on listening to children while they drew, instead of trying to analyse their drawing, is important, as the children's narratives and interpretations of their drawings can give a better picture than the adults' interpretations of the drawings' (2007: 201).

If drawings are used in a thoughtful way they seem a positive approach, relevant to child participants but also to any adult participants in early childhood research such as practitioners, parents or students. But as in every method, we must also consider the limitations, or difficulties, with using drawings as data. Before we offer our own suggestions, take a moment to consider what you think these may be …

Firstly, not all children (or adult participants) may enjoy drawing (Einarsdottir, 2007) or they may not feel they are very good at drawing. Reflect on if you were asked to produce a drawing of friendship, poverty or family as we suggested above. Whatever your age you would have to be both competent and confident that you could physically produce the image you wanted to and you would also have to have the sophistication to be able to represent a complex concept visually. It is also worth considering that the child's understanding may be superior to their drawing ability or vice versa so this might not be the best way to capture their perceptions. If a child is asked to draw in a one-to-one situation with the researcher then they may feel intimidated and scrutinised but if they are asked to draw in a group they may copy others' ideas rather than represent their own (Einarsdottir, 2007). In the same way they may draw whatever they think will make the researcher happy so that we are returning full circle to having to address power issues within the research. Difficulties with using drawings have led some researchers to explore other visual data, such as the use of digital methods, and we will now go on to consider these.

USING DIGITAL METHODS

When we use the term 'digital methods' we are referring to a whole variety of data types; we could be talking about using cameras or video cameras or we could even be referring to the use of freely available data on the Internet such as blogs, forums or social networking sites. In their book *Innovations in Digital Research Methods* Halfpenny and Procter (2015) discuss how more and more 'social science researchers are harnessing innovations in digital technologies to transform their research methods' (2015: 1). Let's look in more detail at three specific areas of digital data which are: (i) videos, (ii) photographs and (iii) the Internet.

Using video can be an effective way of capturing useful data, as Boyd (2014) demonstrated in his research with nursery practitioners. The practitioners wore cameras around their necks as they interacted with young children throughout the day. The practitioners then spent time choosing which clips they wished to discuss with the researcher; they viewed the videos together and reflected on how they had interacted with the children by posing questions or engaging in sustained shared thinking. Boyd (2014: 446–447) found that this methodology worked particularly well because 'it enabled the teachers to be directly involved in the analysis. It allowed repeated viewing and development of analysis to establish shared understanding ... it helped to capture children's actions, expressions and body language.' Child participants could also use digital cameras to record moving images though one issue with this is that if they have not had much experience of filming they might focus on the novelty of the camera and what it can do rather than the focus of the research (Tunstall et al., 2004).

In Tunstall et al.'s research (2004) children were asked to take pictures of rivers to help the researchers develop their understanding of how children understand landscapes and the environment. Taking photos is seen by many authors to be a particularly effective method for children to engage with (Einarsdottir, 2007). It is seen to be particularly advantageous as 'it increases children's power because the data gathering is in part in their hands as they decide what they photograph' (Einarsdottir, 2007: 203). But once again here we must consider if there are any limitations in this approach.

Jorgenson and Sullivan (2010), whilst appreciating the value of utilising strategies and methods that are more compatible with children's developmental needs, also make the important point that 'they also present interpretive challenges insofar as the meanings of the responses are contingent on *how* children construe the research task and *how* they react to the researcher'. Tunstall et al. (2004) also make a really pertinent and interesting point that 'A disadvantage of photography as a research tool could be that it focuses on the visual to the neglect of the other three senses' (2004: 184). We know that young children's optimal learning involves all their senses so it could seem inappropriate to ask them to focus on one only – their sense of sight. Some researchers have tried to address this by asking the children to make audio recordings to accompany tours of their early years settings (Clark, 2005) and which could be used as data alongside the photographs the children had taken. There are different ways that photographs can be used, one of which is a method often called 'photo-elicitation'.

Photo-elicitation has become increasingly popular as a data gathering method in the social sciences and can take many different forms. Participants may be encouraged to take their own photographs, as in Tunstall et al.'s research (2004) or in Einarsdottir's research (2007). Or the researcher may use commercially produced photographs as we did when we were exploring children's understanding of practitioner gender. In both approaches the photographs can provide useful visual clues of the issues being discussed, and a 'coat hanger' for conversations exploring behaviour and viewpoints (Arksey and Knight, 1999: 118). Harper (2002) even suggests that the brain engages in a very different way when photographs are used in interviews:

> The difference between interviews using images and text, and interviews using words alone lies in the ways we respond to these two forms of symbolic representation. This has a physical basis: the parts of the brain that process visual information are evolutionarily older than the parts that process verbal information. Thus images evoke deeper elements of human consciousness that do words; exchanges based on words alone utilize less of the brain's capacity than do exchanges in which the brain is processing images as well as words. These may be some of the reasons the photo elicitation interview seems like not simply an interview process that elicits more information, but rather one that evokes a different kind of information. (2002: 13)

Sampson-Cordle (2001) used photographs in her PhD research. She wished to explore community dynamics so asked a range of participants to take photographs to represent community relationships. She writes 'They created photographs, then wrote about their photos, and finally, held the photos in their hands as they discussed their meanings with the researcher' (abstract). Harper names this approach 'photo feedback' or 'photo self-elicitation' and it is clear to see the links with the Mosaic Approach that we have discussed previously and also how it could be a good model of participatory research.

Photo-elicitation is then a useful method which can be used in a variety of ways to support participants in sharing their views, perspectives and ideas and also to address the power imbalance between researcher and researched. This can especially be seen when participants are facilitated to handle and move around the photographs. Oliffe and Bottorff (2007: 850) suggest that this method 'can yield fascinating empirical data and provide unique insights into diverse phenomena, as well as empowering and emancipating participants by making their experiences visible'. Photographs are of course easily accessible on the Internet alongside many other types of naturally occurring data, which is a form of data we will turn our attention to shortly.

Using digital methods can allow for greater participation from a more diverse range of practitioners regardless of their age. Imagine the possibilities if you wanted to do research with children who had English as an additional language and so had a limited ability to share their ideas with you. The same could be said for children with other additional or special educational needs, such as communication and language difficulties. Just like all children they also 'hold their own views and perspectives, have the right to be heard, and are able to speak for themselves if the right methods are used' (Einarsdottir, 2007: 197).

So we have seen that there are a variety of digital methods that could be used when researching in ECEC. We have also seen that when researching with children it is often useful to use a selection of methods to allow for optimal participation (Barker and Weller, 2003).

TIME TO CONSIDER 

Think about children who have English as an additional language. How might four-year-olds with limited English be encouraged to participate in a piece of research looking to explore young children's understanding of friendship?

HOW CAN NATURALLY OCCURRING DATA BE USED IN ECEC RESEARCH?

We are surrounded by naturally occurring data such as:

- photographs
- newspaper headlines
- blogs
- Internet forums
- films
- advertisements
- magazines

These are just a few sources we have come up with; perhaps you can think of some others. Consider, for example, any professional publications you might regularly read to develop your subject knowledge of ECEC. It would be interesting to review and analyse the use of photographs in these publications over a year to see how children, practitioners or even parents were represented. It would be equally enlightening to review and analyse the headlines on the front cover over a period of time to find out where the main emphasis lies. Silverman (2009) writes about how one of his students successfully defended a PhD thesis which was based on just one page of A4 of newspaper headlines from a local newspaper and how it reported crime. Many people now access such publications online rather than as hard copy and here too there is much potential for data gathering.

One such place a researcher could look is at the abundance of blogs that you have access to as you surf the net; these could be subject-specific such as Early Years forums or more generic such as the very popular Mumsnet for example. Although this is an interesting source it does raise the ethical question of who the data (in this contexts the 'posts') belong to and whether the researcher has any right to analyse them. When they were written the author had not given specific consent to them being used for research purpose (Hookway, 2008). This could also be an issue if a researcher wanted to use videos posted online – though not if they wanted to use commercial films.

Indeed this is what some researchers have done. For example, many have been interested in analysing Disney animation films as data; two such examples are Padilla-Walker et al.'s exploration of prosocial behaviour in Disney films (2013) or Patterson and Spencer's example of exploring gender diversity in Disney animation (2017). These sorts of issues could also be explored by observing people in real life, though of course this would present more ethical challenges.

Silverman (2014), in his quest to compare the use of naturally occurring data with interviews, managed to get ethical approval to sit in on doctor consultations. On one occasion this involved him observing parents of sick children in discussion with the consultant. Sometimes there would be a team of trainee doctors present. The parents who were included in this kind of consultation later reported that they had felt inhibited to ask questions because there were too many professionals in the room. However Silverman found the exact opposite to be true – these parents actually asked many more questions, which he suggested was down to a more informal environment where the trainee doctors were encouraged to ask questions – or were indeed questioned themselves.

Because of the difficulties in the layered meanings of participants' responses, Silverman (2009) would encourage the researcher to look for naturally occurring data, which does not 'ignore the possible disparity between the discourse of actors about some topical issue and the way they respond to questions in a formal context' (Fielding and Fielding, 1986: 21). This quotation is useful when we consider Boyd's research (2014) that we cited in Table 11.1 and how he might have gone about it differently; think about what differences he may have found if he had asked practitioners how they interacted with children rather than asking them to video what was happening as part of their everyday practice. There was probably more possibility that they would reveal what they do rather than what they think they do, or as Pring describes it, 'what is said and what is' (2006: 75), demonstrating how by approaching research in a creative way the researcher may find more efficient ways of answering their research question.

TIME TO CONSIDER

Think about how you would describe a day at work or university to three different people (for example, your partner, your tutor, your boss). Would you describe it in exactly the same way to each person or would you tailor your recount to your audience? Why would you do this? Think about how this relates to how a participant might relate an occasion or a practice to a researcher.

CASE STUDY

Alex: an ECS student

Alex is studying for a degree in Early Childhood Studies. As he is browsing through a selection of electronic journals online he finds an article that particularly grabs his interest. The research article focuses on how children in both Norway and China took the school teddy bear home along with the class diary to record what he got up to (Haldar and Wærdahl, 2009). Alex had read about this practice before and how it supports home–school liaison but he had never before considered how the diary entries, which included both narratives and photographs, could be used as data. He decided he would like to try to replicate this in his own setting to help him gain an understanding of what is important to the families in the community that the setting serves. He puts together a proposal and then meets with his tutor to discuss any ethical issues that need to be considered.

TIME TO CONSIDER

Look back at what you learnt in Chapter 9 (The ethics of research). If you were Alex's tutor what advice might you give him about ethics? Can you think of any other creative ways that Alex could find out about the families and community he works with?

FINAL REFLECTION

In this chapter we have considered various creative approaches to research which are attractive alternatives to the more limited questionnaire, survey, interview, observation menu often associated with research. These alternative, creative methods may possibly be more interesting to read about but it is also important that we maintain the critical idea we discussed in Chapter 3 (Knowledge and truth in research). One way to do so is to keep the following questions in mind when reading a piece of research:

- What do we know about the piece of research's data collection methods? What are the strengths and weaknesses of this?
- What do we know about the study's sample? What are the strengths and weaknesses of this?
- What do we know about the study's ethical considerations? What are the strengths and weaknesses of this?

KEY POINTS 

- Data collection methods in research can encompass much more than the simple word/number approach.
- Sometimes the researcher needs to think creatively in order to allow a diverse range of participants to take part and share their views.
- It is important to look beyond the 'novelty' approach that the researcher may have taken and question the rigour of the methodology and methods adopted.

FURTHER READING 

Haldar, M. and Wærdahl, R. (2009) 'Teddy diaries: a method for studying the display of family life', *Sociology*, 43(6): 1141–50.

Read the journal article that Alex found so interesting and which was the catalyst for his own research. It is about how the diaries that families write in when they take the class-bear home for the weekend were used as data to look at and compare standards of family life in China and Norway.

Hosking, G., Mulholland, L. and Baird, B. (2015) '"We are doing just fine": the children of Australian gay and lesbian parents speak out', *Journal of GLBT Family Studies*, 11(4): 327–50.

Hosking et al. used the Internet to obtain instances where children of gay and lesbian parents spoke of their experiences online.

12

YOUR RESEARCH JOURNEY HAS BEGUN

INTRODUCTION

Think about how your learning has moved on since you first picked up this book. You have collected some useful tools in your researcher toolkit which will support you in engaging with others' research and eventually carrying out your own.

In this chapter we will ...

- Draw together all the key ideas that have been explored throughout the book.
- Ask you to look forward to the next step of your research journey and consider how you can build on this learning.
- Encourage you to think about how you may begin to frame a research question and reflect upon the most appropriate way to try to answer this taking into consideration any ethical issues.
- Challenge you to consider what kind of researcher you want to become.

HOW CAN YOU BUILD ON YOUR LEARNING FROM THIS INTRODUCTION TO RESEARCH?

Let's begin the chapter by reminding you how much you have learnt since you first opened this book. Not only have you developed your understanding about research but you have also acquired a new vocabulary to talk about it and a new ability to be able to critique what you read. Look back at the key points at the end of each chapter to remind yourself of the key messages and consider how you can now build on this knowledge. What do you now know about ...

- the different kinds of research in early childhood
- how to critique others' research
- how knowledge and truth can be defined
- key research terminology
- differences between research 'about' and research 'with' children
- differences between longitudinal and cross-national research
- the importance of ethics in research
- how research is designed
- how to critique creative approaches to research?

And, more importantly, what are you going to do with this newly acquired knowledge?

HOW HAS YOUR LEARNING MOVED ON?

In Chapter 1 we posed three questions for you:

- What do we mean by research?
- In what different ways is research carried out?
- Why is research important in Early Childhood Studies?

Think about your responses to these questions now; you might even wish to jot down a few ideas. This will demonstrate to you how your learning has developed. As you look at the ideas you have jotted down underline some of the key vocabulary you have used. Go back to Chapter 4 (The language of research) – have you included all the words in Table 4.1? If there are any words not included is it because you still do not feel secure about them? We compared learning the language of research with learning a foreign language and hopefully you are now becoming more bilingual as you use these terms confidently. With this new vocabulary should come a new approach to questioning what you read. This new approach to questioning is all about being critical or, as we have already mentioned, asking the 'So What?' question when we read others' research; this will help us ask the 'So What?' question about our own research when we eventually undertake it. Some students can struggle with the idea of asking this question so let us break it down for you to support your thinking. We can explain the 'So What?' question in this context by focusing on the following sub-questions:

- So what is the significance of this?
- So what are the implications of this?
- So why is this important?
- So where does this lead us?

We hope that now you feel confident enough to read others' research and question the text as you read using these sub-questions to support your thinking. If you have engaged well with the activities in this book your understanding in terms of research should really have moved on in many ways

From reading research you are adding to your knowledge and understanding in two different ways. Firstly you are adding to your subject knowledge about young children which will be useful to you regardless of which area you decide to work in with them. Then secondly, you are adding to your understanding of how this research is carried out so that not only can you decide how to conduct your own research but you can decide whether the findings of the research you have read could inform your own practice. Remember Nick in Chapter 2 (Beginning to think critically about research) who was asked by the head teacher to incorporate Brain Gym® into his teaching sessions? We described to you how he searched research literature to find out if there was any evidence offered for its effectiveness or indeed for any alternative programmes. What we didn't tell you in Chapter 2, however, was that Nick eventually decided that, although reading about others' research was interesting and useful for his practice, the most useful thing for him to do was to carry out his own research (which we would call *action research*) to see if such programmes had any impact in the context of his own classroom. Of course he had read Chapter 9 (The ethics of research) and ensured he had all necessary approval and consent before proceeding.

When Keisha carried out research with young children in her early years setting it was because she was concerned about the progress of the handful of children in the group who had English as an additional language; they seemed to be lagging behind the other children and she was concerned that they were not going to be 'school ready'. She was interested to know how they were using the learning environment independently; for example, did they use the number and phonics displays when they were using the mark making table. In fact she found that they were not particularly engaging with the interactive displays and made a point of changing her pedagogy to ensure she modelled how to use them. Furthermore, by concentrating on this small group of children, she made the exciting discovery that some of them were already literate in their first language and they could already read and write when she had assumed that this was something they were going to struggle with.

When Bolshaw et al. (2017) wanted to carry out research with children to find out their perceptions of practitioner gender they were struggling to find an appropriate methodology. By reading up on research that others had conducted such as Einarsdottir (2007) or Clark and Moss (2011), they were able to settle on an appropriate methodology. In much the same way, reading others' research will add to your own knowledge about methodology and therefore help you in devising your own research.

By engaging with scholarly sources we can develop our subject knowledge about children, their families and their communities. We also develop our understanding of research to enable us to carry out our own and so develop our practice and perhaps eventually contribute to theory. But why would we want to carry out research to help us develop our practice? Let us look now at some more specific examples of students carrying out research and consider how they might feel it has been a worthwhile endeavour. These students could choose whether to complete a piece of research and decided that it would be worthwhile in terms of their intended career trajectories.

CASE STUDY

Examples of students carrying out research

Louise and treasure baskets

Louise had become very interested in heuristic play (Goldschmied and Jackson, 2004) and the use of treasure baskets when she had prepared a presentation on this as part of her first year Child Development module. She continued reading about them for her second year Creativity module assignment; at the same time she was also undertaking a placement module in an early years setting and was taken aback by the poor quality of the 'treasure basket' provision and staff understanding of its benefits. Therefore she decided to focus her third year dissertation on this. She gathered her own resources for some parent and baby drop-in sessions and obtained consent to carry out observations and interviews. She was able to use her findings to provide Continuing Professional Development (CPD) for the setting and then subsequently, on graduation, in her role working with parents and young children.

Karim and block play

Karim was fascinated by the block play (Kieff and Wellhousen, 2001) in a setting he had visited. He observed how engrossed the children were and how they were developing their scientific and mathematical knowledge. He knew that he eventually wanted to be a primary school teacher but wanted to ensure that his pedagogy was based on how children learnt best; in other words, he wanted to take the best of early years into formal schooling. He asked the setting if he could return to carry out his research there to make detailed observations of the children's play and learning. He was able to talk about his findings both at his PGCE interview and then at his first teaching post interview. Karim has gone on to develop his research on block play, leading a staff meeting in his school and is presently working on his MA dissertation which is looking at how children can engage in block play in KS1 whilst still meeting the requirements of the National Curriculum.

Hannah and gendered play choices

When she reached the end of the second year of her Early Childhood Studies programme Hannah was still unsure about the career path she wanted to take. At first this meant she was a little unsure about an area to research for her dissertation. She took her tutor's advice to think back over what she had studied so far and decide what she found the most interesting. She decided that she had really enjoyed the Gender module in her second year and in particular when they had looked at children's gender play choices. She therefore decided to do a piece of desk-based research that focused on this. Hannah's first job on graduation was in an FE college working with young people who were training to be Level 2 early years practitioners. She found the research she had done very useful when she was trying to get the young people to challenge their assumptions and think about the best practice when working with young children.

We have seen in this section how student-practitioners feel that engaging in research, even at undergraduate level, had a considerable impact on their professional practice. This is all linked to the idea of being a reflective practitioner and using the lens of others' research to look at how that might relate to what we notice in the setting and then gathering our evidence about what is happening in our own setting.

Use what you have learnt from this introduction to research in ECS to adopt a sceptical lens (Thomas, 2013) when looking at others' research; not that we are encouraging you to be over-critical and over-cynical. But you now certainly have tools in your researcher toolkit and a vocabulary to be able to critique in an effective way. But of course you are not just going to be reading others' research; eventually you are hopefully going to be carrying out your own.

TIME TO CONSIDER

Return to Table 4.1 in Chapter 4 where you had to consider a list of key vocabulary and what your understanding of it was. Choose three to explain to a peer. Think about how your learning has moved on or how your thinking has changed.

HOW DO WE CHOOSE A GOOD AREA TO RESEARCH?

When thinking about a good area for research we can ask ourselves some key questions to help us frame our thinking and suggest a way forward. The key questions could be:

- What am I interested in?
- Is this area of interest manageable?
- Am I able to come up with a good research question?

First let's look at our own interests. By the end of your first year you will have engaged with a wealth of information concerning children, their families and their communities. You will not just have engaged with module content but you will also have done your own reading. One thing we often do with students who have completed a first year module on research and are now preparing to do some desk-based research in their second year is to get them to create a mind map of all the early childhood subject knowledge they have studied so far. If they do this without referencing any notes then they will record the most memorable content, or as we suggested in Chapter 2, the content that resonated with them the most. Next we ask them to take another colour pen and underline or circle any of the content they found most interesting, one colour to indicate what they would like to find out more about and one to indicate anything that they found 'puzzling'. Students who are employed in practice or have placement experience may also indicate anything they have 'noticed' in the setting which would be worth exploring further. By completing this exercise students are already engaging in a more reflective way with the subject knowledge they have covered. By this stage the student may be beginning to get a clear idea of the area they would like to research more – however now they need to ask the big question, 'Is this doable?'

It is all very well to find a compelling area to research but how practical is this? For example, Paul was very interested to find out what and when was the trigger that set children on a trajectory that meant they ended up in the youth justice system; he was particularly interested in the nature versus nurture question. Putting aside the question of ethics here and how he would obtain ethical approval there is the question of how feasible such a piece of research for an undergraduate student could be. For example, when completing a proposal form outlining his research Paul had to say where and how he would gather his data. Suddenly he realised the unfeasibility of his research; he had no contacts whatsoever with people who either worked in the youth justice system or who had been involved with it in another capacity. He quickly realised that although this was an important area to explore, it was not appropriate for him at this stage in his academic career. With support from his tutor he eventually decided he would carry out a desk-based research project that did not require engaging with any participants. Instead he conducted his research by examining the research literature on his chosen area.

We are surrounded by questions; we might spend all day asking them, and certainly if we work with young children we might spend all day trying to answer them. This might lead us to believe that coming up with a question is the easy part of research, but anyone who has agonised over coming up with the perfect research question will quickly tell you this is not the case. Consider the following scenario, in which a second year ECS student catches a tutor at the end of a seminar to run something by them; it is imaginary and yet based on conversations we have had with students over the years.

Student: Can I talk to you about some ideas I have for my third year dissertation? I'm really interested in looking at children who are living in poverty.

Tutor: Why is this area of such interest to you?

Student: Well I enjoyed the discussions we had in Introduction to ECS around this in the first year and then this year we have also looked at it in the Inclusion module. And then I volunteer in a primary school once a week – it seems quite a poor area. And I remember when I was growing up how difficult it was not having much money. I would like to find out how being poor impacts on children's achievement.

The student has clearly engaged well with their modules, has looked for evidence of theory in practice and also has a personal interest. But there are many difficulties with what the student is proposing to do and not something that the tutor can quickly advise on in the few minutes before the next teaching group comes in. They will have to book a tutorial time to discuss in depth the problematic nature of the suggested research. Take a few minutes to consider what the difficulties might be and also what sorts of questions the tutor might ask and what advice they might give.

Although the student has a personal interest she should not minimise the personal impact it may have to revisit an unhappy time in her childhood. Apart from being personally traumatic this could also impact negatively on the academic quality of her work as she engages with her reading, data gathering and analysis in an overly emotive way lacking the ability to stand back and be objective.

The second problem the tutor might raise is about the 'doability' of such a piece of research; if a student wanted to 'measure the impact of poverty' then she would need a measurement tool – so what could this be, how many children would she need as participants and how much time would she need to 'measure' them all. Thirdly, the tutor would raise the question of ethical issues. How would the student identify the 'poor students' in a class and how would their parents feel about their children being identified as 'poor' as well as potentially 'underachieving'?

Finally, the tutor might question why such a piece of research was necessary because it was not particularly addressing any gap in knowledge; the student would only need to consider the research done by the Rowntree Foundation for example, or even Ofsted, to see that there was indeed a link between growing up in poverty and academic achievement. There seems now to be no acceptable rationale for carrying out this research and things are not looking good for the student's proposal.

Hopefully the student has a supportive tutor who can ask the right questions to help the student realise they need to think a little more laterally about what they would like to do. However, tutors themselves remember what it is like to be a student full of ideas and enthusiasm for a piece of research only to have those ideas crushed – even if it is done in a kindly way. The tutor will support the student in changing the focus of their research whilst still being able to explore the area they are interested in. The tutor in this scenario may guide the student to realise that a suitable, and useful, piece of research might be to find out what practitioners consider the barriers to be and explore the strategies they use to attempt to minimise these barriers.

We understand then that when choosing an area to research from the wealth of issues that we could explore in early childhood there will be many factors that influence our choice. Firstly, we may choose a topic because we have found it particularly interesting in our studies and it may even have resonated with our personal life. We must, however, consider whether what we want to do is manageable and doable and then take time to consider what a suitable research question could be.

TIME TO CONSIDER

Time for a bit of role-play! Work with a peer to act out a tutor/student discussion. One of you play the part of the student and tell your 'tutor' an area you have found interesting in your studies so far and would like to explore further. Tell them specifically what your interest is and why. The 'tutor' needs to listen 'critically' and feedback 'kindly'. Think about the problems we considered in the scenario above, such as ethics, 'doability', gaps in knowledge if possible, possible researcher bias and lack of objectivity.

WHAT KIND OF RESEARCHER DO YOU WANT TO BE?

Finally, an important aspect of your continuing research journey is a thoughtful consideration of your growing researcher identity and what sort of researcher you want to become. Included in this will be a reflection on your ethical values as discussed in Chapter 9 (The ethics of research). In addition, you will need to consider how you understand knowledge and truth and how you believe knowledge can be both added to and accessed. Finally, you will need to consider who could be the potential audience for your research. If you can think of no audience is there a danger that your research could be either 'Non-cumulative, failing to progress on the basis of previous research, for ever reinventing the wheel' or 'Ideologically driven, serving the "political purposes" of the researcher rather than the disinterested pursuit of the truth' (Pring, 2006: 158). But before we develop this discussion let's return to our discussion of ethical considerations.

Do you remember in Chapter 9 (The ethics of research) we discussed that as well as having a knowledge of ethical procedures the reflexive researcher will also examine their own ethical values that they are bringing to the research. This will be apparent in how you as a researcher choose an appropriate area to explore, the approach you take to your participants and the approach you take to knowledge and truth.

This will be the least problematic area for you as you will work closely with a supervisor who will both support you in identifying an area but also will ensure you do not become engaged in a research area that is going to be problematic for you. Clough and Nutbrown (2012: 37) use the charming term 'the Goldilocks test' to identify an appropriate research question and your tutor will support you in finding a research area that is 'not too hot' but is 'just right'. They will also support you in finding an appropriate way to approach your participants.

It will be your responsibility though to consider how you are going to view your participants and therefore what you believe they can contribute. For example do you see participants as objects, subjects or social actors in your research and how have you arrived at this viewpoint? Some researchers adopt a stance of seeing participants as merely 'research fodder' (Crow et al., 2006: 86) whereas others will prefer to see participants as co-constructors (Bell, 2013) in helping them answer a research question. How you view them will also impact on how you believe consent should be obtained.

The reflexive researcher will put a lot of thought into how consent is obtained. For example, they will have to decide whether a simple yes and signature on a consent form implies consent is given or whether there is a power imbalance that might imply a more forced consent. You may feel as a student and novice researcher that you have little in terms of power but you only have to consider researching with children or with adults who have little knowledge of the world of Higher Education to realise that you may need to look for ways to 'actively remove the power imbalance' (Karnieli-Miller et al., 2009: 279). The reflexive researcher always has ethics at the forefront of their mind when considering the choice of area to research, how they will approach participants and how they will know they have obtained consent. They will understand that ethics is 'something that you do ... not just an abstract intellectual exercise' (Farrimond, 2013: 3). They will also understand that their consideration of ethics is closely entwined with their approach to knowledge and truth and how they either think they can construct or co-construct valid knowledge.

Thus as a researcher you will need to be aware of the approach you are taking to knowledge and truth. Although this may change depending on the particular question you are answering you may find that you are drawn to a certain kind of research, such as quantitative or qualitative, because of the way you understand the world. Do you understand it in a positivist way and want to 'discover the truth of the world' (Scott and Usher, 1996: 15) or do you think there are 'multiple realities of which some individual knowledge can be acquired' (Krauss, 2005: 757). At the time, regardless of the identity and approach you adopt, you will have to address who you are doing your research for.

As you read around subjects that have interested you, and in particular search peer-reviewed journals, you will notice that you are drawn to a certain way of writing and a certain way of doing research. As other people's research raises questions in your mind then you will be becoming aware of the kinds of research conversations you would like to join, the knowledge you would like to contribute to and the gaps in research you would like to address. It may also be something as simple as knowing you would feel very uncomfortable interviewing participants, it is a highly skilful practice, but would feel confident analysing data from a quantitative questionnaire. We have also had students who have shied away from engaging with any human participants at all and have preferred to undertake more desk-based research or what Roberts-Holmes (2018: 62) might call 'research by proxy' or may also be called a 'meta-study'; this has not disadvantaged them in any way. On the contrary they have been able to demonstrate exemplary research skills and an excellent ability to analyse the information they have gathered. They are also making apparent in this way that they believe knowledge can be added to by gathering together fragments of knowledge to make new knowledge. They may do this either quantitatively or qualitatively.

We have discussed elsewhere how your approach to knowledge and truth will influence whether you choose a qualitative or quantitative approach. Though of course we have also explained how this will also depend on the question you decide to ask and therefore the best way to answer it. At the same time there is a close relationship between question and method as the type of question you want to ask will be influenced both by how you are drawn to different questions and the way you see the world.

Each researcher will have an idea of the audience they are trying to reach. For example, they may be trying to join the conversation of others working in that field or they may be more concerned with impacting on practice and therefore reaching practitioners. Often research can be accused of not being accessible; for example we cited Pring's (2006) example in Chapter 4 (The language of research). Do you remember how he criticised educational research for being, at times 'inaccessible in esoteric journals and in opaque language' (p. 158). We are sure that as a student you may feel at times that the researcher has deliberately written up their work in a way to confuse and irritate you. You will need to decide if you want to be a researcher who writes in such a way as to be accessible to participants and that your findings will be additionally presented in a format that is appropriate to practitioners in the workplace through Continuing Professional Development (CPD).

You might be thinking at this stage that the only kind of researcher you want to be is one who passes the research assignment! But knowing your researcher identity, however fledgling it might be, and reflecting where you stand in terms of ethical considerations, your approach to knowledge and truth and who you would want to read your research and how this might impact on how you write it, are all important considerations. We have already discussed how no research is value-free; as both a reader of research and eventually a researcher you are adding your own values to the mix so it is important to be transparent about what these are. This will help you not only with carrying out and writing up your own research eventually but also to engage with others' research critically.

TIME TO CONSIDER

We have given you lots to think about in this section so take some time now to gather your thoughts. See if you can complete Table 12.1 and discuss your responses with a peer.

Table 12.1 How you are developing a researcher identity

How do you view participants?
How would you define knowledge?
How do you think you can obtain knowledge?
What kind of audience would you like to read your research?

CASE STUDY

Oscar: a work-based student

Oscar has been working in early childhood for two years and is entering the third year of an Early Childhood Studies degree. One of the things he is particularly interested in is the very few male early years practitioners he has come across in the profession so he decides this would be an interesting and important area to explore. He considers the questions you have also addressed in Table 12.1. He believes that his participants (male practitioners) have something very important to share with him and he knows the questions he asks them will be informed by his own experiences so he is looking to co-construct some knowledge with them. He doesn't believe he will discover the definite answer to the practices of men working in early childhood because he understands that the information he will discover will be context-bound but he does think that by asking these men questions about their pedagogical practices that he will be able to add to his own knowledge in some way. He also believes he will add to others' knowledge and wants to ensure that the findings are accessible to other practitioners.

FINAL REFLECTION

We hope you have enjoyed this journey into research and are as excited about research as we are. At times we know we will have confused and irritated you; at least we hope we have, because we are convinced this is a sign of learning. To now move forward in your research journey read extensively around the areas you find interesting, noticing how others have carried out research in this area and considering how you could join in this conversation.

KEY POINTS

- You have acquired a new vocabulary to articulate your views about research and also you have a developing ability to critique and not accept all pieces of research at face value.
- There are many considerations to take into account when choosing a suitable area for research; this includes accessibility, 'doability' and the ethical issues that we looked at in detail in Chapter 9 (The ethics of research).
- The reflexive researcher has to examine their own identity before embarking on research and decide what kind of researcher they aspire to be.

FURTHER READING 

Roberts-Holmes, G. (2018) *Doing Your Early Years Research Project: A Step by Step Guide*, 4th edn. London: Sage.

Now that you are beginning your early years research journey, you will find this book really useful when considering how you would go about conducting your own study.

Murkerji, P. and Albon, D. (2018) *Research Methods in Early Childhood*, 3rd edn. London: Sage.

This is another book that you will benefit from reading when it comes to planning and carrying out your own pieces of research within early childhood.

REFERENCES

Ainsworth, M.D. (1964) 'Patterns of attachment behavior shown by the infant in interaction with his mother', *Merrill-Palmer Quarterly of Behavior and Development*, 51–8.

Ainsworth, M., Blehar, M., Waters, E. and Wall, S. (2015) *Patterns of Attachment: A Psychological Study of the Strange Situation*. Hove: Psychology Press.

Alderson, P. (2001) 'Research by children', *International Journal of Social Research Methodology*, 4: 139–53.

Alderson, P. and Morrow, V. (2011) *The Ethics of Research with Children and Young People: A Practical Handbook*. London: Sage.

Alexander, P.A., Winters, F., Loughlin, S.M. and Grossnickle, E. (2012) 'Students' conceptions of knowledge, information, and truth', *Learning and Instruction*, 22(1): 1–15.

Allen, G. (2011) *Early Intervention: The Next Steps*. London: Cabinet Office.

Altman, W.H.F. (2013) *Plato the Teacher: The Crisis of the Republic*. Lanham, MD: Lexington Books.

ARACY (Australian Research Alliance for Children and Youth) (2007) *National indigenous education: An overview of issues, policies and the evidence base*. Available at: www.aracy.org.au/publications-resources/command/download_file/id/115/filename/National_indigenous_education_-_An_overview_of_issues,_policies_and_the_evidence_base.pdf (accessed 2 January 2018).

Arksey, H. and Knight, P. (1999) *Interviewing for Social Scientists*. London: Sage.

Ashby, A., Richardson, J.T.E and Woodley, A. (2011) 'National student feedback surveys in distance education: an investigation at the UK Open University', *Open Learning*, 26(1): 5–25.

Ashcroft, J. (2017) 'Do boys' attitudes to reading differ to those of girls? A study into the views of reading within a year three class', *The STeP Journal*, 4(1): 2–14.

Attride-Stirling, J. (2001) 'Thematic networks: an analytic tool for qualitative research', *Qualitative Research*, 1(3): 385–405.

Australian Bureau of Statistics (2017) *Preschool Education, Australia, 2016*. Available at: www.abs.gov.au/ausstats/abs@.nsf/mf/4240.0 (accessed 2 January 2018).

Baistow, K. (2000) 'Cross-national research: what can we learn from inter-country comparisons?', *Social Work in Europe*, 7(3): 8–13.

Baldock, P., Fitzgerald, D. and Kay, J. (2005) *Understanding Early Years Policy*. London: Sage.

Bandura, A., Ross, D. and Ross, S.A. (1961) 'Transmission of aggression through imitation of aggressive models', *Journal of Abnormal and Social Psychology*, 63: 575–82.

Barker, J. and Weller, S. (2003) "Is it fun?" Developing children centred research methods', *International Journal of Sociology and Social Policy*, 23(1): 33–58.

Batada, A. Seitz, Wootan, M.G. and Story, M. (2008) 'Nine out of 10 food advertisements shown during Saturday morning children's television programming are for foods high in fat, sodium, or added sugars, or low in nutrients,' *Journal of the American Dietetic Association*, 108(4): 673–8.

BBC News (2008) '1957: BBC fools the nation'. Available at: http://news.bbc.co.uk/onthisday/hi/dates/stories/april/1/newsid_2819000/2819261.stm (accessed 2 January 2018).

BBC News (2011) 'Weaning before six months "may help breastfed babies"'. Available at: www.bbc.co.uk/news/health-12180052 (accessed 2 January 2018).

BBC News (2015) 'Smacking children "creates cycle of violence"'. Available at: www.bbc.co.uk/news/uk-scotland-34878521 (accessed 2 January 2018).

Bell, K. (2013) 'Participants' motivations and co-construction of the qualitative research process', *Qualitative Social Work*, 12(4): 523–39.

Bergström, K., Jonsson, L. and Shanahan, H. (2010) 'Children as co-researchers voicing their preferences in foods and eating: methodological reflections', *International Journal of Consumer Studies*, 34: 183–9.

Berkowitz, D. and Schwartz, D.A. (2016) 'Miley, CCN and The Onion: When fake news becomes realer than real', *Journalism Practice*, 10(1): 1–17.

Bertram, T. and Pascal, C. (2002) *Early Years Education: An International Perspective*. Available at: www.nfer.ac.uk/research/centre-for-information-and-reviews/inca/TS%20Early%20Years%20Education%202002.pdf (accessed 2 January 2018).

Bhopal, R., Vettini, A., Hunt, S., Wiebe, S., Hanna, L. and Amos, A. (2004) 'Review of prevalence data in, and evaluation of methods for cross cultural adaptation of, UK surveys on tobacco and alcohol in ethnic minority groups', *British Medical Journal*, 328(7431). doi: https://doi.org/10.1136/bmj.37963.426308.9A.

Bogdan, R.C. and Biklen, S.K. (1998) *Qualitative Research for Education: An Introduction to Theory and Methods*, 3rd edn. Boston, MA: Allyn and Bacon.

Bolshaw, P., Josephidou, J. and O'Connor, S. (2017) 'Exploring children's perceptions of the gendered nature of the early years workforce', *69th Annual OMEP World Conference*. Conference Centre Tamaris, Opatija, 20–24 June.

Booktrust (2017) *About Bookstart Corner*. Available at: www.bookstart.org.uk/professionals/bookstart-corner/about/ (accessed 2 January 2018).

Boseley, S. (2011) *Six months of breastmilk alone is too long and could harm babies, scientists now say*. Available at: www.theguardian.com/lifeandstyle/2011/jan/14/six-months-breast-feeding-babies-scientists (accessed 2 January 2018).

Bowlby, J. (1952) *Maternal Care and Mental Health*. Geneva: WHO.

Boyd, P. (2014) 'Learning conversations: teacher researchers evaluating dialogic strategies in early years settings', *International Journal of Early Years Education*, 22(4): 441–56.

Boyland, E., Harrold, J., Kirkham, T. and Halford, J. (2011) 'The extent of food advertising to children on UK television in 2008', *International Journal of Pediatric Obesity*, 6(5–6): 455–61.

Bracken-Roche, D., Bell, E., Macdonald, M.E. and Racine, E. (2017) 'The concept of "vulnerability" in research ethics: an in-depth analysis of policies and guidelines', *Health Research Policy and Systems*, 15(8).

Bradbury-Jones, C. and Taylor, J. (2015) 'Engaging with children as co-researchers: challenges, counter-challenges and solutions', *International Journal of Social Research Methodology*, 18(2): 161–73.

Bradshaw, J., Ager, R., Burge, B. and Weater, R. (2009) *PISA 2009: Achievement of 15-year-olds in England*. Available at: www.nfer.ac.uk/publications/npdz01/npdz01.pdf (accessed 2 January 2018).

Braun, V. and Clarke, V. (2013) *Successful Qualitative Research*. London: Sage.

British Educational Research Association (BERA) (2011) *Ethical Guidelines for Educational Research*. London: BERA.

British Psychological Society (BPS) (2014) *Code of Human Research Ethics*, 2nd edn. Leicester: BPS.

Brookfield, S. (2015) 'Teaching students to think critically about social media', *New Directions for Teaching and Learning*, 144: 47–56.

Bruce, T. (2011) *Early Childhood Education*, 4th edn. Abingdon: Hodder.

Bruner, J.S. (1960) *The Process of Education*. Cambridge, MA: Harvard University Press.

Bruner, J.S. (1968) *Toward a Theory of Instruction*. New York: W.W. Norton & Company.

Callanan, M., Anderson, M., Haywood, S., Hudson, R. and Svetlana Speight, S. (2017) *Study of Early Education and Development: Good Practice in Early Education Research Report*. NatCen Social Research. Available at: www.foundationyears.org.uk/files/2017/01/SEED-Good-Practice-in-Early-Education.pdf (accessed 2 January 2018).

Carr, L.T. (1994) 'The strengths and weaknesses of quantitative and qualitative research: what method for nursing?', *Journal of Advanced Nursing*, 20: 716–21.

Cheng, J.H.S. and Marsh, H. (2010) 'Are differences between universities and courses reliable and meaningful?', *Oxford Review of Education*, 36(6): 693–712.

Christensen, P. and Prout, A. (2002) 'Working with ethical symmetry in social research with children', *Childhood*, 9(4): 477–97.

Clark, A. (2005) 'Listening to and involving young children: a review of research and practice', *Early Child Development and Care*, 175(6): 489–505.

Clark, A. and Moss, P. (2005) *Spaces to Play: More Listening to Young Children Using the Mosaic Approach*. London: National Children's Bureau.

Clark, A. (2017) *Listening to Young Children: A Guide to Understanding and Using the Mosaic Approach*, 3rd edn. London: National Children's Bureau/Jessica Kingsley.

Clark, A. and Moss, P. (2011) *Listening to Young Children: The Mosaic Approach*. London: National Children's Bureau.

Clough, P. and Nutbrown, C. (2012) *A Students' Guide to Methodology*, 3rd edn. London: Sage.

Coady, M. (2010) 'Ethics in early childhood research', in G. MacNaughton, S.A. Rolfe and I. Siraj-Blatchford (eds), *Doing Early Childhood Research*, 2nd edn. Maidenhead: Open University Press. pp. 73–84.

Cooper, L. and Harlow, J. (2018) 'Physical development', in J. Johnston, L. Nahmad-Williams, R. Oates and V. Wood (eds), *Early Childhood Studies: Principles and Practice*, 2nd edn. Oxon: Routledge.

Corsaro, W.A. (2015) *The Sociology of Childhood*. London: Sage.

Corsaro, W.A. and Molinari, L. (2017) 'Entering and observing children's worlds: a reflection on a longitudinal ethnography of early education in Italy', in P. Christensen and A. James (eds), *Research with Children: Perspectives and Practices*. London: Falmer Press. pp. 179–200.

Cossar, J., Brandon, M. and Jordan, P. (2013) '"You've got to trust her and she's got to trust you": children's views on participation in the child protection system', *Child & Family Social Work*, 21(1): 103–12.

Creswell, J.W. (2014) *Research Design: Qualitative, Quantitative, and Mixed Methods Approaches*. London: Sage.

Creswell, J.W. and Plano Clark, V.L. (2011) *Designing and Conducting Mixed Methods Research*, 2nd edn. London: Sage.

Crotty, M. (1998) *The Foundations of Social Research: Meaning and Perspective in the Research Process*. London: Sage.

Crow, G., Wiles, R., Heath, S. and Charles, V. (2006) 'Research ethics and data quality: the implications of informed consent', *International Journal of Social Research Methodology*, 9(2): 83–95.

Cullen, K. (2011) *Introducing Child Psychology: A Practical Guide*. London: Icon Books.

Cutcliffe, J.R. and McKenna, H.P. (2002) 'When do we know that we know? Considering the truth of research findings and the craft of qualitative research', *International Journal of Nursing Studies*, 39(6): 611–18.

Dalrymple, T. (2013) *The New Vichy Syndrome*. London: Encounter.

David, T., Goouch, K., Powell, S. and Abott, L. (2003) *Birth to Three Matters: A Review of the Literature*. Research Report 444. Nottingham: DfES.

Dearden, L., Sibieta, L. and Sylva, K. (2010) 'From birth to age 5: evidence from the Millennium Cohort Study', in A. Goodman and P. Gregg (eds), *Poor Children's Educational Attainment: How Important Are Attitudes and Behaviour?* York: Joseph Rowntree Foundation. pp. 18–25.

Dearden, L., Sibieta, L. and Sylva, K. (2011) 'The socioeconomic gradient in early child outcomes: evidence from the Millennium Cohort Study', *Longitudinal and Life Course Studies*, 2(1): 19–40.

Declerq, B., Ebrahim, H., Koen, M., Martin, C., van Zyl, E., Daries, G., Oliver, M., Venter, R., Ramabenyane, M. and Sibeko, L. (2011) 'Levels of well-being and involvement of young children in centre-based provision in the Free State Province of South Africa', *South African Journal of Childhood Education*, 1(2): 64–80.

Demack, S. and Stevens, A. (2013) *Evaluation of Bookstart England: Bookstart Corner*. Available at: http://booktrustadmin.artlogic.net/usr/resources/1133/bookstart-corner-final-report-full-version-with-appendices.pdf (accessed 2 January 2018).

Department for Children, Schools and Families (DCSF) (2008a) *The Play Strategy*. Available at: http://webarchive.nationalarchives.gov.uk/20130401151715/www.education.gov.uk/publications/eOrderingDownload/The_Play_Strategy.pdf (accessed 2 January 2018).

Department for Children, Schools and Families (DCSF) (2008b) *Customer Voice Research: Play*. Available at: http://dera.ioe.ac.uk/11356/1/DCSF-RW082.pdf (accessed 2 January 2018).

Department for Education (DfE) (2011) *Early Years Evidence Pack*. Available at: www.gov.uk/government/publications/early-years-evidence-pack (accessed 23 April 2018).

Department for Education (DfE) (2013) *Evaluation of the Free School Meals Pilot*. Available at: www.gov.uk/government/uploads/system/uploads/attachment_data/file/184047/DFE-RR227.pdf (accessed 2 January 2018).

Department for Education (DfE) (2017a) *Statutory Framework for the Early Years Foundation Stage*. Available at: www.foundationyears.org.uk/files/2017/03/EYFS_STATUTORY_FRAMEWORK_2017.pdf (accessed 2 January 2018).

Department for Education (DfE) (2017b) *Study of Early Education and Development*. Available at: www.seed.natcen.ac.uk/ (accessed 2 January 2018).

Department for Education and Skills (DfES) (2001) *National Standards for under 8s Day Care and Childminding*. Nottingham: DfES Publications.

Dobbs, T.A., Smith, A. and Taylor, N.J. (2006) '"No, we don't get a say, children just suffer the consequences": children talk about family discipline', *The International Journal of Children's Rights*, 14(2): 137–56.

Doherty, J. and Hughes, M. (2014) *Child Development: Theory and Practice 0–11*, 2nd edn. Harlow: Pearson Education.

Donaldson, J.F. and Graham, S. (1999) 'A model of college outcomes for adults', *Adult Education Quarterly*, 50(1): 24–40.

Donaldson, M. (1978) *Children's Minds*. Glasgow: Fontana.

Early Childhood Studies Degree Network (ECSDN), the Association for Professional Development in Early Years (TACTYC) and the Sector Endorsed Foundation Degree in Early Years (SEFDEY) (2017) *Briefing and Response to Organisation for Economic Cooperation and Development (OECD), International Early Learning Study (IELS)*. Available at: http://tactyc.org.uk/wp-content/uploads/2016/04/ECSDN-TACYTC-and-SEFDEY-Joint-Response-to-International-Early-Learning-Study-Final-Corrected.docx (accessed 2 January 2018).

Early Education (2012) *Development Matters in the Early Years Foundation Stage (EYFS)*. Available at: www.gov.gg/CHttpHandler.ashx?id=104249&p=0 (accessed 2 January 2018).

Ecker, U.K.H., Lewandowsky, S., Chang, E.P and Pillai, R. (2014) 'The effects of subtle misinformation in news headlines', *Journal of Experimental Psychology*, 20(4): 323–35.

Economic and Social Research Council (2011) *Evidence Briefing: Longitudinal Studies. Child Development and Social Mobility*. Available at: www.esrc.ac.uk/files/news-events-and-publications/evidence-briefings/longitudinal-studies-child-development-and-social-mobility/ (accessed 2 January 2018).

Education Endowment Foundation (2016) *Magic Breakfast Evaluation: Report and Executive Summary*. Available at: https://educationendowmentfoundation.org.uk/public/files/Projects/Evaluation_Reports/EEF_Project_Report_Magic_Breakfast.pdf (accessed 2 January 2018).

Educational Kinesiology Foundation (2016) *Brain Gym® International*. Available at: www.braingym.org/ (accessed 2 January 2018).

Edward, A. (2010) 'Qualitative designs and analysis', in G. MacNaughton, S.A. Rolfe and I. Siraj- Blatchford (eds), *Doing Early Childhood Research*, 2nd edn. Maidenhead: Open University Press. pp. 155–76.

Edwards, C., Gandini, L. and Forman, G. (1998) *The Hundred Languages of Children: The Reggio Emilia Approach – Advanced Reflections*, 2nd edn. Westport, CT: Ablex Publishing.

Einarsdottir, J. (2007) 'Research with children: methodological and ethical challenges', *European Early Childhood Education Research Journal*, 15(2): 197–211.

Eisenstadt, N. (2011) *Providing a Sure Start: How Government Discovered Early Childhood*. Bristol: Policy Press.

Ely, M. (1991) *Doing Qualitative Research: Circles within Circles*. London: Falmer Press.

Eron, L.D. (1997) 'Spare the rod and spoil the child?', *Aggression and Violent Behaviour*, (4): 309–11.

Ertl, H. (2006) 'Educational standards and the changing discourse on education: The reception and consequences of the PISA study in Germany', *Oxford Review of Education*, 32(5): 619–34.

European Early Childhood Education Research Association (EECERA) (2014) *Ethical Code for Early Childhood Researchers*. Available at: www.becera.org.uk/docs/EECERA_Ethical_Code.pdf (accessed 23 April 2018).

Fargas-Malet, M., McSherry, D., Larkin, E. and Robinson, C. (2010) 'Research with children: methodological issues and innovative techniques', *Journal of Early Childhood Research*, 8(2): 175–92.

Farrimond, H. (2013) *Doing Ethical Research*. Basingstoke: Palgrave Macmillan.

Fewtrell, M., Wilson, D.C., Booth, I. and Lucas, A. (2011) 'When to wean? How good is the evidence for six months' exclusive breastfeeding', *British Medical Journal*, 342(7790): 209–12.

Field, F. (2010) *The Foundation Years: Preventing Poor Children Becoming Poor Adults. The Report of the Independent Review on Poverty and Life Chances*. Available at: http://webarchive.nationalarchives.gov.uk/20110120090128/http:/povertyreview.independent.gov.uk/media/20254/poverty-report.pdf (accessed 2 January 2018).

Fielding, N.G. and Fielding, J.L. (1986) *Linking Data*. London: Sage.

Fisher, J. (2016) *Interacting or Interfering? Improving Interactions in the Early Years*. Maidenhead: Open University Press.

Fisher, R. (1998) 'Thinking about thinking: developing metacognition in children', *Early Child Development and Care*, 141(1): 1–15.

Flewitt, R. (2005) 'Conducting research with young children: some ethical considerations', *Early Child Development and Care*, 175(6): 553–65.

Ford, K. (2011) 'I didn't really like it, but it sounded exciting: Admission to hospital for surgery from the perspectives of children', *Journal of Child Health Care*, 15: 250–60.

Frankfort-Nachmias, C. and Nachmias, C. (1992) *Research Methods in the Social Sciences*. London: Edward Arnold.

Fraser, S. (2004) 'Situating empirical research', in S. Fraser, V. Lewis, S. Ding, M. Kellett and C. Robinson (eds), *Doing Research with Children and Young People*. London: Sage. pp. 15–16.

Gabriel, N. (2010) 'Adults' conceptions of childhood', in R. Parker-Rees, C. Leeson, J. Willan and J. Savage (eds), *Early Childhood Studies*, 3rd edn. Exeter: Learning Matters. pp. 137–51.

Gauntlett, D. (2007) *Creative Explorations: New Approaches to Identities and Audiences*. London: Routledge.

Goffman, E. (1990) *The Presentation of Self in Everyday Life*. Harmondsworth: Penguin.

Goldacre, B. (2009) *Bad Science*. London: HarperCollins.

Goldschmied, E. and Jackson, S. (2004) *People under Three: Young Children in Day Care*, 2nd edn. London: Routledge.

Goldstein, H. (2004) 'International comparisons of student attainment: some issues arising from the PISA study', *Assessment in Education Principles Policy and Practice*, 11(3): 319–30.

Gorard, S. (2004) *Combining Methods in Educational and Social Research*. Maidenhead: Open University Press.

Government of Western Australia (2017) *On-Entry Assessment Programme*. Available at: www.det.wa.edu.au/educationalmeasurement/detcms/navigation/on-entry/ (accessed 2 January 2018).

Haldar, M. and Wærdahl, R. (2009) 'Teddy diaries: a method for studying the display of family life', *Sociology*, 43(6): 1141–50.

Halfpenny, P. and Procter, R. (2015) *Innovations in Digital Research Methods*. London: Sage.

Harden, R.M. and Stamper, N. (1999) 'What is a spiral curriculum?', *Medical Teacher*, 21(2): 141–3.

Harms, T. and Clifford, R. (1980) *The Early Childhood Environment Rating Scale*. New York, NY: Teachers College Press.

Harper, D. (2002) 'Talking about pictures: a case for photo elicitation', *Visual Studies*, 17(1): 13–23.

Hattingh, A. and de Kock, D.M. (2008) 'Perceptions of teacher roles in an experience-rich teacher education programme', *Innovations in Education and Teaching International*, 45(4): 321–32.

Hawkins, S.S., Cole, T.J. and Law, C. (2009) 'An ecological systems approach to examining risk factors for early childhood overweight: findings from the UK Millennium Cohort Study', *Journal of Epidemiology and Community Health*, 63(2): 147–55.

Haynes, L., Service, O., Goldacre, B. and Torgerson, D. (2012) *Test, Learn, Adapt: Developing Public Policy with Randomised Controlled Trials*. Available at: www.gov.uk/government/uploads/system/uploads/attachment_data/file/62529/TLA-1906126.pdf (accessed 2 January 2018).

HM Government (2010) *The United Nations Convention on the Rights of the Child: How Legislation Underpins Implementation in England*. Available at: www.gov.uk/government/uploads/system/uploads/attachment_data/file/296368/uncrc_how_legislation_underpins_implementation_in_england_march_2010.pdf (accessed 2 January 2018).

Hogan, D. (2005) 'Researching "the child" in developmental psychology', in S. Greene and D. Hogan (eds), *Researching Children's Experience: Approaches and Methods*. London: Sage. pp. 22–41.

Hookway, N. (2008) '"Entering the blogosphere": some strategies for using blogs in social research', *Qualitative Research*, 8(1): 91–113.

House of Commons (2017) *Children's Wellbeing and Mental Health: Schools*. Available at: https://hansard.parliament.uk/commons/2017-01-10/debates/51DC0042-ED3A-43CD-BCD7-1458748A4394/Children%E2%80%99SWellbeingAndMentalHealthSchools (accessed 2 January 2018).

Hyatt, K.J. (2007) 'Brain Gym®: building stronger brains or wishful thinking?', *Remedial and Special Education*, 28(2): 117–24.

Ingleby, E. (2012) *Early Childhood Studies: A Social Science Perspective*. London: Bloomsbury.

Institute of Education (2011) *Impact of the Millennium Cohort Study: November 2011*. Available at: www.cls.ioe.ac.uk/library-media/documents/Impact%20case%20studies%20-%20Millennium%20Cohort%20Study%20-%20November%202011.pdf (accessed 2 January 2018).

Institute of Education (2015) *Welcome to the Millennium Cohort Study*. Available at: www.cls.ioe.ac.uk/page.aspx?&sitesectionid=851&sitesectiontitle=Welcome+to+the+Millennium+Cohort+Study (accessed 2 January 2018).

James, A. and Prout, A. (1997) *Constructing and Reconstructing Childhood: Contemporary Issues in the Sociology Study of Childhood*. Abingdon: Routledge.

Johnson, S. and Antill, M. (2011) *Impact Evaluation of the Millennium Cohort Study*. Available at: www.esrc.ac.uk/files/research/research-and-impact-evaluation/milennium-cohort-study-impact-evaluation/ (accessed 2 January 2018).

Jones, P. (2010) *Rethinking Childhood: Attitudes in Contemporary Society*. London: Continuum.

Jorgenson, J. and Sullivan, T. (2010) 'Accessing children's perspectives through participatory photo interviews', *Forum: Qualitative Social Research*, 11(1).

Kanes, C., Morgan, C. and Tsatsaroni, A. (2014) 'The PISA mathematics regime: knowledge structures and practices of the self', *Educational Studies in Mathematics*, 87(2): 145–65.

Kanyal, M. (2014) *Children's Rights 0–8: Promoting Participation in Education and Care*. Abingdon: Routledge.

Kara, H. (2015) *Creative Research Methods in the Social Sciences: A Practical Guide*. Bristol: Policy Press.

Karet, N. (2013) *BBC Trust Review of the BBC's Children's Services*. Available at: http://downloads.bbc.co.uk/bbctrust/assets/files/pdf/our_work/childrens_services/audience_research.pdf (accessed 2 January 2018).

Karnieli-Miller, O., Strier, R. and Pessach, L. (2009) 'Power relations in qualitative research', *Qualitative Health Research*, 19(2): 279–89.

Kaufman, N.H. and Rizzini, I. (2009) 'Closing the gap between rights and realities of children's lives', in J. Qvortrup, W.A. Corsaro, and M. Honig (eds), *The Palgrave Handbook of Childhood Studies*. Basingstoke: Palgrave Macmillan. pp. 422–34.

Kehily, M. (2009) 'Understanding childhood: an introduction to some key themes and issues', in M. Kehily (ed.), *An Introduction to Childhood Studies*. Maidenhead: Open University Press/McGraw-Hill Education. pp. 1–16.

Kellert, M. (2005) *Children as Active Researchers: A New Research Paradigm for the 21st Century? NCRM Methods Review Papers NCRM/003*. Available at: https://wiki.inf.ed.ac.uk/pub/ECHOES/Participatory/Kellet2006.pdf (accessed 2 January 2018).

Kieff, J. and Wellhousen, K. (2001) *A Constructivist Approach to Block Play in Early Childhood*. Albany, NY: Delmar Cengage Learning.

Kilderry, A. (2015) 'The intensification of performativity in early childhood education', *Curriculum Studies*, 47(5): 633–52.

Knowland, V., Purser, H. and Thomas, M. (2015) 'Cross-sectional methodologies in development psychology', in J.D. Wright (ed.) *International Encyclopaedia of the Social and Behavioural Sciences*. Oxford: Elsevier. pp. 354-360.

Krauss, S.E. (2005) 'Research paradigms and meaning making: a primer', *The Qualitative Report*, 10(4): 758–70.

Kumar, R. (2014) *Research Methodology: A Step-by-Step Guide for Beginners*, 4th edn. London: Sage.

Laevers, F. (2005) *Well-Being and Involvement in Care Settings. A Process-Oriented Self-Evaluation*. Available at: www.kindengezin.be/img/sics-ziko-manual.pdf (accessed 2 January 2018).

Lave, J. and Wenger, E. (1991) *Situated Learning*. Cambridge: Cambridge University Press.

Law, J. (2001) *After Method: Mess in Social Science Research*. London: Routledge.

Lewin, K. (1943) 'Forces behind food habits and methods of change', *Bulletin of the National Research Council*, 108: 35–65.

Lewis, J. (2003) 'Design issues', in J. Ritchie and J. Lewis (eds), *Qualitative Research Practice: A Guide for Social Science Students and Researchers*. London: Sage.

Liddell, C. and Kruger, P. (1987) 'Activity and social behavior in a crowded South African township nursery: some effects of crowding', *Merrill-Palmer Quarterly*, 33: 195–211.

Lindon, J. (2012) *Understanding Child Development 0–8 Years*. Abingdon: Hodder Education.

Little, H., Wyver, S. and Gibson, F. (2011) 'The influence of play context and adult attitudes on young children's physical risk-taking during outdoor play', *European Early Childhood Education Research Journal*, 19(1): 113–31.

Livingstone, S. (2003) 'On the challenges of cross-national comparative media research', *European Journal of Communication*, 18(4): 477–500.

Lobe, B., Livingstone, S. and Haddon, L. (2007) *Researching Children's Experiences Online across Countries: Issues and Problems in Methodology*. Available at: www.lse.ac.uk/media@lse/research/EUKidsOnline/EU%20Kids%20I%20(2006-9)/EU%20Kids%20Online%20I%20Reports/D41_ISBN.pdf (accessed 2 January 2018).

LoDolce, M.E., Harris, J.L. and Schwatrz, M.B. (2013) 'Sugar as part of a balanced breakfast? What cereal advertisements teach children about healthy eating', *Journal of Health Communications*, 18(11): 1293–309.

Lundy, L., McEvoy, L. and Byrne, B. (2011) 'Working with young children as co-researchers: an approach informed by the United Nations Convention on the Rights of the Child', *Early Education and Development*, 22(5): 714–36.

Mackenzie, N. and Knipe, S. (2006) 'Research dilemmas: paradigms, methods and methodology', *Issues in Educational Research*, 16(2): 193–205.

Mackinder, M. (2017) 'Footprints in the woods: "tracking" a nursery child through a Forest School session', *Education 3–13*, 45(2): 176–90.

Macpherson, P. and Tyson, E. (2008) 'Ethical issues', in S. Elton-Chalcraft, A. Hansen and S. Twiselton (eds), *Doing Classroom Research: A Step-by-Step Guide for Student Teachers*. Maidenhead: Open University Press. pp. 55–69.

Maggetti, M., Radaelli, C. and Gilardi, F. (2012) *Designing Research in the Social Sciences*. London: Sage.

Maguire-Fong, M. (2015) *Teaching and Learning with Infants and Toddlers: Where Meaning-Making Begins*. New York: Teachers College Press.

McGarrigle, J. and Donaldson, M. (1974) 'Conservation accidents', *Cognition*, 3: 341–50.

Meehan, C. (2016) 'Every child mattered in England: but what matters to children?', *Early Child Development and Care*, 186(3): 382–402.

Melhuish, E. (2016) 'Longitudinal research and early years policy development in the UK', *International Journal of Child Care and Education Policy*, 10(3). DOI 10.1186/s40723-016-0019-1.

Melhuish, E., Ereky-Stevens, K., Petrogiannis, K., Ariescu, A., Penderi, E., Rentzou, K., Tawell, A., Leseman, P. and Broekhuizen, M. (2015) *A Review of Research on the Effects of Early Childhood Education and Care (ECEC) on Child Development*. Available at: http://ecec-care.org/fileadmin/careproject/Publications/reports/new_version_CARE_WP4_D4_1_Review_on_the_effects_of_ECEC.pdf (accessed 2 January 2018).

Messenger-Davies, M. (2008) *Children, Media and Culture*. Maidenhead: Open University Press.

Miao, Z., Reynolds, D., Harris, A. and Jones, M. (2015) 'Comparing performance: a cross-national investigation into the teaching of mathematics in primary classrooms in England and China', *Asia Pacific Journal of Education*, 35(3): 392–403.

Miles, M.B. and Huberman, M. (1994) *Qualitative Data Analysis: An Expanded Sourcebook*. London: Sage.

Ministry of Health (1959) *The Welfare of Children in Hospital* (the Platt Report). London: HMSO.

Moore, S., Neville, C., Murphy, M. and Connolly, C. (2010) *The Ultimate Study Skills Handbook*. Maidenhead: Open University Press/McGraw-Hill Education.

Morrison, K. (2013) 'Interviewing children in uncomfortable settings: 10 lessons for effective practice', *Educational Studies*, 39(3): 320–37.

Morton, E. (2011) 'Breast is not best', Available at: www.thesun.co.uk/archives/health/308539/breast-is-not-best/ (accessed 2 January 2018).

Moss, P., Dahlberg, G., Grieshaber, S., Mantovani, S., May, H., Pence, A., Rayna, S., Swadener, B. and Vandenbroeck, M. (2017) 'The Organisation for Economic Co-operation and Development's International Early Learning Study: opening for debate and contestation', *Contemporary Issues in Early Childhood*, 17(3): 343–51.

Murray, J. (2012) 'Performativity cultures and their effects on teacher educators' work', *Research in Teacher Education*, 2(2): 19–23.

National Children's Bureau (2015) *What Is Research*. Available at: www.ncb.org.uk/pear/research-and-public-health/what-is-research (accessed 6 October 2016).

National Evaluation of Sure Start (NESS) Team (2012) *The Impact of Sure Start Local Programmes on Seven Year Olds and Their Families*. Available at: www.ness.bbk.ac.uk/impact/documents/DFE-RR220.pdf (accessed 2 January 2018).

National Institute for Health and Care Excellence (NICE) (2008) *Maternal and Child Nutrition*. Available at: www.nice.org.uk/guidance/ph11/resources/maternal-and-child-nutrition-pdf-1996171502533 (accessed 2 January 2018).

Newby, P. (2014) *Research Methods for Education*. Abingdon: Routledge.

Nutbrown, C. (2012) *Foundations for Quality: The Independent Review of Early Education and Childcare Qualification* (the Nutbrown Review). Runcorn: Department for Education Publications.

Ofcom (2014) *Children's Online Behaviour: Issues of Risk and Trust. Qualitative Research Findings*. Available at: www.ofcom.org.uk/__data/assets/pdf_file/0028/95068/Childrens-online-behaviour-issues-of-risk-and-trust.pdf (accessed 2 January 2018).

Oliffe, J.L. and Bottorff, J.L. (2007) 'Further than the eye can see? Photo elicitation and research with men', *Qualitative Health Research*, 17(6): 850–58.

Opie, C. (2007) *Doing Educational Research*. London: Sage.

Organisation for Economic Co-operation and Development (OECD) (2006) *Starting Strong II*. Paris: OECD Publishing.

Organisation for Economic Co-operation and Development (OECD) (2009) *PISA 2009 Results: Executive Summary*. Available at: www.oecd.org/pisa/pisaproducts/46619703.pdf (accessed 2 January 2018).

Organisation for Economic Co-operation and Development (OECD) (2011) *PISA In Focus 8: Do Students Today Read for Pleasure?* Available at: www.oecd-ilibrary.org/docserver/download/5k9h362lhw32-en.pdf?expires=1497019828&id=id&accname=guest&checksum=11A4C71EEBC784DCC0026317E0C80C75 (accessed 2 January 2018).

Organisation for Economic Co-operation and Development (OECD) (2012a) *Research Brief: Research in ECEC Matters*. Available at: www.oecd.org/education/school/49322250.pdf (accessed 2 January 2018).

Organisation for Economic Co-operation and Development (OECD) (2012b) *Research Brief: Working Conditions Matter*. Available at: www.oecd.org/edu/school/49322754.pdf (accessed 2 January 2018).

Organisation for Economic Co-operation and Development (OECD) (2012c) *Starting Strong III*. Paris: OECD Publishing.

Organisation for Economic Co-operation and Development (2012d) *International Comparison: Longitudinal Research*. Available at: www.oecd.org/education/school/49322823.pdf (accessed 2 January 2018).

Organisation for Economic Co-operation and Development (OECD) (2014) *PISA 2012 Results in Focus: What 15-Year-Olds Know and What They Can Do with What They Know*. Available at: www.oecd.org/pisa/keyfindings/pisa-2012-results-overview.pdf (accessed 2 January 2018).

Organisation for Economic Co-operation and Development (OECD) (2015) *Starting Strong IV*. Paris: OECD Publishing.

Organisation for Economic Co-operation and Development (OECD) (2016) *PISA 2015 Results in Focus*. Available at: www.oecd.org/pisa/pisa-2015-results-in-focus.pdf (accessed 3 July 2017).

Organisation for Economic Co-operation and Development (OECD) (2017a) *What We Do and How*. Available at: www.oecd.org/about/whatwedoandhow/ (accessed 2 January 2018).

Organisation for Economic Co-operation and Development (OECD) (2017b) *The International Early Learning and Child Well-being Study – The Study*. Available at: www.oecd.org/edu/school/the-international-early-learning-and-child-well-being-study-the-study.htm (accessed 2 January 2018).

Organisation for Economic Co-operation and Development (OECD) (2017c) *What Is PISA?*. Available at: www.oecd.org/pisa/aboutpisa/ (accessed 2 January 2018).

Osgood, J. (2011) *Narratives from the Nursery: Negotiating Professional Identities in Early Childhood*. Abingdon: Routledge.

Padilla-Walker, L.M., Coyne, S.M., Fraser, A.M. and Stockdale, L.A. (2013) 'Is Disney the nicest place on earth? A content analysis of prosocial behavior in animated Disney films', *Journal of Communication*, 63(2): 393–412.

Pascal, C. and Bertram, T. (2009) 'Listening to young citizens: The struggle to make real a participatory paradigm in research with young children', *European Early Childhood Education Research Journal*, 17(2): 249–62.

Patterson, G. and Spencer, L.G. (2017) 'What's so funny about a snowman in a tiara? Exploring gender identity and gender nonconformity in children's animated films', *Queer Studies in Media & Popular*, 2(1): 73–93.

Pence, A. (2017) 'Baby PISA: dangers that can arise when foundations shift', *Journal of Childhood Studies*, 41(3): 54–8.

Penn, H. (2008) *Understanding Early Childhood: Issues and Controversies*. Maidenhead: Open University Press.

Penny, A. and Rice, H. (2012) *Childhood Bereavement Network*. Available at: www.childhoodbereavementnetwork.org.uk/research/gaps-in-research.aspx (accessed 2 January 2018).

Piaget, J. (1971) *Biology and Knowledge*. Chicago, IL: University of Chicago Press.

Piaget, J. (2002) *Language and Thought of the Child*, 3rd edn. London: Routledge Classics.

Pink, S. (2006) *Doing Visual Ethnography: Images, Media and Representation in Research*, 2nd edn. London: Sage.

Poulton, R., Moffitt, T.E. and Silva, P.A. (2015) 'The Dunedin Multidisciplinary Health and Development Study: overview of the first 40 years, with an eye to the future', *Social Psychiatry and Psychiatric Epidemiology*, 50(5): 679–93.

Powell, M.A. and Smith, A.B. (2009) 'Children's participation rights in research', *Childhood*, 16(1): 124–42.

Pring, R. (2006) *Philosophy of Educational Research*, 2nd edn. London: Continuum.

Prosser, J. and Loxley, A. (2010) 'The application of visual methodology in the exploration of the visual culture of schools', in D. Hartas (ed.), *Educational Research and Enquiry: Qualitative and Quantitative Approaches*. London: Continuum.

Punch, K. (2014) *Introduction to Social Research: Quantitative and Qualitative Approaches*, 3rd edn. London: Sage.

Punch, S. (2002) 'Research with children: the same or different from research with adults?', *Childhood*, 9(3): 321–41.

Quality Assurance Agency (QAA) (2014) *Subject Benchmark Statement: Early Childhood Studies*. Available at: www.qaa.ac.uk/en/Publications/Documents/SBS-early-childhood-studies-14.pdf (accessed 2 January 2018).

Quigley, M., Kelly, T. and Sacker, A. (2007) 'Breastfeeding and hospitalization for diarrheal and respiratory infection in the United Kingdom Millennium Cohort Study', *Pediatrics*, 119(4): 837–42.

Rabiee, P., Sloper, P. and Beresford, B. (2005) 'Doing research with children and young people who do not use speech for communication', *Children & Society*, 19(5): 385–96.

Randall, D., Anderson, A. and Taylor, J. (2016) 'Protecting children in research', *Journal of Child Health Care*, 20(3): 344–53.

Rawle, T. (2013) 'Air pollution now leading cause of lung cancer'. Available at: www.express.co.uk/life-style/health/437473/Air-pollution-now-leading-cause-of-lung-cancer (accessed 2 January 2018).

Roberts, H., Smith, S. and Bryce, C. (1995) *Children at Risk? Safety as a Social Value*. Buckingham: Open University Press.

Roberts-Holmes, G. (2018) *Doing your Early Years Research Project*, 4th edn. London: Sage.

Robertson, J. (1958) *Young Children in Hospital*. London: Tavistock Publications.

Rodd, J. (2013) 'Reflecting on the pressures, pitfalls and possibilities for examining leadership in early childhood within a cross-national research collaboration', in E. Hujala, M. Waniganayake and J. Rodd (eds), *Researching Leadership in Early Childhood Education*. Tampere: Tampere University Press. pp. 31–46.

Russell, J.B. (1997) *Inventing the Flat Earth: Columbus and Modern Historians*. Westport, CT: Greenwood Press.

Sabates, R. and Dex, S. (2012) *Multiple Risk Factors In Young Children's Development. CLS Cohort Studies Working paper 2012/1*. Available at: www.cls.ioe.ac.uk/shared/get-file.ashx?id=1327&itemtype=document (accessed 2 January 2018).

Sabri, D. (2013) 'Student evaluations of teaching as 'Fact-Totems': the case of the UK National Student Survey', *Sociological Research Online*, 18(4).

Sammons, P., Siraj-Blatchford, I., Sylva, K., Melhuish, E., Taggart, B. and Elliot, K. (2005) 'Investigating the effects of pre-school provision: using mixed methods in the EPPE research', *International Journal of Social Research Methodology*, 8(3): 207–24.

Sammons, P., Toth, K., Sylva, K., Melhuish, E., Siraj, I. and Taggart, B. (2015) 'The long-term role of the home learning environment in shaping students' academic attainment in secondary school', *Journal of Children's Services*, 10(3): 189–201.

Sampson-Cordle, A.V. (2001) 'Exploring the relationship between a small rural school in Northeast Georgia and its community: an image-based study using participant-produced photographs'. PhD dissertation, Athens, GA.

Save the Children (2000) *Children and Participation: Research, Monitoring and Evaluation with Children and Young People*. Available at: www.savethechildren.org.uk/sites/default/files/docs/children_and_partipation_1.pdf (accessed 10 July 2017).

Save the Children (2015) *The Power of Reading: How the Next Government Can Unlock Every Child's Potential through Reading*. Available at: www.savethechildren.org.uk/sites/default/files/images/The_Power_of_Reading.pdf (accessed 10 July 2017).

Schuller, T., Wadsworth, M., Bynner, J. and Goldstein, H. (2012) *The Measure of Well-Being: the Contribution of Longitudinal Studies*. Available at: www.ons.gov.uk/ons/guide-method/user-guidance/well-being/publications/the-contribution-of-longitudinal-studies.pdf (accessed 2 January 2018).

Schweinhart, L.J. (2005) *The High/Scope Perry Preschool Study Through Age 40*. Available at: http://www.peelearlyyears.com/pdf/Research/INTERNATIONAL%20Early%20Years/Perry%20Project.pdf (accessed 14 May 2018).

Schweinhart, L. (2016) 'Use of early childhood longitudinal studies by policy makers', *International Journal of Child Care and Education Policy*, 10(6): DOI: 10.1186/s40723-016-0023-5.

Scott, D. and Usher, R. (1996) *Understanding Educational Research*. Abingdon: Routledge.

Sherbert Research (2017) *Methodologies*. Available at: http://sherbertresearch.com/methodologies/ (accessed 2 January 2018).

Sheridan, S., Giota, J., Han, Y. and Kwon, J. (2009) 'A cross-cultural study of preschool quality in South Korea and Sweden: ECERS evaluations', *Early Childhood Research Quarterly*, 24(2): 142–56.

Shi, L. (2006) 'Students as research participants or as learners?', *Journal of Academic Ethics*, 4(1): 205–20.

Silverman, D. (2009) *Doing Qualitative Research*, 3rd edn. London: Sage.

Silverman, D. (2014) *Interpreting Qualitative Data*. London: Sage.

Silverman, D. (2016) *Qualitative Research*. London: Sage.

Siraj-Blatchford, I. (2009) 'Conceptualising progression in the pedagogy of play and sustained shared thinking in early childhood education: a Vygotskian perspective', *Education and Child Psychology*, 26 (2): 77–89.

Siraj-Blatchford, I., Sylva, K., Muttock, S., Gilden, R. and Bell, D. (2002) *Researching effective pedagogy in the early years*. Available at: http://dera.ioe.ac.uk/4650/1/RR356.pdf (accessed 2 January 2018).

Slee, P. and Shute, R. (2003) *Child Development: Thinking about Theories*. London: Arnold.

Smith, A.B. (2011) 'Respecting children's rights and agency: theoretical insights into ethical research procedures', in D. Harcourt, B. Perry and T. Waller (eds), *Researching Young Children's Perspectives*. Abingdon: Routledge. pp. 11–25.

Smith, J.K. and Hodkinson, P. (2008) 'Relativism, criteria, and politics', in N.K. Denzin and Y.S. (eds), *Collecting and Interpreting Qualitative Materials*. London: Sage. pp. 401–34.

Smith, M. (2017) 'How left or right-wing are the UK's newspapers?' Available at: https://yougov.co.uk/news/2017/03/07/how-left-or-right-wing-are-uks-newspapers/ (accessed 2 January 2018).

Smith, P. and Connolly, K.J. (1980) *The Ecology of Preschool Behaviour*. Cambridge: Cambridge University Press.

Southall, D.P., Plunkett, M.C.B., Banks, M.W., Falkov, A.F. and Samuels, M.P. (1997) 'Covert video recordings of life-threatening child abuse: lessons for child protection', *Pediatrics*, 100(5): 735–60.

Spaulding, L., Mostert, P. and Mean, A. (2010) 'Is Brain Gym® an effective educational intervention', *Exceptionality*, 18(1): 18–30.

Spock, B. (1946) *The Common Sense Book of Baby and Child Care*. New York: Duell, Sloan and Pearce.

Strike, K.A. (2006) 'The ethics of educational research', in J.L. Green, G. Camilli and P.B. Elmore (eds), *Handbook of Complementary Methods in Education Research*. New York: Routledge.

Sumsion J., Harrison, L., Presss, F., McLeod, S., Goodfellow, J. and Bradley, B. (2011) 'Researching infants' experiences of early childhood education and care', in D. Harcourt, B. Perry and T. Waller (eds), *Researching Young Children's Perspectives: Debating the Ethics and Dilemmas of Educational Research with Children*. Abingdon: Routledge. pp. 113–27.

Sylva, K., Melhuish, E., Sammons, P., Siraj-Blatchford, I., Taggart, B. and Elliot, K. (2003) *The Effective Provision of Pre-School Education (EPPE) Project: Findings from the Pre-school Period*. Available at: http://generic.surestart.org/pdfdir/news6.pdf (accessed 14 May 2018).

Sylva, K., Melhuish, E., Sammons, P., Siraj-Blatchford, I. and Taggart, B. (2004) *The Effective Provision of Pre-School Education (EPPE) Project: Final Report*. Nottingham: DfES Publications.

Sylva, K., Melhuish, E., Sammons, P., Siraj-Blatchford, I. and Taggart, B. (2010) *Early Childhood Matters: Evidence from the Effective Pre-School and Primary Education Project*. London: Routledge.

Taggart, B., Sylva, K., Melhuish, E., Sammons, P. and Siraj, I. (2015) *Effective Pre-school, Primary and Secondary Education Project (EPPSE 3–16+)*. Available at: http://dera.ioe.ac.uk/23344/1/RB455_Effective_pre-school_primary_and_secondary_education_project.pdf (accessed 14 May 2018).

Tayler, K. and Price, D. (2016) *Gender Diversity and Inclusion in Early Years Education*. Abingdon: Routledge.

Taylor, A. (2011) 'Coming, ready or not: Aboriginal children's transition to school in urban Australia and the policy push', *International Journal of Early Years Education*, 19(2): 145–61.

The Children's Society (2016) *The Good Childhood Report 2016*. Available at: www.childrenssociety.org.uk/sites/default/files/pcr090_mainreport_web.pdf (accessed 2 January 2018).

The Lullaby Trust (2017) 'Our history: how it all began'. Available at: www.lullabytrust.org.uk/about-us/who-we-are/our-history-2/ (accessed 2 January 2018).

Thomas, G. (2013) *How to Do Your Research Project*. London: Sage.

Thomson, P. (2015) 'Why is this reading so hard?', *Patter*, 13 April. Available at: http://patthomson.net/2015/04/13/why-is-the-reading-so-hard/ (accessed 2 January 2018).

Thomson, R. and Holland, J. (2003) 'Hindsight, foresight and insight: the challenges of longitudinal qualitative research', *International Journal of Social Research Methodology*, 6(3): 233–44.

Thomson, R. and Kehily, M. with Hadfield, L. and Sharpe, S. (2008) *The Making of Modern Motherhood*. The Open University. Available at: http://www3.open.ac.uk/events/0/200873_43860_o1.pdf (accessed 2 January 2018).

Tickell, C. (2011a) *The Early Years Foundation Stage (EYFS) Review: Report on the Evidence*. Available at: www.gov.uk/government/uploads/system/uploads/attachment_data/file/516537/The_early_years_foundation_stage_review_report_on_the_evidence.pdf (accessed 2 January 2018).

Tickell, C. (2011b) *The Early Years: Foundations for Life, Health and Learning*. Available at: www.gov.uk/government/uploads/system/uploads/attachment_data/file/180919/DFE-00177-2011.pdf (accessed 2 January 2018).

Tisdall, K., Davis, J. and Gallagher, M. (2009) *Researching with Children and Young People*. London: Sage.

Tompsett, H., Ashworth, M., Atkins, C., Bell, L., Gallagher, A., Morgan, M. and Wainwright, P. (2009) *The Child, the Family and the GP: Tensions and Conflicts of Interest in Safeguarding Children*. Available at: http://lx.iriss.org.uk/sites/default/files/resources/DCSF-RBX-09-05.pdf (accessed 2 January 2018).

Trinch, S. and Snajdr, E. (2017) 'What the signs say: gentrification and the disappearance of capitalism without distinction in Brooklyn', *Journal of Sociolinguistics*, 21(1): 64–89.

Tunstall, S., Tapsell, S. and House, M. (2004) 'Children's perceptions of river landscapes and play: What children's photographs reveal', *Landscape Research*, 29(2): 181–204.

UK Longitudinal Studies Centre (2017) *Longitudinal FAQs*. Available at: www.iser.essex.ac.uk/ulsc/longitudinal-faqs (accessed 2 January 2018).

Unicef (2007) *Child Poverty in Perspective: An Overview of Child Well-being in Rich Countries*. Available at: www.unicef.org/media/files/ChildPovertyReport.pdf (accessed 2 January 2018).

Unicef (2013) *Child Well-Being in Rich Countries: A Comparative Overview*. Available at: www.unicef-irc.org/publications/683/ (accessed 2 January 2018).

Unicef (2015a) *The State of the World's Children 2015: Executive Summary*. Available at: www.unicef.org/publications/files/SOWC_2015_Summary_and_Tables.pdf (accessed 2 January 2018).

Unicef (2015b) *Breastfeeding*. Available at: www.unicef.org/nutrition/index_24824.html (accessed 2 January 2018).

Unicef (2017a) *How We Protect Children's Rights with the UN Convention on the Rights of the Child*. Available at: www.unicef.org.uk/what-we-do/un-convention-child-rights/ (accessed 2 January 2018).

Unicef (2017b) *Longitudinal Research for Children*. Available at: www.unicef-irc.org/research/276/ (accessed 2 January 2018).

United Nations (UN) (1989) *United Nations Convention on the Rights of the Child*. Treaty no. 27541. Available at: https://downloads.unicef.org.uk/wp-content/uploads/2010/05/UNCRC_united_nations_convention_on_the_rights_of_the_child.pdf?_ga=2.119561160.1753319808.1496413662-596175726.1496413662 (accessed 2 January 2018).

University of Leeds (2015) *Evaluating Information*. Available at: https://library.leeds.ac.uk/tutorials/evaluating/ (accessed 2 January 2018).

Veale, A. (2005) 'Creative methodologies in participatory research with children', in S. Greene and D. Hogan (eds), *Researching Children's Experience*. Thousand Oaks, CA: Sage.

Vygotsky, L. (1978) *Mind in Society: The Development of Higher Psychological Processes*. Cambridge, MA: Harvard University Press.

Waller, T. (2014) 'Voices in the park: researching the participation of young children in outdoor play in early years settings', *Management in Education*, 28(4): 161–6.

Warin, J. (2000) 'Gender consistency at the start of school', *Sex Roles*, 42(3-4): 209–31.

Warin, J. (2011) 'Ethical mindfulness and reflexivity: managing a research relationship with children and young people in a fourteen year qualitative longitudinal research (QLR) study', *Qualitative Inquiry*, 17(9): 805–14.

Watkins, D.C. (2012) 'Qualitative research: the importance of conducting research that doesn't "count"', *Health Promotion Practice*, 13(2): 153–8.

Watson, J.B. and Rayner, R. (1920) 'Conditioned emotional reactions', *Journal of Experimental Psychology*, 3(1): 1–14.

Westwood, J. (2014) 'Childhood in different cultures', in T. Maynard and S. Powell (eds), *An Introduction to Early Childhood Studies*. London: Sage. pp. 11–21.

White, H., Sabarawal, S. and de Hoop, T. (2014) *Randomized Controlled Trials (RCTS): Methodological Briefs – Impact Evaluation No. 7*. Available at: www.unicef-irc.org/publications/752/ (accessed 10 July 2017).

Whitebread, D. and Jarvis, P. (2013) *Too Much Too Soon: Reflections Upon the School Starting Age*. Available at: www.toomuchtoosoon.org/uploads/2/0/3/8/20381265/scm_submission_-_school_starting_age_.pdf (accessed 2 January 2018).

Williams, A.F. and Prentice, A. (2011) 'Scientific advisory committee on nutrition replies to Mary Fewtrell and colleagues', *British Medical Journal*, 342(7794): 400

Wilson, G. (2001) 'Power and translation in social policy research', *International Journal of Social Research Methodology*, 4(4): 319–26.

Woodhead, M. (1996) 'In search of the rainbow: pathways to quality in large scale programmes for young disadvantaged children', *Early Childhood Development: Practice and Reflections*, 7. The Hague: Bernard van Leer Foundation.

Woodhead, M. and Faulkner, D. (2008) 'Subjects, objects or participants? Dilemmas of psychological research with children', in P. Christiansen and A. James (eds), *Research with Children: Perspectives and Practices*. London: Falmer Press. pp. 10–39.

World Health Organisation (WHO) (2015) 'Up to what age can a baby stay well nourished by just being breastfed?' Available at: www.who.int/features/qa/21/en/ (accessed 2 January 2018).

Young Lives (2017a) *Young Lives – A Multi-Disciplinary Longitudinal Study of Child Poverty*. Available at: www.younglives.org.uk/sites/www.younglives.org.uk/files/GuidetoYLResearch-S1-StudyOverview.pdf (accessed 2 January 2018).

Young Lives (2017b) *What Can Comparative Country Research Tell Us About Child Poverty?* Available at: www.younglives.org.uk/sites/www.younglives.org.uk/files/GuidetoYLResearch-S2-WhyComparativeResearch.pdf (accessed 2 January 2018).

Zhou, D. (2009) 'A review of sandplay therapy', *International Journal of Psychological Studies*, 1(2): 69–72.

INDEX

Note: Tables are indicated by page numbers in bold print. The letter "*b*" after a page number refers to bibliographical information in a "Further Reading" section.

accessibility of research 158
accuracy of information 20
adverts 138, 139
aggression 58
Ainsworth, M.D. et al 32, 115
Alderson, P. 72, 116, 117
Alderson, P. and Morrow, V. 76
Alexander, P.A. et al 37, 39*b*
Allen Review 83
Ashcroft, J. 4
Association for Professional Development in Early Years (TACTYC) 100
assumptions 16–17
attachment theory 32, 115
audience 158
audio recordings 143
Australia: school readiness 102–3
authors, credentials of 23

Baldock, P. et al 5
Bandura, A. 58, 59, 63
Batada, A. et al 25
BBC children's brands 76
BBC News 18
behaviourism 59
Bennet, T. 27*b*
Bertram, T. and Pascal, C. 97
Bhopal, R. et al 101
blogs 145–6
Bobo doll experiment 58
Bolshaw, P. et al 151
Bookstart Corner programme 90–92
Bowlby, J. 32
Boyd, P. 139, 143, 146
Boyland, E. et al 25
Bradbury-Jones, C. and Taylor, J. 76
Brain Gym 26, 151
Braun, V. and Clarke, V. 35–6, 43, 124–5, 127
breastfeeding, research on 17–18
British Educational Research Association (BERA) 110, 111
British Psychological Society 111
Bronfenbrenner 71
Brookfield, S. 16–18, 34
Bruner, J.S. 33, 47

Canada 96
changing views of children 54–5
  case study 62–3
child conferencing 73
Childhood (journal) 47
childhood poverty 99
childhood as preparation for adulthood 55
children as active participants 66–79, 119
  access 77
  benefits **72**
  case study: Xander 77–8
  co-constructors of research 116
  methods 72–6
  recruitment 77
  remuneration 76–7
children as objects of research 55–62
children as researchers 66–7
Children's Society: *The Good Childhood Report* 61
children's views 9, 61, 66, 68, 71–5, 119, 144–5
  mosaic approach (Clark and Moss) **73–4**
China 105
citations 23
Clark, A. 79*b*, 142, 143
Clark, A. and Moss, P. 72, 73–4, 74–5, 77, 151
Clough, P. and Nutbrown, C. 156
Coalition government 6, 83, 84
cohort studies 82
collages 139–40

common sense 30, 34
  case study 38
communities of practice 45
comparative investment in ECEC 96
Contemporary Issues in Early Childhood (journal) 47
Continuing Professional Development 152, 158
Corsaro, W.A. 77–8
Corsaro, W.A. and Molinari, L. 88
Cossar, J. et al 61
covert methods 114, **115**
creative approaches 137–48
Creswell, J.W. 31, 128, 130
critical realism 35–6
critical thinking
  asking questions 150
  and assumptions 16–17
  case study: Nick 26–7, 151
  demonstrating 25
  four steps (Brookfield) **17**–18
  quality of information: markers 19–23, **24**
cross-national research 5, 7–8, 95–106
  case study: Harry 104–6
  differing values 102
  ethnocentrism 102–3
  language and translation 101
  longitudinal research 99
  strengths and limitations **104**–6
  usefulness 96–7
  Young Lives 99
cross-sectional research 82–3
Crotty, M. 31

Daily Express 16
Daily Mail, The 21
Dalrymple, T. 34–5
Dearden, L. et al 86, 91
deception in research 117
Denmark 96
desk-based research 157
digital methods 142–5
  case study 147
Dimbleby, Richard 22
disciplines in early childhood research 23, **126**
disrespectful methods 116–**17**
dissertations 3
Dobbs, T.A. et al 9
Donaldson, M. 56–7
drawings 138, 139, 141–2
drop-out of participants 88, 89
Dunedin Study 83
Dyer, C. 121*b*

Early Childhood Education and Care (ECEC) 2
Early Childhood Studies Degree Network (ECSDN) 100
Early Years Evidence Pack 11
Early Years Foundation Stage (EYFS) 68–9, 116
Ecker, U.K.H. et al 16
Economic and Social Research Council (ESRC) 82
Education Endowment Foundation 6
Edward, A. 50
Effective Provision of Pre-School Education (EPPE) Project 6, 11, 54, 83, 84, 90, 116
Einarsdottir, J. 72, 141, 142, 143, 144, 145, 151
Eisenstadt, N. 84–5, 88
Elementary Education Act (1870) 9
email interviews 132
empowerment of children 69
ethics of research 109–120
  codes of ethics 110
  covert methods 114, **115**
  disrespectful methods 116–**17**
  ethical compliance 111–12
  ethical considerations at different stages **112–13**
  harm 110–111
  informed consent 66, 100, 114, 118, 120, 157
  meaning of 'ethics' 109–110
  researchers with professional background (case study) 113–14
  risk/benefit equation 114, **115**
  values 112, 156–7
European Early Childhood Education Research Association 111, 113

Fargas-Malet, M. et al 142
Fenwick, S. 51*b*
Fewtrell, M. et al 17, 18
Field, Frank 91
field notes 132
Fielding, N.G. and Fielding, J.L. 146
films 146
Finland 97, 102
Fisher, J. 141
Fisher, R. 33, 34
Flewitt, R. 118
focus groups 132
Ford, K. 139
Fraser, S. 3
free school meals 5–6
funding 96
  longitudinal research 88–9

gatekeeping 48–9
Gauntlett, D. 139
gendered assumptions 152
Goffman, Erving 139
Goldacre, B. 20, 27*b*, 131
Goldschmied, E. and Jackson, S. 10, 152

Goldstein, H. 105
Google 37
Google Scholar 20, 23
GPs and views of children 9
graduate leadership in nurseries 8
group interviews 132
Guardian, The 18, 21

Haldar, M. and Wærdahl, R. 101, 147, 148*b*
Halfpenny, P. and Procter, R.: *Innovations in Digital Research Methods* 143
Harden, R.M. and Stamper, N. 47
Harper, D. 144
Hattingh, A. and de Kock, D.M. 139–40
Haynes, L. et al 90
health organisations 86
Hedges, H. and Cullen, J. 39*b*
Hogan, D. 60, 64*b*
Hosking, G. et al 148*b*
Hughes, M. 57
Hyatt, K.J. 26–7

importance of research 8–10
information
  assumptions 16–17
  critical thinking 16–17
  and Internet 37
  key terms 19
  markers of quality 19–23, **24**, 37
    case study: Nick 26–7
  popular sources 19
  provenance of author 23
  relevance 23–4
  resonance 20
  style 22
  subjective information 20–21
  timeliness 21–2
  truthfulness and integrity 20–21
informed action 18
informed consent 66, 100, 114, 118, 157
  case study 120
Institute of Education 86, 87
integrity 20
interests of researchers 153–4
International Early Learning and Child Well-being Study (IELS) 100, 104
International Leadership Research Forum (ILRF) 97
Internet 37, 143, 145–6
interviews 130, 132
  with children 141
  group interviews 132
  and photo-elicitation 144

Johnson, S. and Antill, M. 87, 91–2, 93*b*
Jones, P. 55
Jorgenson, J. and Sullivan, T. 143
journal articles, peer reviewed 19, 21
Journal of Early Childhood Research 47
journals 47–8

Kara, H. 137–8
Kehily, M. 23, 60
Kellert, M. 66–7, 70, 71
key person scheme 10–11
Kieff, J. and Welhousen, K. 152
Kilderry, A. 131
knowledge
  and common sense 34
  definitions of 33–4, 36
  and reading research 151
  and truth 33–5, 127, 157
knowledge creation 2–3

Labour government 67
Laevers, F. 62
language in cross-national research 101–2
language learning 42
large-scale programme evaluations 5, 6
Lave, J. and Wenger, E. 45, 46, 48
Leeds University 24
Lewis, J. 118
Liddell, C. and Kruger, P. 103
Lindon, J. 57, 59, 62, 63
listening to children 119, 142
Livingstone, S. 96
Lobe, B. et al 3
LoDolce, M.E. et al 139
longitudinal research 5, 6–7, 81–92
  case study: Pooja 90–92
  cross-national 99
  definitions 82
  drop-out of participants 88, 89
  funding 88–9
  influences of 86–7
  insight into societal changes 87
  limitations 88
  Making of Modern Motherhood (Thomson, R. et al) 87–8
  Perry Preschool Project 89, 90
  small-scale studies 88
Longitudinal Studies Centre 82
Lundy, L. et al 68, 79*b*

McGarrigle, j. and Donaldson, M. 57
Mackenzie, N. and Knipe, S. 125, 127
Macpherson, P. and Tyson, E. 110, 119
mapping 74
market research 75
Meehan, C. 141
Melhuish, E. 84, 85, 86, 93*b*
Melhuish, E. et al 11, 13*b*
methodology 124–5
  and paradigms 125
methods of data collection
  benefits and limitations **132**–3, 139

case study 133
choosing methods 140–41
considering practicalities 154
creative approaches 137–48
qualitative and quantitative 127–8, 130–31
translated data 101–2
words and numbers 129–30
Mexico 97
Miao, Z. et al 105, 106
Miles, M.B. and Huberman, M. 129
Millennium Cohort Study (MCS) 6–7, 99
influence 86–7
models 138, 139
Moore, S. et al 23
Morgan, B. 121*b*
Morrison, K. 49
Mosaic Approach (Clark and Moss) 73–4, 76–7
Moss, P. et al 100
Mukherji, P. and Albon, D. 135*b*

National Children's Bureau 3
National Evaluation of Sure Start (NESS) 84–5
National Institute for Health and Care Excellence (NICE) 86
National Student Survey (NSS) 130–31
naturally occurring data 145–6
neuroscience and brain research 5
New Zealand 83
newspapers 21, 87
Nuremberg Code 110, 118
Nutbrown Review 11

objective information 21
observations 50, 73, 129, 132
covert observations 114, 115, 117
with interviews 130
of play 152
Ofcom 75
Office of National Statistics (ONS) 99
Oliffe, J.L. and Bottorff, J.L. 144
Opening Windows programme 74–5
Organisation for Economic Co-operation and Development (OECD) 9, 12*b*, 82, 87, 96, 104, 106, 107*b*
definition of early childhood research 3
Starting Strong II 96
Starting Strong III 104

Padilla-Walker, L.M. et al 146
Panorama (BBC) 22
paradigmatic assumptions 16–17
paradigms 47, 125
parents' perspectives in research 74
participants, views of 156–7
Pascal, C. and Bertram, T. 72, 74–5
passivity of children 60, 62, 66
past experiences of childhood 70
Patterson, G. and Spencer, L.G. 146
PDF documents 22
peer-reviewed articles 19, 21
Penn, H. 54, 55, 57, 58, 60, 65, 66, 67
Penny, A. and Rice, H. 61
performativity culture 131
Perry Preschool Project 89, 90, 96
photography 113–14, 138, 139
photo-elicitation 143–4
photos taken by children 74, 143
physical punishment 9
Piaget, J. 46, 47, 56–8, 63
Pink, S. 138
Plato 35
Platt Report 63
play 67–8, 74
heuristic play 152
sand play 133
space for 103–4
Play Strategy, The (DCSF) 67–8
policy research 5–6
Powell, M.A. and Smith, A.B. 61
power imbalance 116, 117
practicalities of research 154, 155
practitioners' perspectives 74
Pring, R. 49, 146, 156, 158
Programme for International Student Assessment (PISA) 4, 100, 104–5
Prosser, J. and Loxley, A. 138, 141
Punch, K. 69, 77, 111, 112, 117, 125, 126, 128, 142

quantitative and qualitative research 4–5, 127–8
choice of 158
combined data 130–31
questionnaires 132, 141
Quigley, M. et al 86

Rabiee, P. et al 75
randomised controlled trials (RCTs) 89
reading research 151
realism 35
reflexivity 156–7
Reggio Emilia 73
relativism 35
reliability of information 20
research, choice of area of 153–5
research in controlled environments 58–60, **59**
research designs
choices 123–4
types of research 5
research examples
Hannah and gendered play choices 152
Karim and block play 152

Louise and treasure baskets: heuristic play 152
research language *see* terminology
'research', meaning and nature of 2–4, 44
research questions 154–5
research 'with' children *see* children as active participants
researcher identity 156–9, **158**
resonance 20
rights of children 67, 69
risk/benefit equation 114, **115**
risks, exposure to 7
Roberts, H. et al 71
Roberts-Holmes, G. 51*b*, 110, 116, 119, 127, 157
Robertson, J. 63
Rodd, J. 97
role play 74

Sabates, R. and Dex, S. 7
Sammons, P. et al 90, 91
samples 46
Sampson-Cordle, A.V. 144
Save the Children 8, 69, 71
schema 46
school readiness 102–3, 151
Scientific Advisory Commission on Nutrition (SACN) 18
search engines 2
Sector Endorsed Foundation Degree in Early Years (SEFDEY) 100
sensitive areas of research 60–61
separation from parents 62–3
Sherbert Research 67, 72, 73, 75–6
Sheridan, S. et al 104
Shi, L. 140
signs 128, 139
Silverman, D. 43, 116, 145, 146
Siraj-Blatchford, I. et al 126
Smith, A.B. 9, 60, 61
Smith, J.K. and Hodkinson, P. 31
Smith, M. 21
Smith, P. and Connolly, K.J. 103
'social science', meaning of 125–6
socialisation 70–71
South Africa 86, 103
Southall, D.P. et al 114, 121
Spaulding, L. et al 26, 27
spiral curriculum 47
Spock, B.: *Common Sense Book of Baby and Child Care* 30, 34
standardised tests 58
staff-child ratio 11
stages of development 56
starting age of compulsory school 97, 102
Statutory Framework for Early Years Foundation Stage (2017) 10
stereotyping 117
Study of Early Education and Development (SEED) 85–7
style of information 22
subjective information 20–21
Sumsion, J. et al 78
Sun, The 17, 18
Sure Start Local Programmes (SSLP) 85, 90
surveys 130, 132
Sustained Shared Thinking (SST) 126
Sweden 97
Sylva, K. et al 6, 11, 54, 81, 84, 116, 128

Taggart, B. et al 11
Tayler, K. and Price, D. 31
Taylor, A. 102–3
television: food advertisements 25
terminology 41–51
  building a glossary 44–**5**
  case study: Joel 50
  key vocabulary **43**, 44
  language as barrier 48–9
  shared vocabularies 45–7
texting 17
Thomas, G. 43, 45, 153
Thompson, P. 42
Thomson, R. et al 87–8, 89
Thomson, R. and Holland, J. 88–9
Tickell, C. 10–11
timeliness of information 21–2
Tisdall, K. et al 8–9, 96
Tobin, J. et al 107*b*
Tompsett, H. et al 9
tours 74
'traditional paradigm of childhood' 55
triangulation 43
Tronick et al 59–60
truth
  and common sense 30, 34
  critical realism 35–6
  definitions 30–**31**
  evolving truth 30
  factors in understanding **33**
  and integrity 20–21
  and knowledge 33–5, 127, 157
  and *post-truth* 29
  relativism 35
  realism 35
  and research 36–8
  and research into attachment theory 32
Tunstall, S. et al 143–4
types of research 4–8

UK
  child wellbeing 98, 100
  investment in ECEC 96
  ranking for mathematics 105

UK Longitudinal Studies Centre 82
Unicef 7–8, 82, 86, 98
United Nations Convention on the Rights of the Child (UNCRC) 67, 68

video 114, 120, 138, 139, 143
visual imagery 138–9
  examples 138, **139**
vocabulary *see* terminology
vulnerability of children 70

Walker, J. et al 134*b*
Waller, T. 77–8
Warin, J. 109, 118, 139
Watson, J.B. and Raynor, R. 59
wellbeing 9, 62
  in hospital 62–3
  International Early Learning and Child Well-being Study (IELS) 100
  play space 103–4
  ranking of countries by Unicef 98
Westwood, J. 55, 102
Wikipedia 23
Wilson, G. 101–2
Woodhead, M. 103
Woodhead, M. and Faulkner, D. 57, 58, 59, 64*b*, 65–6, 71, 115
World Health Organisation (WHO) 18, 86

YouGov UK 21
Young Lives study 99